ANTHROPOSOPHIA

Rudolf Joseph Lorenz Steiner
February 27, 1861 – March 30, 1925

FROM THE WORKS OF DR. RUDOLF STEINER

ANTHROPOSOPHIA

THE DIVINE FEMININE TRINITY

Dr. Douglas J. Gabriel

Our Spirit, LLC
2024

OUR SPIRIT, LLC

P. O. Box 355
Northville, MI 48167

www. ourspirit. com
www. neoanthroposophy. com
www. gospelofsophia. com
www. eternalcurriculum. com

2024 Copyright © by Our Spirit, LLC

All rights reserved. No part of this publication may
Be reproduced, stored in a retrieval system, or transmitted,
in any form or by any means, electronic, mechanical,
recording, photocopying, or otherwise, without prior written
permission of the publisher.

ISBN: 978-1-963709-02-5

CONTENTS

The Enigma of the Being Anthroposophia	1
The Realm of 'The Mothers'	29
Anthroposophia and *The Riddles of Philosophy*	31
The Three Elemental Worlds as "The Mothers"	40
Primacy of The Mothers	43
A Condensed Version of *The Riddles of Philosophy*	44
Goethe's *Faust* and The Mothers	93
The New Isis Myth	115
America's Wooden Doll of Anthroposophy	119
The Mysteries of Sophia	121
Rudolf Steiner on the Significance of the Feminine	131
The Enigma of the Being Anthroposophia	137
The Triple Goddess	147
Why Sophia is Not the Holy Spirit	154
The Mother of the Divine Feminine Trinity	181
The Daughter of the Divine Feminine Trinity	219
The Holy Sophia of the Divine Feminine Trinity	253
Further Reflections	259
Sophiology and the Children of Wisdom	263
Sophiologists—Lovers of Sophia	274

Bibliography	327
About Dr. Rudolf Steiner	333
About the Author, Dr. Douglas Gabriel	335
Translator's Note	337

The Enigma of the Being Anthroposophia

Many anthroposphists have tried to create and maintain a relationship with Anthroposophia, a Being they are told by Rudolf Steiner is vitally important to their spiritual development, and yet they cannot wrap their minds around how to develop this relationship. On the one hand, Steiner tells his students to focus on this Being to advance their personal spiritual development, and on the other hand they are told the Mysteries of Anthroposophia (Sophia-Wisdom) will only be fully revealed in the future. This has led to much speculation, that often goes nowhere. Just as soon as a spiritual scientist thinks she has understood Anthroposophia, a new dimension opens, and all previous parameters of Sophia must be redefined. Pretty soon, it is hard to distinguish the difference between Anthroposophia, Sophia, the Sophia of Christ, the Holy Spirit, the Archangel (Archai) Michael, the Holy Sophia, the Mother of Jesus, The Mothers, the Kyriotetes, or the Heavenly Sophia. It seems that these seemingly different being's influences overlap and that they must either work together, share the same duties, or perhaps in some cases, are the same being.

The importance Steiner places on the Archai Michael, our current Spirit of the Times (Zeitgeist), must be balanced with the roles of Anthroposophia. This doesn't seem logical until one realizes that Archai Michael is a 'Son of Sophia,' one of the highest emissaries of the Heavenly Sophia (Kyriotetes - Spirits of Wisdom). Time Spirit Michael is also the emissary of Christ and referred to as the 'countenance of Christ' and the Archangel of the Sun. The confusion continues to mount as the aspirant tries to understand and commune with Anthroposophia, until she notices the simple answer which is spelled out by Steiner without any dogma or doctrine concerning the way to imagine and communicate with Sophia. The answers to the mysteries of Anthroposophia are clearly found in Steiner's work; but the formulation of a specific explanation of the threefold nature of Anthroposophia, the Heavenly Sophia (Kyriotetes), and The Mothers is not found in any one lecture or book. Once an understanding of The Mothers is added to the better known aspects of Anthroposophia—the Earthly Sophia and the Heavenly Sophia—then a clear imagination arises of a divine feminine trinity in the form of Mother (The Mothers), Daughter (Kyriotetes-Heavenly Sophia), and Anthroposophia.

This Divine Feminine Trinity can be found throughout Steiner's Anthroposophy if the aspirant of spiritual science looks hard enough. It is important to remember that Dr. Steiner said Anthroposophy was brought to him by Anthroposophia.

Through Steiner's injunction to 'let Anthroposophia in,' the anthroposophic student is told to develop a relationship with a Spiritual Being who knows us better than we know ourselves. Anthroposophia should become our counselor and the objective reflection of our own personal self-development. Interaction with this Being will help the aspirant take each new step of self-development. Anthroposophia is the midwife of the soul that births the 'Virgin Sophia,' the purified higher nature of the soul. Once the Virgin Sophia, as the Bride of the Lamb, is prepared and has passed the requisite initiations, the soul can alchemically wed the spirit, like Sophia to Christ—Sophia Christos, Cosmic Wisdom to Cosmic Love. Then, the true heart of the soul becomes a place for the Christened spirit to dwell.

Let's read in Steiner's own words a few descriptions of this being Anthroposophia.

***The Anthroposophic Movement*, Rudolf Steiner, VII, *Third Stage: The Present Day—Life-Conditions of the Anthroposophical Society*, Dornach, June 16, 1923, GA 258**

"The Anthroposophists of today must not suppose that they have simply the same obligations as those people will one day have, who believe in Anthroposophy, when Anthroposophists are reckoned by millions, and not by thousands. When a few thousands are forerunners in a movement, these thousands are under a far greater, a multiple degree of obligation. They are under the obligation namely, in all and every detail to exercise greater courage, greater energy, greater patience, greater tolerance and, above all things, greater truthfulness. And in this third period the test was laid in particular on *truthfulness* and on *earnestness*. What in a way was necessary, was that the thing should grow up, which formed the theme of discussion on one occasion during the course delivered to the Theologians. It was spoken of then. *That* was what there should have been amongst the little band of Anthroposophists, and *that* is what must come: namely, a feeling, a kind of sense, that Anthroposophy—quite apart from the existence of Anthroposophists—must be looked upon as an independent living Being in itself; as something, so to speak, that goes about amongst us, and to which we are *responsible at* every moment of our lives. It was said in this lecture to the theologians in so many words: *Anthroposophy* is herself an invisible person, going about amongst visible people, and to whom, so long as they are only a little number, they owe the very greatest responsibility,—something, that must really be treated as an invisible person, actually living amongst us, who must be consulted in every single action of life, as to what *she* says to it."

The Being of Anthroposophy, Rudolf Steiner, February 3, 1913, Berlin, GA 145 *

"We know that we are living in an age when the Spirit-Self [Manas] is being prepared; and that, although we are still deeply involved in the development of the Consciousness-Soul, the evolution of the Spirit-Self is being prepared. For we are living in the period of the Consciousness-Soul [1,414 AD-3,574 AD], and looking towards the preparation of the Period of the Spirit-Self [3,574 AD-5,734 AD], in much the same way as the Greeks lived in the Intellectual-Soul Period [747 BC-1,414 AD] the soul of the higher feelings, and looked towards the dawning of the Consciousness-Soul. And just as the Greeks founded philosophy which (in spite of Paul Deussen 1. and others) first existed amongst the Greeks, just as the Greeks founded it during the unfolding of the Intellectual-Soul (or the Higher-Feeling-Soul), when man was still directly experiencing the lingering influence of the *objective* Sophia. just as philosophy then arose and developed in such a way that Dante could look upon it as a real concrete, *actual being*, who brought him consolation after Beatrice had been torn from him by death; so we are living now in the midst of the Consciousness-Soul Period, and are looking for the dawn of the Period of the Spirit-Self, and know that something is once more becoming *objective* to man; which, however, is also carrying forward through the coming times that which man has won while passing through the Period of the Consciousness-Soul.

"What is it that has to be evolved? What has to come to development is the presence of a *new* Sophia. But man has learnt to relate this Sophia to his Consciousness-Soul, and to experience her as directly related to man's being. This is taking place during the Period of the Consciousness-Soul. Thereby this

Sophia has become the being who directly enlightens human beings. For after she has entered into man, she must go outside him taking with her his being, and represent it to him *objectively* once more. In this way did Sophia once enter the human soul and arrive at the point of being so intimately bound up with it that a beautiful love-poem, like that of Dante's 2. could be made about her—*Sophia will again become objective*; but she will take with her that which man is—and represent herself objectively in this form—now not merely as Sophia, but as Anthroposophia—as the Sophia who, after passing through the human soul, through the being of man, henceforth bears that being within her, and thus stands before the enlightened person as once the objective being Sophia stood before the Greeks. This is the progress of the history of human evolution in relation to the spiritual facts under consideration.

"And now I leave it to all those, who wish to examine the matter very minutely, to see how it may also be shown in detail from the destiny of *Sophia, Philosophia and Anthroposophia*, how humanity evolves progressively through the soul principles which we designate the Intellectual-Soul (the soul of the higher feelings), the Consciousness-Soul and the Spirit-Self [Manas]. People will learn how deeply established in the collective being of mankind is that which we have in view through our Anthroposophy. What we receive through Anthroposophy is the essence of ourselves; which first floated towards man in the form of a celestial goddess with whom he was able to come into relationship with, that lived on as Sophia and [then] Philosophia, and which man will again bring forth out of himself, putting it before him as the fruit of true self-knowledge in Anthroposophy. We can wait patiently till the world is willing to prove how deeply founded down to the smallest details is what we have to say.

"For it is the essence of Theosophy or Anthroposophy that its own being consists of what is man's being, and the nature of its efficacy is that man receives and discovers from Theosophy or Anthroposophy what he himself *is*, and has to put it before himself because he must exercise self-knowledge.

"This once floated toward us in the form of a celestial goddess with whom we were able to enter into relationship. This divine being lived on as Sophia and Philosophia, and now we can once again bring her out of ourselves and place her before us as the fruit of true anthroposophical self-knowledge. We can wait patiently until the world is willing to test the depth of the foundations of what we have to say, right down to the smallest details. It is the essence of anthroposophy that its own being consists of *the being of the human,* and its effectiveness, its reality, consists in that we receive from anthroposophy what we ourselves are and what we must place before ourselves, because we must practice self-knowledge.

"Sophia must become present again. But we must learn to relate this Sophia to the Consciousness-Soul, bring her down directly to human beings. And thereby Sophia becomes the being who directly enlightens human beings. After Sophia has entered human beings, she must take their being with her and present it to them outwardly, *objectively*. Thus, Sophia will be drawn into the soul and become inwardly connected. Thus, she will present herself not only as Sophia, but as Anthroposophia—as the Sophia who, after passing through the human soul—*through the very being of the human being*—henceforth bears that being within her. And in this form she will confront enlightened human beings as the *objective* being Sophia who once stood before the Greeks."
A lecture given during the first general meeting of the Anthroposophical Society in Berlin

1. Paul Jakob Deussen (1845-1919) was a German professor of philosophy at University of Kiel and academic researcher of the history and cultures, languages, and literature of the Indian subcontinent. In regards to the Greek origins of Philosophy Rudolf Steiner adds the following:

> "We may even say: Ancient Greek history is, essentially, the gradual loss of primeval wisdom. If we study the philosophers before Socrates, namely Heraclitus, Thales, Anaximenes, Anaxagoras, the philosophers of the tragic epoch, as Nietzsche called them—I have dealt with them in my book *Riddles of Philosophy*, and have tried to give as good as possible a picture, from an external standpoint—if we study these philosophers (but the external writings tell us very little about them), we shall find again and again that the passages which have remained like an oases in a desert, re-echo a great, encompassing wisdom and knowledge which existed in the remote past of human evolution. The words of Heraclitus, of Thales, Anaxagoras and Anaximenes, appear to us as if humanity had, as it were, forgotten its primeval wisdom and only remembered occasionally some fragmentary passages."
>
> Rudolf Steiner, Dornach, Oct. 17, 1919, GA 191

2. Dante Alighieri (Italian poet: c. 1265–September 14, 1321) His *Divine Comedy* originally called *Comedia* (modern Italian: *Commedia*) that led Giovanni Boccaccio to herald it *Divina*, is widely considered one of the most important poems of the Middle Ages and the greatest literary work in the Italian language. A central figure in the *Divine Comedy* is his Florentine muse Beatrice di Folco Portinari. Regarding her, Dante said they first met when he was but nine years old, while she was eight, and he claimed to have fallen in love with her "at first sight." Dante's creations with Beatrice in mind served as classic examples of Courtly Love, a literary genre developed earlier in the French and Provençal Troubadour poetry of prior centuries. Dante's experience of such chaste love inspiration was perhaps typical amongst poets; but his expression of it was unique, not to mention his departure from Latin; choosing instead to write in the Italian vernacular. Consequently

the immeasurable impact of Dante in the literature and language of Italy is akin to the impact of Shakespeare in England or Goethe in Germany; in fact, in Italy he is often referred to as *il Sommo Poeta* ('the Supreme Poet'). It was in the name of this Courtly Love that Dante left his imprint on the *dolce stil nuovo* ('sweet new style'; a term invented by Dante himself), and he would join other contemporary poets and writers in exploring never-before-emphasized aspects of love (*Amore*). By his own account, his love for Beatrice would be his reason for writing poetry and even for living. When Beatrice died in 1290, at the young age of 25, she became the core inspiration for the *Divine Comedy*. In many of his poems, Beatrice is depicted as a semi-divine muse, watching over him constantly and providing him with both spiritual instruction and stern admonitions. In light of this, Dante Alighieri can be considered as representative example, for that time period, of the Intellectual-Soul (Higher-Feeling-Soul) as referred to above by Rudolf Steiner.

The Temple Legend, Rudolf Steiner, Part II, Lecture XII, Concerning the Lost Temple and How it is to be Restored (In connection with the Legend of the True Cross, or Golden Legend) II, Berlin, May 22, 1905, GA 93

"We find the same medieval tendency as manifested in the Knights Templars, in two Round Tables as well, that of King Arthur, and that of the Holy Grail. In King Arthur's Round Table can be found the ancient universality, whereas the spirituality proper to Christian knighthood had to be prepared in those who guarded the Mystery of the Holy Grail. It is remarkable how calmly and tranquilly medieval people contemplated the developing power (fruit) and outward form of Christianity.

"When you follow the teaching of the Templars, there at the heart of it is a kind of reverence for something of a feminine nature. This femininity was known as the Divine Sophia, the Heavenly Wisdom. Manas is the fifth principle. the Spirit-Self of man, that must be developed; for which a temple must be built. And, just as the pentagon at the entrance to Solomon's Temple characterizes the fivefold human being, this female principle similarly typifies the wisdom of the Middle Ages. This wisdom is exactly what Dante sought to personify in his Beatrice. Only from this viewpoint can Dante's *Divine Comedy* be understood. Hence you find Dante, too, using the same symbols as those which find expression in the Templars, the Christian knights, the Knights of the Grail, and so on. Everything which is to happen [in the future] was indeed long since prepared for by the great initiates, who foretell future events, in the same way as in the *Apocalypse*, so that souls will be prepared for these events.

"According to legend we have two different currents when humanity came to the Earth: the children of Cain, whom one of the Elohim begat through Eve, the children of the Earth, in whom we find the great arts and external sciences. That is one of the currents; it was banished, but is however to be sanctified by Christianity, when the fifth principle comes into the world. The other current is that of the children of God, who have led man towards an understanding of the fifth principle. They are the ones that Adam created. Now the sons of Cain were called upon to create an outer sheath, to contain what the sons of God, the Abel-Seth children, created.

"In the Ark of the Covenant lies concealed the Holy Name of Yahveh. However, what is needed to transform the world, to create the sheath for the Holy of Holies, must be accomplished again through the sons of Cain. God created man's physical body, into which man's ego works, at first destroying this temple. Man can only rescue himself if he first builds the house to carry him across the waters of the emotions, if he builds Noah's Ark for himself. This house must set man on his feet again. Now those who came into the world as the children of Cain are building the outward part, and what the children of God have given is building the inner part. These two streams were already current when our race began ... [Gap in text]

"So we shall only understand theosophy when we look upon it as a testament laying the ground for what the Temple of Solomon denotes, and for what the future holds in store. We have to prepare for the New Covenant, in place of the Old Covenant. The old one is the Covenant of the creating God, in which God is at work on the Temple of Mankind. The New Covenant is the one in which man himself surrounds the divine with the Temple of Wisdom, when he restores it, so that this 'I' will find a sanctuary on this Earth when it is resurrected out of matter, set free.

"So profound are the symbols, and so was the instruction, that the Templars wanted to be allowed to confer upon mankind. The Rosicrucians are none other than the successors to the Order of the Templars, wanting nothing else than what the Templars did, which is also what theosophy desires: they are all at work on the great Temple of Humanity."

The Christian Mystery, **Rudolf Steiner, Lecture II,** ***The Medieval View of the World in Dante's Divine Comedy,*** **Düsseldorf, February 11, 1906, GA 97**

"Today we'll consider one of the greatest works in world literature, Dante's *Divine Comedy*. We have to understand that to gain even a little insight into this work we must go back to the 13th and 14th centuries. Goethe has Faust say:

> 'The spirit of our times, as you will say,
> is basically just the gentlemen's own mind
> acting as mirror for the times.'

"When someone wants to discuss a work written in earlier times he usually does so from his own point of view, finding in it the things that come from his own subjective feelings.

"In the case of Dante's *Divine Comedy* we can see how hard it is to go back to the Middle Ages in one's mind... Today people have simply no idea that people in his day still saw something of the spirit in everything material. For them, nothing was wholly physical and nothing purely spiritual. Interweaving matter and spirit was something entirely natural for them. If we enter into such a way of thinking we are alive to the feelings out of which the *Divine Comedy* was written. It is pointless to fight over whether Beatrice was just a symbol or Dante's lover. The two are not contradictory. Beatrice was a real person, and she also stood for all that is spirit. For someone not lead astray by learning—*she was the true personification of Theologia.*

"Let us consider the atmosphere in mind and spirit in which the work evolved. It gives sublime expression to 13th and 14th century strict Christian Catholicism; before the Church came to be divided. People like Cardinal Nicholas of Cusa [1401–August 11, 1464], whose thinking was that of scholasticism. Dante was a student of scholasticism. He saw the world the way his teacher Thomas Aquinas did [c. 1225–March 7, 1274].

"What was the mission of Christianity? It was to create a new basic religious approach. Before that, a girdle of religious views spread around the whole world. Christianity brought a different basic approach to religion...

"...Anyone wishing to understand the medieval view of the ideal Church must organize himself in a higher way so that he may see its original image in the other world. Dante used the views of the heavenly hierarchies held by Dionysius the Areopagite for this. Dionysius wrote of a ranking order of Angels

[Sons of Twilight], Archangels [Spirits of Fire], Principalities [Archai; Spirits of Time], Powers [Exusiai/Elohim; Spirits of Form], Virtues [Dynamis; Spirits of Movement], Dominions [Kyriotetes; Spirits of Wisdom], Thrones [Spirits of Will], Cherubim [Spirits of Harmony], Seraphim [Spirits of Love]. The ranks in the temporal hierarchy of the Church were meant to reflect those heavenly hierarchies. Dante wrote of the hierarchies in symbolic form in the Garden of Eden.

"Then Beatrice took on the role of guide. We distinguish between a female element in the soul, which is inner soul nature, and a male element, which is the spiritual principle in the universe that impregnates the soul. The female soul draws us upwards. ["The Eternal Feminine draws us upwards." Goethe, *Faust*] Medieval alchemists called the female aspect of the human being the 'Lilium.' This is also why Goethe spoke of the 'beautiful Lily' in his *Tale*. [*The Green Snake and the Beautiful Lily*] In the Dantean way of thinking Beatrice represents the edifice of scholastic theology.

"Spirits of the Moon who had broken their spiritual vows were first of all brought before Beatrice. They had broken their vow to serve only the spiritual and had fallen back into sensuality. In ancient Greek theosophy Mercury was still the spirit who had a role to play when the ancient Atlanteans advanced to a concept of the I. The earliest Atlanteans were not yet conscious of the I. The personal comes under the sign of the god Mercury, Hermes. Man came to the personal level when he fell into I-nature, egotism. This also made us into people who want to have possessions and is the reason why Mercury was also the god of merchants.

"On Jupiter Dante found the princes who exercised justice. Something very important occurred on the Sun. Dante was shown the true nature of eternity on the Sun; how to see the day known as the Day of Judgement. The Day of Judgement changes everything. Two people made their appearance—Thomas Aquinas and King Solomon. Thomas Aquinas represented life in terms of Christianity, of the *New Testament*, and King Solomon was the teacher of the *Old Testament*.

"Christians saw the priesthood as a physical expression of what the Christ meant to them in spiritual development. After life on Earth the Christ had gone away and was now triumphant in the fixed star heaven. Someone who has prepared his spiritual embryo here on Earth so that he has spiritual vision is able to see the Christ in the fixed-star heaven. The disciple who had been most profoundly initiated, John, appeared as the teacher of this view. Only the Christ and Mary were able to take their bodies up into the fixed star heaven. A master also has his body fully in hand. Just as people are learning to master their passions with moral ideas in our present civilization, so does someone who has reached a higher level truly learn to control the physical body. Jesus and Mary had hallowed their physical body to such a degree that they were able to take it with them to the highest regions.

"Then St. Bernard 1. became the guide for the higher regions where God is beheld and one enters wholly into the divine self. There Dante went beyond the teachings of the Church. He saw the three cycles, the threefold original essence of the world, Father, Son and Holy Spirit. They are called Brahma, Vishnu and Shiva in Indian religion. Here the Trinitarian nature of the universe became apparent, with Dante rising to pure vision in the spirit, to contemplation.

"In the end we are shown how we live, move and are in God but must not presume to understand God. In the end, Dante only wrote of growing certainty in the human ability to recognize God. For him, this work was the drama of the world seen from the other side."

Note:

1. Bernard of Clairvaux, O. Cist. (Latin: Bernardus Claraevallensis; 1090–August 20, 1153), venerated as Saint Bernard, was an abbot, mystic, healer, co-founder of the Knights Templar, and a major leader in the reformation of the Benedictine Order through the nascent Cistercian Order. Saint Bernard founded the Abbey of Clairvaux within a remote glen in France known as the Val d'Absinthe, about 9 miles southeast of Bar-sur-Aube. In the year 1128, Bernard attended the Council of Troyes, during which he wrote the Rule of the Knights Templars, which soon became an ideal of Christian nobility. The origin of the cult of the veneration of the Virgin Mary can be traced back to Saint Bernard.

   "Looking back at the three great Cultural Periods which Spiritual Science shows us in our Present Earth-cycle, we find that the third ends about the seventh or eighth century B.C., and the fourth with the beginning of the fifteenth century A.D. At this point there lies, not far behind us, an important, significant transition in the soul-life of civilized humanity. Usually it is hardly touched upon in history—and why? There, too, is the dread of self-knowledge, and also of knowledge of the human soul. An interesting example of the time antecedent to the change can be found in accounts of a personality such as St. Bernard of Clairvaux. St. Bernard, perhaps the most outstanding personality of the twelfth century, and indeed of the age with which the fourth Post-Atlantean Period of civilization came to an end, manifested a structure of soul which after the fifteenth century was no longer possible in Europe. Nowadays it is very hard to describe this, because the preconditions for forming the right conceptions are altogether lacking; but I advise you to read accounts of the life of St. Bernard so as to see the impression he made on other people. Reading these accounts, one says to oneself: By the side of these, what are the

Gospel stories of Miracles? The few sick folk healed by Christ Jesus himself—according to the *Gospels*—are a trifle compared with the astonishing wonder-working activities of St. Bernard! The number of people of whom it is said that he made the blind to see and lame to walk, is beyond all comparison with the number of similar cases reported in the *Gospels*. The accounts of the impression made by his preaching gives one the feeling that what he said acted as a widespread, intensely active spiritual aura. In the words of this man there lived a reality of which we can have no conception at the present day. If one tried to describe all the effects produced by his personality, people would simply not believe it for there is no possibility nowadays of giving an adequate idea of how he was then regarded. To penetrate to the inner structure of his soul, is, as I have said, difficult today, because, even in our own circle, the conditions for it are wanting."

Rudolf Steiner, Lecture Berlin, July 16, 1918 (GA 181)

Brunetto Latini, Rudolf Steiner, Lecture, Dornach, January 30, 1915, GA 161

"…Man, to begin with, on the Earth, is for himself the only example—the only document he has brought over from the spiritual world. Therefore he must pass through this—*the document of his own being*. He must go through himself. This was always known to those who experienced anything of Initiation. Thus it was known to Brunetto Latini, teacher and friend of Dante. Moreover, it is characteristic how Brunetto Latini's Initiation, as we may call it, was eventually brought about. It happened by a particular event. That is what frequently occurs. Fundamentally speaking, everyone who sets his foot on the path of spiritual science is waiting for the portal of the spiritual world to be opened to him sooner or later, as indeed it will be. It may be—indeed it often is so—that the entry to the spiritual world takes place by degrees. Then we grow slowly into the spiritual world. Nevertheless, very, very frequently it happens that the world is opened to us as by a kind of shock which breaks in upon our life—by a sudden and unexpected event.

"Thus, as Brunetto Latini himself relates, he had been sent as ambassador to the ruler of Castile. On his way back he learned that his party, the Guelphs, had been expelled from Florence. Florence had utterly changed during his absence. This message brought him into confusion. Such confusion of our state of soul which is suited to the outer physical world, often goes hand-in-hand with what becomes the starting-point for an entry into the spiritual world.

"Brunetto Latini goes on to relate how as a result of his confusion, instead of riding home, he rode into a neighboring forest, quite unaware of what he was doing (or so at any rate he afterwards believed when he looked back on it). Then, when he came to himself, he had a strange and unwanted impression. He saw no longer the ordinary world of the physical plane around him; but something that looked like an immense mountain. He did not come to himself again in that consciousness which normally confronts the physical world. He came to consciousness over against quite another world than that which was physically there around him. There was an immense mountain; but these things were such that they came and went—came into being and passed away again. There at the side of the mountain stood a woman, according to whose commands that which arose, arose, and that which passed away, passed away again.

"Brunetto Latini now beheld the laws and principles of Nature's working in the forms of Imagination. All Nature's laws—the living and creative essence of Nature herself—came before him in an Imagination, in the figure of a woman who gave her orders for all these things to arise and pass away again.

"We must imagine ourselves living in the time of the thirteenth, fourteenth century, when the natural scientific way of thought was slowly entering. In later times, men spoke abstractly of the 'Laws of Nature'; they would on no account imagine that there was any reality of being behind the totality of Nature's laws. Brunetto Latini, however, saw it in the form of Imagination, as a woman, out of whose spirit proceeded all that was subsequently felt as the abstract Laws of Nature, like a Word that held sway throughout Nature, which stood before him in living Imagination.

"This woman, he relates, then bade him deepen the forces of his soul; so would he enter more and more deeply into himself. Here it is interesting. Raying out over him her forces, as it were, she gives him the possibility to enter more and more deeply into himself. He dives down into his own being, and the sequence he now indicates is indeed, under certain conditions, the true sequence of Initiation.

"The first thing, he tells us, which he now learned to know were the forces of the soul. Diving down into himself, man does indeed learn to know what otherwise remains unconscious in him—the forces of his soul. This recognition of his own soul-forces is a thing from which man will often flee, when he draws near to it. For when we perceive the forces of the soul, it often seems to us that we say to ourselves: 'What an unsympathetic soul that is!' We do not like this feeling, any more than the worthy professor did when he saw his own form, which was distasteful to him. We do not want to see. For with the chorus of the soul's forces we often see many a thing we have within us; which we by no means attribute to ourselves in ordinary life. We see it as something that is at work in the totality of our own being—

enhancing our being, or making it smaller; making us of greater or lesser value for the Universe.

"Thus, to begin with, we rise into the soul-forces. At the next stage, we experience the four temperaments. There it becomes clear to us how we are woven together, of the choleric, melancholic, sanguine, and phlegmatic, and how this weaving together lies deeper down than the soul-forces.

"Then, when we have gone through the temperaments, we come to what may be called the five senses—*in the occult sense.* For in the way man ordinarily speaks of the five senses, he only knows them from outside. You cannot learn to know the senses inwardly till you have descended through the temperaments into the deeper regions of your own self. Then you behold the eyes, the ears, the other senses from within. You experience your own eyes, for instance, or your ears—*feeling them from within.* You must imagine it thus. Just as you came into this hall through this door, and perceived the objects and persons that were already here, so when you undergo this descent into yourself you come into the region of your eyes or your ears. There you perceive how the forces are working from within outward, to bring about your seeing and your hearing. You perceive an altogether complicated world, of which a man who only knows the outer physical plane has no idea at all.

"Some, no doubt, will say: 'Maybe, but this world of the eyes and the ears will not impress me greatly. The world of the physical plane which I have around me here is great, and the world of the eyes and ears is very small. I should be gazing into a minute world.'

"That, however, is Maya [illusion]. What you envisage when you are within your ears or within your eyes is far greater, fuller in content, than the outer physical world. *You have a far more abundant world around you there.*

"Then and then only, when you have gone through this region, you come into the realm of the four elements. We have already spoken of all the properties of the several elements; but it is only at this stage that you feel really within them—within the earthy, the watery, the airy, and the element of warmth.

"Man ordinarily knows his senses from without. Here now he learns to know them from within. Consciously entering into the eye from within, he then breaks through the eye, and breaking through the eye comes into the four elements. But he can likewise break through the ear, or the sense of taste.

"By these four elements he is perpetually surrounded, only he does not know what they are inwardly. He cannot see it with outer organs of sense. He must first get out of the sense-organs—albeit, get out of them *from within*. He must leave them again, as though by a gateway. He must get out, through his eye or his ear. So he slips through—through the eye, through the ear—and comes into the region of the elements. And in the region of the elements he learns to know all the spiritual beings who are living there—the manifold Nature-spirits, and Beings who belong to the Hierarchies nearest to man.

"Then, going on and on, he comes into the region of the seven Planets. He is already farther outside, and learns to know what is creatively connected with man, in the Great Universe (Macrocosm). And then at last he has to cross *Oceanos*—the 'Great Ocean,' as it has always been called.

> The Soul-forces
> The Four Temperaments
> The Five Senses
> The Four Elements
> The Seven Planets
> The Ocean.

"What does this passing through the Ocean signify? Man can approach the planets while with the last portion of his soul's being he still remains within the physical. But when he thus goes inward through the gates of the senses, eventually he must take with him the very last relics of his soul, so that he may consciously enter the condition in which he is normally only in sleep. Ordinarily, when he is with the planets, he still remains in the body with a portion, as it were, with a fragment of his soul. But when he draws even this last out of the body, it seems to him as though he were floating through *the Universal Ocean of Spiritual Being.*

"All this, Brunetto Latini undergoes. He tells how he undertook one after another of these steps, at the behest of the woman who appeared to him in his Imaginative cognition. Then she instructed him that he must go still farther. This, however, was at a particular moment, which again is highly characteristic.

"Think of the situation. Perplexed, at a loss on account of what has happened in his paternal city, he rides into a forest. He comes to himself again; but this awakening leads him not into the physical world. It leads him through all the regions which we have here described. Then, however, the moment arises when, not by accident, not by mere chance—*but by the definite summons of this woman he sees himself in the forest once more.* Having undergone all these things, having passed through the soul-forces and the temperaments and through the senses outward into the elemental world, where he already perceived abundant spiritual life; having perceived the seven planets, and through them the higher Hierarchies, circle on circle; having felt himself at length not on the solid ground but swimming as it were, swimming through the Great Ocean; now he awakens again in the physical world.

"That is the very significant thing we recognize in all these Initiations. The disciple passes through a complete cycle and returns again into the physical world.

"Having lived through all this, Brunetto Latini feels himself once more in his forest. Now he is really surrounded by all that is physically about him. And presently the woman is there again at his side; albeit he now has the physical forest around him. She tells him to ride on towards the right, and she gives him instruction on how he shall come to *Philosophy* and to the *four Virtues* of man, and to the knowledge of *the God of Love*."

Towards the end of Steiner's life, he often referred to Anthroposophia as the living being who fills Anthroposophy with the wisdom (Sophia) of Christ. He even equates Anthroposophia with the Spirits of Wisdom, who some now know as the 'Daughter.' Anthroposophia seems to have the power and characteristics of the Beings of Wisdom (Kyriotetes). In one way of looking at it, you could say that the Cosmic Being of Wisdom fills Anthroposophia just as Christ fills the Holy Spirit. Again, this points in the direction of a Divine Feminine Trinity and the co-equal power shared by the three members of the Trinity.

What we receive through Anthroposophy is the essence of ourselves, which in former times descended to man in order to manifest itself as a celestial goddess with whom he was able to find a personal relationship, who lived as the Sophia, as Philo-Sophia, and to whom he will give birth again out of himself, placing her before him as the fruit of true self-knowledge in Anthroposophy. For the being of anthroposophy is such that its own being consists in that which constitutes the essence of man's being and the nature of its influence is that man receives in Anthroposophy what he himself is; and that he must place this before him—*through the practice of self-knowledge.*

The mysteries of Sophia are spoken of by Rudolf Steiner in ways that no one fully understands. The nature of Anthroposophia as a truly human being is referred to again and again. What he insinuates is that the 'human' being of Anthroposophia is essentially a template to serve the collective consciousness of humanity as it develops over the course of history. This is what makes Anthroposophia so 'human' in every way except for not having a physical body. Anthroposophia seems to 'defy' space and time as She is present to every human who is progressing on their personal spiritual path. She works with each individual and is personally present for each person. She is intimately concerned with our personal advancement and takes our hand and shows us the way. These characteristics are inexplicable to the rational mind, and yet Steiner focuses on his students becoming aware of all aspects of the workings of this being.

The Anthroposophic Movement, Rudolf Steiner, VII, *The Consolidation of the Anthroposophic Movement,* Dornach, June 16, 1923, GA 18

"…Irrespective of the fact that individual anthroposophists exist, a feeling should have developed, and must develop, among them that Anthroposophia exists as a separate being, who moves about among us, as it were, towards whom we carry a responsibility in every moment of our lives. Anthroposophia is actually an invisible person who walks among visible people and towards whom we must show the greatest responsibility for as long as we are a small group. Anthroposophia is someone who must be understood as an invisible person, as someone with a real existence, who should be consulted in the individual actions of our lives. Thus, if connections form between people—friendships, cliques and so on—at a time when the group of anthroposophists is still small, it is all the more necessary to consult and to be able to justify all one's actions before this invisible person."

***Perception of the Nature of Thought*, Rudolf Steiner, Dornach, January 10, 1915, GA 161**

"Thus, we are living today in the midst of the Consciousness-Soul Period [1,414 AD-3,574 AD];, looking towards the dawn of the age of the Spirit-Self [E. European Period 3,574 AD-5,734 AD]; and we know that something is separating itself off from man, something which will, however, carry through the times that are to come what man has won as the fruit of passing through the Consciousness-Soul Period. What is it that has to be developed? What must be developed is without doubt the presence once again amongst mankind of a 'Sophia.' But man has learnt to relate this 'Sophia' to his Consciousness-Soul, to bring her into direct relationship with human beings. This has taken place during the Consciousness-Soul Period, and the Sophia has thereby become the being who explains man as such. Once she has entered into man, she must take his being with her and place it objectively before him from without. Thus the Sophia enters into the human soul and separates it again, but she will take with her man's essential being and place it objectively before him—now not merely as the 'Sophia' but as Anthroposophia, as the Sophia who, after passing through the human soul, through man's being, henceforth bears this being of man within her and thus appears before an enlightened human being as once the Sophia stood as an objective being before the Greeks."

***The Christmas Foundation Conference*, Part II, *The Proceedings of the Conference*, Rudolf Steiner, Lecture IV, *The Laying of the Foundation Stone*, GA 260**

"For decades it has been possible to perceive this threefoldness of man which enables him in the wholeness of his being of spirit, soul and body to revive for himself once more in a new form the call 'Know thyself.' For decades it has been possible to perceive this threefoldness. But only in the last decade have I myself been able to bring it to full maturity while the storms of war were raging. I sought to indicate how man lives in the physical realm in his system of metabolism and limbs, in his system of heart and rhythm, in his system of thinking and perceiving with his head. Yesterday I indicated how this threefoldness can be rightly taken up when our hearts are enlivened through and through by Anthroposophia.

"We may be sure that if man learns to know in his feeling and in his will what he is actually doing when, as the Spirits of the Universe enliven him, he lets his limbs place him in the world of space, that then—not in a suffering, passive grasping of the Universe but in an active grasping of the world in which he fulfils his duties, his tasks, his mission on the earth—that then in this active grasping of the world he will know the being of all-wielding love of man and Universe which is one member of the All-World-Being.

"We may be sure that if man understands the miraculous mystery holding sway between lung and heart—expressing inwardly the beat of universal rhythms working across millennia, across the aeons of time to ensoul him with the Universe through the rhythms of pulse and blood—we may hope that, grasping this in wisdom with a heart that has become a sense organ, man can experience the divinely given universal images as out of themselves they actively reveal the cosmos. Just as in active movement we grasp the all-wielding love of worlds, so shall we grasp the archetypal images of world existence when we sense in ourselves the mysterious interplay between universal rhythm and heart rhythm, and through this the human rhythm that takes place mysteriously in soul and spirit realms in the interplay between lung and heart.

"And when, in feeling, the human being rightly perceives what is revealed in the system of his head, which is at rest on his shoulders even when he walks along, then, feeling himself within the system of his head and pouring warmth of heart into this system of his head, he will experience the ruling, working, weaving thoughts of the Universe within his own being.

"Thus he becomes the threefoldness of all existence: Universal Love reigning in Human Love; Universal Imagination reigning in the forms of the human organism; Universal Thoughts reigning mysteriously below the surface in Human Thoughts. He will grasp this threefoldness and he will recognize himself as an individually free human being within the reigning work of the gods in the Cosmos, as a cosmic human being, an individual human being within the cosmic human being, working for the future of the universe as an individual human being within the cosmic human being. Out of the signs of the present time he will re-enliven the ancient words: 'Know thou thyself!'

"The Greeks were still permitted to omit the final word, since for them the human self was not yet as abstract as it is for us now that it has become concentrated in the abstract ego-point or at most in thinking, feeling and willing. For them human nature comprised the totality of spirit, soul and body. Thus the ancient Greeks were permitted to believe that they spoke of the total human being, spirit, soul and body, when they let resound the ancient word of the Sun, the word of Apollo: 'Know thou thyself!'

"Today, re-enlivening these words in the right way out of the signs of our times, we have to say: Soul of man, know thou thyself in the weaving existence of spirit, soul and body. When we say this, we have understood what lies at the foundation of all aspects of the being of man. In the substance of the Universe there works and is and lives the spirit which streams from the heights and reveals itself in the human head; the force of Christ working in the circumference, weaving in the air, encircling the Earth, works and lives in the system of our breath; and from the inmost depths of the Earth rise up the forces which work in our limbs. When now, at this moment, we unite these three forces, the forces of the heights, the forces of the circumference, the forces of the depths, in a substance that gives form, then in the understanding of our soul we can bring face to face the Universal Dodecahedron with the Human Dodecahedron. Out of these three forces: out of the spirit of the heights, out of the force of Christ in the circumference, out of the working of the Father, the creative activity of the Father that streams out of the depths, let us at this moment give form in our souls to the Dodecahedral Foundation Stone which we lower into the soil of our souls so that it may remain there a powerful sign in the strong foundations of our soul existence and so that in the future working of the Anthroposophical Society we may stand on this firm Foundation Stone.

"Let us ever remain aware of this Foundation Stone for the Anthroposophical Society, formed today. In all that we shall do, in the outer world and here, to further, to develop and to fully unfold the Anthroposophical Society, let us preserve the remembrance of the Foundation Stone which we have today lowered into the soil of our hearts. Let us seek in the threefold being of man, which teaches us love, which teaches us the Universal Imagination, which teaches us the Universal Thoughts; let us seek, in this threefold being, the substance of Universal Love which we lay as the foundation, let us seek in this threefold being the archetype of the Imagination according to which we shape the Universal Love within our hearts, let us seek the power of thoughts from the heights which enable us to let shine forth in fitting manner this dodecahedral Imagination which has received its form through love! Then shall we carry away with us from here what we need. Then shall the Foundation Stone shine forth before the eyes of our soul, that Foundation Stone which has received its substance from Universal Love and Human Love, its picture image, its form, from Universal Imagination and Human Imagination, and its brilliant radiance from Universal Thoughts and Human Thoughts, its brilliant radiance which whenever we recollect this moment can shine towards us with warm light, with light that spurs on our deeds, our thinking, our feeling and our willing.

"The proper soil into which we must lower the Foundation Stone of today, the proper soil consists of our hearts in their harmonious collaboration, in their good, love-filled desire to bear together the will of Anthroposophy through the world. This will cast its light on us like a reminder of the Light of Thought that can ever shine towards us from the Dodecahedral Stone of Love which today we will lower into our hearts."

With the being of Anthroposophia we find a clear and detailed biography of one of the three aspects of the Divine Feminine Trinity. Through developing a relationship with the being Anthroposophia, the Wisdom of Christ unfolds revealing the cosmic workings of the Son (Elohim) and the Daughter (Kyriotetes). The evolving spiritual scientist needs the Holy Spirit to reveal the nature of the Cosmic Christ through the being of Anthroposophia in the realm of the Spirit-Self. Likewise, through Sophia (Beings of Wisdom) the nature of the Son of God is revealed through the Archangel (Archai) Michael in the realm of the Life-Spirit. Then, through the Mother, the Father God is revealed by the Archai in the realm of Spirit-Human. Anthroposophia has the task of bringing us to the understanding of the other members of both the Male and Female Trinities. Through Anthroposophia, we come to communicate with the higher realms, discern wisdom and know the beings who inhabit those realms.

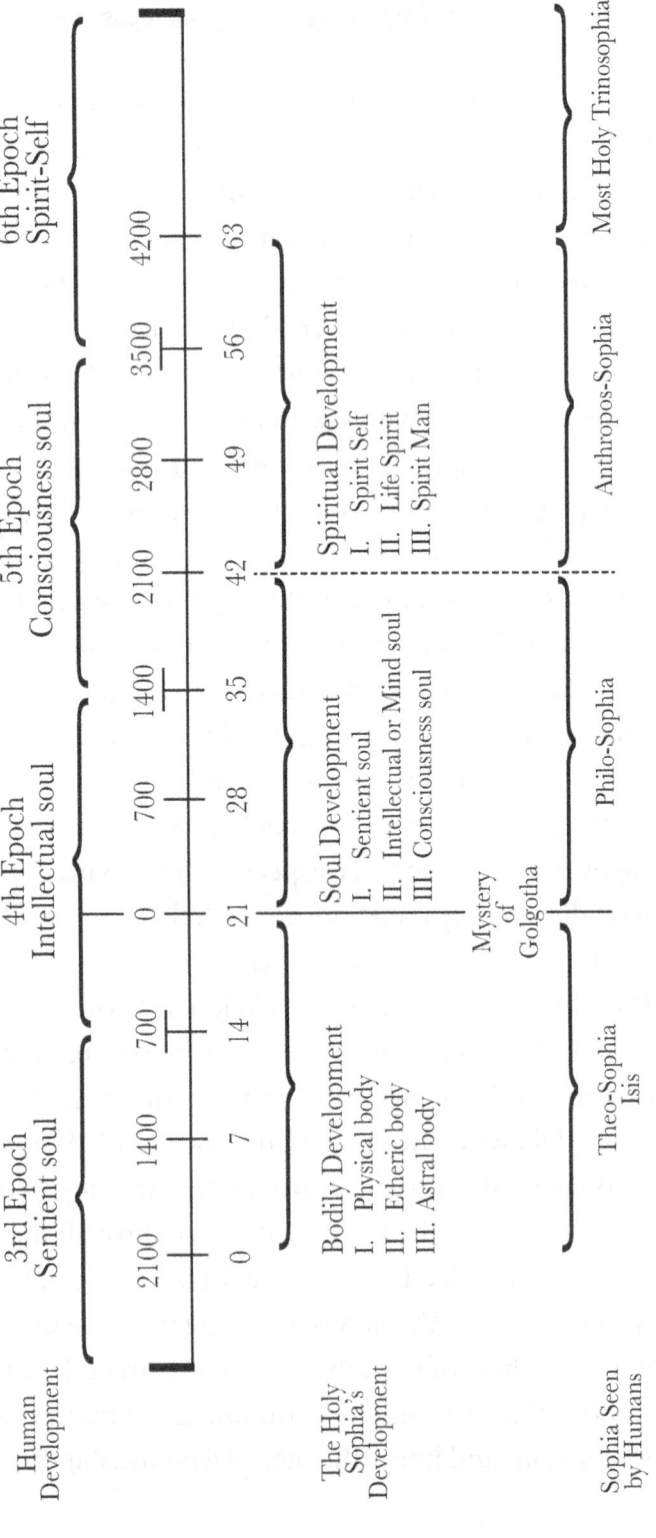

The Realm of 'The Mothers'

A great deal of confusion hovers around Steiner's references to the three elemental worlds; often they are conflated with elemental beings, elemental forces, and the etheric formative forces. Out of a need for clarification about this most important area of Steiner's cosmology, this chapter offers a summary of Steiner's indication on the topic and some responses from some of his students.

Oskar Kurten's 2018 book, *Symphonies of Creation: The Primal Elementary Kingdoms in the Work of Rudolf Steiner* does a marvelous job presenting a description of the three elemental kingdoms, taken directly from the works of Rudolf Steiner. Other books have recently been published concerning this topic that have caused great confusion and are in error—according to Steiner's own words. These elemental realms have seldom ever been addressed by anthroposophists and therefore Kurten's book is one of the only attempts to comprehensively present this topic. The topic is difficult, and Kurten's book is difficult to read and comprehend. Thus, we have summarized some of the major points of the book to clarify what Rudolf Steiner was indicating concerning elemental kingdoms (worlds, realms, beings).

Just as confusing, and perhaps more debated, is the topic of the 'The Mothers' that Steiner speaks about repeatedly in his lectures on Goethe's *Faust*. Even though he is quite clear about who The Mothers are and what functions they play in human life, their existence is debated and often dismissed as an aspect of Anthroposophia that is 'forbidden' to discuss. When the debate reaches fever pitch, one side reminds the other that Steiner indicated there is a 'Being' called Anthroposophia, whose genesis and nature is described in *The Riddles of Philosophy* and then the discussion goes off the rails.

Once Anthroposophia is given her rightful place and the 'Heavenly Sophia' (the combined beings of the Kyriotetes, the Beings of Wisdom), who most Anthroposophists will acknowledge as a key component of Steiner's cosmology, is added to the overall picture, we are one step away from the obvious reality that The Mothers, Anthroposophia, and the Heavenly Sophia comprises a 'Trinity of the Feminine Divine.' We have placed before the reader a comprehensive presentation of the Divine Feminine Trinity, as a coequal being with the Divine Male Trinity (Father, Son, and Holy Spirit), in our trilogy called, *The Gospel of Sophia* by Tyla Gabriel.

The three elemental worlds are understood as the realms of 'The Mothers,' the student of Spiritual Science can then see the cosmological importance of the place of the spiritual hierarchies in human development from the view of Anthroposophia. Reading Steiner's summary of *The Riddles of Philosophy*, as presented below, will demonstrate the proper place of Anthroposophia, The Mothers, and the elemental realms. Reading the summary of Kurten's book, also presented below, will underscore Steiner's idea that The Mothers comprise the three elemental kingdoms. When the full picture arises, the debate could be over. Steiner implies that Sophia is a threefold being who is the helper of the Christ, even throughout the Pre-Earthly Deeds of Christ. The threefold Sophia is known as The Mothers, the Daughter, and Holy Sophia (Anthroposophia). This revelation has been placed in the works of Dr. Steiner for those with 'eyes to see' and 'ears to hear.'

Anthroposophia and
The Riddles of Philosophy

Many spiritual scientists heartily embrace Rudolf Steiner's injunctions to seek the Being of Anthroposophia in their personal spiritual development but are quite confused who this being is or where they can find Her. One of the best places to find a description of the Being Anthroposophia is in the book, *The Riddles of Philosophy*, Steiner's sweeping philosophic picture of the development of human thinking.

Anthroposophia is not given that name in the book, but Steiner makes it clear that the development of human thinking is also the development of the Being Anthroposophia. As Steiner describes the historical thought processes of philosophers, he points out that a being develops alongside philosophy in stages of about six or seven hundred years. Four stages of this evolution of thought are described in detail, outlining the nature of the growing Being Anthroposophia.

We are not concerned with producing a full expose on the Being Anthroposophia in this book because we have previously discussed her at length in the trilogy of books, *The Gospel of Sophia*. Accepting the reality of a Being who 'passes through you' every time you advance in spiritual development is somewhat understandable as a personal experience. Steiner calls Anthroposophia the "midwife of the soul" who helps lead us to the spirit. In *The Gospel of Sophia,* we call this third person of the Divine Feminine Trinity the Holy Sophia (Anthroposophia).

Another aspect of the Divine Feminine Trinity is also described in detail by Rudolf Steiner throughout his books and lectures. The Being of Wisdom/Sophia (Sophia means wisdom), the leader of the Kyriotetes (Spirits of Wisdom), descended along with the Being of Love (Christ), the leader of the highest ranks of the Elohim. Heavenly Sophia, from the Kyriotetes, descended as far as the Angel realm whereas Christ descended from the Holy Trinity into the ranks of the Kyriotetes and down to the Elohim, ultimately ending in the human realm. In *The

Gospel of Sophia, the Kyriotetes (Spirits of Wisdom) are referred to as the Daughter of Sophia (Daughter of The Mothers). Rudolf Steiner and Sergei O. Prokofieff call Her the Heavenly Sophia from the Kyriotetes (Spirits of Wisdom).

Rudolf Steiner's many descriptions of this Being are scattered throughout his works and some anthroposophists understand the significance of this cosmic piece of the puzzle. The Being of Wisdom (Sophia of the Kyriotetes) has created the wisdom we can find in Nature, and the wisdom found in the constitution of the human body. Wisdom prevails throughout the Cosmos as the activity of the Heavenly Sophia, the leader of the Beings of Wisdom (the Daughter of The Mothers) who finds Her place in anthroposophical cosmology alongside Christ during His descent into the human realm. Students of Spiritual Science eventually put together all of the references concerning Anthroposophia, the Heavenly Sophia, and The Mothers, and it adds up to a threefold Being of Wisdom who Steiner openly described but did not name as a Divine Feminine Trinity.

When it comes to understanding the nature of the Sophia that Steiner calls The Mothers, many anthroposophists part ways with Rudolf Steiner and refuse to consider the indications where he describes three distinct 'beings of wisdom' that manifest in his anthroposophical cosmology. The problem for most anthroposophists is that Steiner does not give a name to two of the three beings in the Divine Feminine Trinity. Steiner names Anthroposophia and describes her (without naming her) in *The Riddles of Philosophy*.

Rudolf Steiner also clearly names the three previous incarnations of the Earth—Old Saturn, Old Sun, and Old Moon—as the three Greek gods Zeus, Chronos, and Chthon who created 'fire, air, and water' just as the Old Saturn incarnation of the Earth created warmth, the Old Sun incarnation created air, and the Old Moon incarnation created water. Zeus rules the ether, Chronos rules space, and Chthon rules matter. These three Mothers (who Steiner calls The Mothers) created all that is in the outer world. These Three Mothers created the earthly substance which gives humanity a firm world to 'come up against' to discover their true nature.

Spiritual Scientific Notes on Goethe's Faust, **Volume II, Rudolf Steiner, Lecture IV,** *Faust and the 'Mothers,'* **Dornach, November 2, 1917, GA 273**

"Moreover, when we take our Earth upon which we are still evolving, and about which we cannot speak as of something completed, and when we look from this Earth to Old Saturn, Old Sun, and Old Moon, there we find the 'Mothers' that figure in another form in the Greek Mysteries under names Proserpina, Demeter, and Rhea. For all the forces that are in Old Saturn, Old Sun, and Old Moon are still working—working on into our own time. And those forces that are physical are but the shadow, the image, of what is spiritual. Everything physical is a mere picture of the spiritual."

The human being finds himself as the 'world serpent' interwoven with the creation of The Mothers from the past (Old Saturn, Old Sun, Old Moon) wrestling with the present and trying to get back to The Mother's home through the process. Steiner tells us in *The Riddles of Philosophy* that the thinking human being finds himself identified with Ophioneus, the giant who wrestles with the cosmic serpent.

The soul also feels that it cannot know anything of its own origin at first, because it sees itself in the midst of a world in which The Mothers work in conjunction with Ophioneus. It feels itself in a world in which the perfect and the imperfect are joined together. Ophioneus is twisted into the soul's own being.

This "soul's own being" is the human ego that must balance the past, present and the future in all considerations by wrestling with the imperfect and carrying it back to its origins in the perfect—The Mothers. This wrestling is actually a description of the development of 'world serpent thinking' that exists in both realms of the perfect and imperfect. Thinking is both the lawfulness of the outer world of nature and the lawfulness found in the human soul and spirit. Thinking is the bridge between The Mothers of the past (Old Saturn, Old Sun, Old Moon) and the human being's astral body, etheric body, and physical body, which were donated by The Mothers during Old Saturn, Old Sun, and Old Moon.

The ego of the human being was donated by Christ during the Earth incarnation and is represented by the giant Ophioneus wrestling with the serpent. Often, the serpent represents wisdom and self-awareness, much like the Tree of Knowledge was the home of the serpent of the knowledge of good and evil.

The Mothers are also portrayed in the Greek goddesses Erebus, Nyx, and Hemera. Greek gods derive from primal Greek goddesses and thus it was understood that The Mothers were divine beings who could 'give birth' and create fire (warmth), air, and water (fluids). Do not imagine that a Greek god was strictly 'male.' Many Greek divinities were both male and female, like Hemera and Eros.

The Mothers

Zeus	Space	Saturn
Chronos	Time	Sun
Chthon	Matter	Moon

Rudolf Steiner goes to great lengths in *The Riddles of Philosophy* to give numerous names to The Mothers so there would be no mistaking the fact that they are *feminine* in nature.

Here are some of the names Steiner uses to describes The Mothers:

- Three Mothers of the world's origin
- The Mothers
- Primeval Mothers
- Original Causes
- Spirit, soul, and matter

- Fire, air, water
- Good Mothers of all origin
- Primordial Mothers
- Perfect good
- Beneficial world processes

Rudolf Steiner clearly described two Sophia's—Anthroposophia and the Being of Wisdom (Kyriotetes). Once we add the picture of the Primal Mother—The Mothers—it is obvious that Steiner taught that Sophia is three distinct beings joined in a trinity of beings. Some scholars call them—the Mother, the Daughter, and the Holy Sophia. The descriptions presented below are a compilation of the ideas found in *The Riddles of Philosophy* that clearly describe both the evolving Being of Anthroposophia (also called Holy Sophia) and the Primal Mother(s). Together, we have the first theological, sophiological, and philosophical definition of a Divine Feminine Trinity that is directly linked to the Divine Male Trinity of Father, Son, and Holy Spirit (Father God, Jesus Christ, the Holy Spirit).

The evolving human thinking that Steiner calls the Being of Anthroposophia, as described in *The Riddles of Philosophy*, places the Greek thinker in the temple of the Primal Mother or the Temple of Wisdom (Sophia). This Temple of Wisdom was created by the donations and sacrifices of the divine hierarchies in the three prior stages of the Earth—Old Saturn, Old Sun, and Old Moon. The Temple of Wisdom (Sophia) is where the Greek thinker began the awakening of the forces of the human ego—the human thinker—as it wrestled to understand the outer world, which was for the most part a complete mystery. The wisdom of the world was taught to the thinker through completely immersing the thinker in The Mothers.

All that arose from the gifts of the divine in the past were seen as the wisdom of The Mothers. The Greek 'thinker' needed to distinguish himself as separate from the world of The Mothers if they were to become independent thinkers. Thus, the Giant Ophioneus, who represents the human ego, had to wrestle self-knowledge from The Mothers from the world of wisdom around them.

In mythology, Ophioneus wrestled with the serpent but today the thinking human being (ego) wrestles with the outside world and attempts to tame its forces for the 'Good.' Ophioneus represents the modern philosopher trying to tame the forces of the serpent (dragon) found in the astral body of desires. If those astral forces are tamed, the philosopher then can become like Asclepius, the great healer who tamed the serpent Ophiuchus and was raised into the starry heavens as his own constellation. The Greeks looked to the starry heavens as a Temple of Wisdom that taught them the virtues of the archetypes found in the stories describing the characters who had been raised up into that divine realm. Asclepius wrestled with the serpent and was bitten by it, but finally he learned to hear the language the serpent spoke, thus making him *filled with the wisdom of the gods*.

The human ego can also wrestle with the astral body of desires and learn to tame its wild fury into calm wisdom and thereby be raised into the heavens as a new archetype. The taming of the astral body of desires is accomplished by understanding and refining the astral body so that it can become a new supersensible organ that can perceive spiritual realities. These new organs not only perceive the moral world order, but also allow the philosopher to perceive the world of the gods—the divine realms. Sometimes this is called 'seeing the astral light'; and at other times it is called the capacity of Moral Imagination.

Imagination is a new way of seeing with new sense organs that must be developed through higher thinking, love, and moral action. Asclepius brought the healing arts to Greece through the practice of interpreting dreams that would arise while a person slept in the healing temple. The archetypes would speak to the person while asleep and the priests would translate the dreams. This was a passive form of seeing into the spiritual world where thinking was unawakened and sleepy.

In today's world, we must consciously develop the higher capacities of thought that Steiner describes as the fourth stage of the evolution of Anthroposophia (Holy Sophia) in *The Riddles of Philosophy*. Steiner calls this consciousness 'thinking about thinking' which is a new stage of philosophical development that helps build the strength to wrestle with the serpent of wisdom. Observing the process of thinking itself leads the philosopher to the Asclepian personal ego that is coming towards the individual from the outer world. The world (Primal Mother—The Mothers) brings the revelation of the true nature of the human ego, but it is the wrestling with wisdom (serpent) that brings the possibility that one can 'write your destiny in the stars' as the Greek gods, goddesses, heroes, and heroines did.

For the Greek thinker, there was wisdom written in the starry constellations that tell them about the Primal Mother. All around us, the Mother speaks through the wisdom of nature. When we can hear the language of the serpent (wisdom), just like Eve in the Garden of Eden, we can then discern good from evil and possess the ego awareness necessary to act with morality and love. The true philosopher (philo-lover, Sophia-wisdom = lover of wisdom) loves the Primal Mother (Mother Sophia) and works together with the Being Anthroposophia (Holy Sophia) to bring down the Wisdom of the highest Being of the Kyriotetes (the Daughter of Sophia/Heavenly Sophia) into all that he thinks, feels, and wills.

When thinking (Mother), feeling (Daughter), and willing (Holy Sophia) come together in unity, the philosopher reaches the objective stage to begin a true schooling in how to write his or her own moral destiny into the stars. The Temple of Wisdom of the Primal Mother then becomes the Invisible College for the budding student of Anthroposophia (Holy Sophia).

The Invisible College has been called many names: Shambhala, the etheric realm, Tushita Heaven, the realm of spiritual economy, the Akashic realm, the White Island, among many others. This Temple of Wisdom is the place that initiates go to work on building the edifices of the Future Jupiter incarnation of the Earth [Planetary Condition]. Each moral thought, feeling, or action, brings another 'perfect stone' to the construction of this new Invisible College which is a future 'heaven' for Angels.

The Temple of Wisdom was built for humanity by The Mothers; but now it is time for humanity to build an Invisible College where every spiritual thinker can add their gifts of wisdom, beauty, and goodness. Initiates can even visit this Invisible College in the daytime through meditation, prayer, and other methods that carry the initiate across the threshold between the physical and spiritual worlds.

The Temple of Wisdom is readily found in the astral body which shines with twinkling starlight. Once the astral light is tamed and insight is received from the Primal Mother and the Being of Anthroposophia, the aspirant can then attempt to bring the cosmic wisdom that descended with the highest Being of Wisdom (Daughter) back to its rightful home in the starry heavens. The 'Knowledge of Good and Evil' becomes the content of the lessons of the Invisible College, which are taught to the aspirant by the spiritual beings of the Cosmos. The Daughter (Wisdom) is returned to her Mother through the help of the Being of Anthroposophia (Holy Sophia) who is the midwife of the human soul birthing its higher spirit.

The Being of Anthroposophia (Holy Sophia) evolves alongside each aspirant, thrilled with each new step in learning gained through study in the Invisible College. This type of learning is imprinted into the etheric body of the human being, which receives the teachings of the Invisible College like a hungry soul receiving spiritual nourishment.

The Invisible College contains the wisdom that is imprinted in the etheric body of the individual, and it contains the personal moral efforts of the past, present, and future. The astral body connects to space, whereas the etheric body connects to time and is not bound by past, present, or future. The etheric body is a perfect image of cosmic forces that seem to be eternal. The truth of wisdom, the lawful processes of the Cosmos, and the moral edifices of the future are already imprinted into the living etheric body of the aspirant. The teachings of the Invisible College provide new lessons that will lead us into the future as the thinking philosopher learns to enkindle the light of Imagination with wise, moral pictures that are archetypes worthy to take their place in the starry halls of the Invisible College which create the very environment of the Future Jupiter stage of evolution. The Invisible College can be seen with supersensible organs of perception as the manifestation of the etheric body of the Cosmos.

The final stage of philosophical development involves transformation of the human physical body, following the taming of the astral body of desires and the development of an understanding of the etheric body of time. This can only be accomplished when the Divine Plan of Creation from the Being of Wisdom (Daughter of Sophia) is unfolded. This process of ascension begins with the philosopher; thinking about thinking' and developing Moral Imagination that acknowledges the gifts of The Mothers (Primal Mother).

Once higher feelings have been refined into Moral Inspirations, that are enkindled by the highest Being of Wisdom (Daughter of the Primal Mother), the Being of Anthroposophia (Holy Sophia) is there to guide our way into the Invisible College where the School of the Archangel [Archai] Michael, our current Time Spirit, can be found in the etheric realm surrounding the Earth. Ultimately, knowing all three Sophia's (Mother, Daughter, Holy Sophia) brings us into divine resonance with Christ/Sophia, or what Steiner called—*the Sophia of Christ*.

The Invisible College (Temple of Wisdom/Shambhala) constitutes the three future stages of human spiritual evolution—Future Jupiter, Future Venus, and Future Vulcan which are nurtured by the Being of Anthroposophia (Holy Sophia), the highest Being of Wisdom (Daughter of Sophia), and the Primal Mother (Mother Sophia).

The Primal Mother (Mother Sophia) is hidden from the thinking individual at this time in evolution and her true nature is obscured from materialistic thinkers. It takes a path of self-development that leads to a comprehensive worldview (cosmology) to integrate the Wisdom of The Three Sophias with modern scientific thinking. Once the Primal Mother has finally been recognized and the highest Being of Wisdom (Heavenly Sophia) is found throughout all nature; then, the Being of Anthroposophia can lead us from the Temple of Wisdom to the new temple, often called, the Invisible College (New Jerusalem), the future home of the spirit of humanity.

The Three Elemental Worlds as "The Mothers"

The creative, shape-giving activity of the elementary kingdoms is the basis of all phenomena through which 'being' comes into manifestation. It is important not to confuse elementary kingdoms with elemental beings who are at work as forces of nature, even though there is a close connection between these two kinds of beings. We must therefore distinguish between being a kingdom in the usual sense and being incarnated in a kingdom in the esoteric sense.

As beings of a particular kind, minerals, plants, animals, and human beings each comprise a kingdom of their own. Among these earthly creations, only the human being is incarnated in the strictest sense. Human beings awaken through their physical-mineral body to self-awareness. Only human beings are completely incarnated in the mineral kingdom. Humans have risen beyond the mineral, plant, and animal kingdoms because they have an ego-consciousness with a soul developing into a spiritual being—an Angel.

Only when human beings have learned to understand and manipulate plant life in the same way as we manipulate things today in the dead mineral kingdom, will we be incarnating into the plant kingdom in a similar fashion. We will reach this level of consciousness during the Future Jupiter stage of Earth's planetary incarnations. During the Future Venus stage, human beings will understand and master the nature of animal sentience, and thereby will be incarnating in the animal kingdom. Finally, in Future Vulcan, we will fully understand the nature of the human being and only then will be incarnating fully into the human kingdom.

The Spirit World encompasses the two higher stages of form, the rupa and arupa planes. The Spirit World is divided into seven regions, of which the arupa plane forms the three higher regions, and the rupa plane the four lower regions. The Spirit World is composed of living thought-beings. The thought substance of which these beings of the Spirit World consist, contains the forces that give what manifests in the astral and physical world its form. This thought-substance is the bearer of 'divine thought' that is the foundation of the world; the substance into which the gods implanted their intentions and goals for the formation of the world. The Spirit World thus reveals itself as a world of formative thought-forms creating structures and forming substances.

The arupa world is the world of Intuition, the actual Akashic Chronicle. The rupa world, also called the mental or heavenly world, is the world of Inspiration, the world of the 'harmony of the spheres' reveals itself as a sounding world. Only on the rupa plane do the thought seeds of arupa take shape as specific thought forms, as thought-archetypes. The rupa world is the world of formed thoughts, the world of archetypes or the realm of forms.

The surrounding sense world, excluding humans, is not the immediate expression and activity of divine-spiritual beings but of lower supersensory beings which the gods have detached from themselves, and which they use to bring to manifestation their thoughts from the past. These are the beings of the world of the elements.

The Spiritual World is the primordial world sufficient unto itself; the other two (soul and physical) emerge from it by a process of densification, as it were, and eventually dissolves back into it again.

The human being lives as a god-permeated being in a god-unpermeated world. Only in such a world, devoid of gods, could humanity advance from a dim consciousness to bright, free self-awareness and to its own free intelligence and free will. Everything that appears on the physical plane in sense-perceptible form is a condensed image of what is pre-figured as thought-form in this first region of archetypes.

The three elementary kingdoms are the form-creating thought-seed beings of the arupa plane which give everything that is physically shaped its sense-perceptible form. The first elementary kingdom consists of the formless thought-seed beings of the highest, the seventh region, of Spirit Land, which gives rise to what is mineral and manifested in physical, material form.

Humanity, also, once lived in the first elementary kingdom: during the Old Saturn period. In addition to his physical body, he received the etheric body and thus lived a plant-like existence in the second elementary kingdom during Old Sun. In the Old Moon phase, with the integration of the astral body into his being, humans rose to the animal level and therefore lived in the third elementary kingdom. And, by being endowed during Earth existence with the Ego-component, the human being entered the fourth elementary kingdom. Thus, the beings and forces of the elementary kingdoms are the foundation for the evolution of all beings and worlds. No true understanding of the world is possible without an understanding of the elementary kingdoms.

The Archai work formatively at the physical level using the forces of the first elementary kingdom; the Archangels work at the etheric level using forces of the second elementary kingdom; and, the Angels at the astral level use forces of the third elementary kingdom.

We can imagine the elementary kingdoms as thought-seed entities flowing in the elemental world as: points of energy, thought-figures, or thought-forms, without independence and without impetus of their own for their activity. The formative forces of these thought-seed entities are used by the Angels, Archangels, and Archai in order to create formed structures in the soul, etheric, and physical worlds.

The first elementary kingdom works through sound and tone; the second through light; the third through fire; the fourth through air as the Ego shapes itself. The first elementary kingdom acts formatively through life-ether; the second through sound-ether; the third through light-ether; and the fourth through warmth-ether.

Elemental beings absorb into their nature the cosmic thoughts of the elementary kingdom that rays into and becomes one with them and are thus able to unfold their activity together with them. Elemental beings shape the phenomena of the physical world by using the elementary kingdom forces of cosmic thought. If we are to speak at all of what is behind physical reality, then we must speak of the objective weaving of thought, of the objective world of thought—*the elementary kingdoms.*

The activity of thinking, the connecting and separating of ideas, does not take place in the physical body but in the etheric or elemental body. When we live in the elemental world, thoughts become living beings.

As a secretion of the beings of the third hierarchy and of the Elohim, the elemental beings have no independence of their own. They consist, so to speak, only of body and soul; they have no essential spiritual core. The elemental beings are usually categorized as: fire/salamanders, air/sylphs, water/undines, and earth/gnomes.

The human physical body is fashioned and maintained by the first elementary kingdom, the etheric body by the second, and the astral body by the third elementary kingdom.

We can also regard the elemental world in its three aspects as the totality of etheric beings that bring to manifestation in physical, etheric, and astral forms the formative forces of cosmic thought from the three elementary kingdoms.

Primacy of The Mothers

Once we have clearly defined the elemental realms and the realms of The Mothers, it is easy to see they are one and the same. The Mothers created Old Saturn, Old Sun, and Old Moon. The Elohim created the fourth elemental realm as a recapitulation of The Mothers and then added the human Ego-consciousness.

Even though Steiner did not name Anthroposophia in *The Riddles of Philosophy*, he defined Her so well that it is unmistakable what he was indicating. So too, Steiner did not name The Mothers as the third member of the Divine Feminine Trinity. He described and defined them clearly; but more than likely the world was not ready to hear about the Divine Feminine Trinity during his time.

A Condensed Version of *The Riddles of Philosophy*

The following is taken from the text of *The Riddles of Philosophy* (GA 18) and was condensed and summarized to highlight the descriptions of the Being Anthroposophia. The sweeping images of the evolution of thinking are profound and quite unique in its philosophical approach to thinking. Rudolf Steiner's incredible insight into the mind of the ancients is unparalleled and the development of thinking over the entire course of history is made understandable through his wisdom.

Familiarity with Steiner's anthroposophical cosmology is necessary to fully comprehend the ramifications of the evolution of philosophy through the Being Anthroposophia. Though not named in the book, the Being Anthroposophia is the mirror image of the collective development of human thinking throughout history, and on into the future. These passages are a rare description of Anthroposophia, and once the reader truly beholds her visage the philosophical romance with Wisdom will deepen and reward the soul for its efforts.

Four distinctly discernible epochs in the evolution of the philosophical struggle of mankind presented themselves to the philosopher's view. He had to recognize the difference of these epochs as distinct as the difference of species in the realm of nature. This observation led him to acknowledge in the realm of the history of man's philosophical development the existence of objective spiritual impulses following a definite law of evolution of their own, independent of the individual men in whom they are observed. The achievements of these men as philosophers thus appear as the manifestation of these impulses that direct the course of events under the surface of external history.

It can be shown that in the evolutionary course of the philosophical struggle of mankind, periods are distinguishable, each of which lasts between seven and eight centuries. In each of these epochs there is a distinctly different impulse at work, as if it were under the surface of external history, sending its rays into the human personalities and thus causing the evolution of man's mode of philosophizing while taking its own definite course of development. In the following, due to the importance of the concepts that are so fundamental to our subject the complete chapter is given without quotation marks, preceded and followed by a triangle.

$$\Delta$$

The Riddles of Philosophy, Pt. I, Rudolf Steiner, II, *The World Conception of the Greek Thinkers*, 1894, GA 18

With Pherekydes of Syros, who lived in the sixth century B.C., a personality appears in the Greek intellectual-spiritual life in whom one can observe the birth of what will be called in the following presentation, "a world and life conception." What he has to say about the problems of the world is, on the one hand, still like the mythical symbolic accounts of a time that lies before the striving for a scientific world conception; on the other hand, his imagination penetrates through the picture, through the myth, to a form of reflection that wants to pierce the problems of man's existence and of his position in the world by means of *thoughts*. He still imagines the earth in the picture of a winged oak around which Zeus wraps the surface land, oceans, rivers, etc., like a woven texture. He thinks of the world as permeated by spiritual beings of which Greek mythology speaks.

But Pherekydes also speaks of three principles of the world: Of Chronos, of Zeus and of Chthon.

Throughout the history of philosophy there has been much discussion as to what is to be understood by these three principles. As the historical sources on the question of what Pherekydes meant to say in his work, *Heptamychos,* are contradictory, it is quite understandable that present-day opinions also do not agree. If we reflect on the traditional accounts of Pherekydes, we get the impression that we can really observe in him the beginning of philosophical thought but that this observation is difficult because his words have to be taken in a sense that is remote from the thought habits of the present time; its real meaning is yet to be determined. [1]

Pherekydes arrives at his world picture in a different way from that of his predecessors. The significant fact is that he feels man to be a *living soul* in a way different from earlier times. For the earlier world view, the word, "soul," did not yet have the meaning that it acquired in later conceptions of life, nor did Pherekydes have the idea of the soul in the sense of later thinkers. He simply *feels* the soul-element of man, whereas the later thinkers want to speak clearly about it (in the form of thought) and they attempt to characterize it in intellectual terms. Men of earlier times do not as yet separate their own soul experience from the life of nature. They do not feel that they stand as a special entity beside nature. They experience *themselves* in nature as they experience lightning and thunder in it, the drifting of the clouds, the course of the stars or the growth of plants. What moves man's hand on his own body, what places his foot on the ground and makes him walk, for the prehistoric man, belongs to the same sphere of world forces that also causes lightning, cloud formations and all other external events. What he at this stage feels, can be expressed by saying,

"Something causes lightning, thunder, rain, moves my hand, makes my foot step, moves the air of my breath within me, turns my head." If one expresses what is in this way experienced, one has to use words that at first hearing seem to be exaggerated. But only through these exaggerations will it be possible to understand what is intended to be conveyed.

A man who holds a world picture as it is meant here, experiences in the rain that falls to the ground the action of a force that we at the present time must call "spiritual" and that he feels to be of the same kind as the force he experiences when he is about to exert a personal activity of some kind or other. It should be of interest that this view can be found again in Goethe in his younger years, naturally in a shade of thought that it must assume in a personality of the eighteenth century. We can read in Goethe's essay, *Nature*:

> She (nature) has placed me in life; she will also lead me out of it. I trust myself into her care. She may hold sway over me. She will not hate her work. It was not I who spoke about her. Nay, what is true and what is false—everything has been spoken by her. Everything is her fault, everything her merit.

To speak as Goethe speaks here is only then possible if one feels one's own being imbedded in nature as a whole and then expresses this feeling in *thoughtful reflection*. As Goethe thought, so man of an earlier time felt without transforming his soul experience into the element of thought. He did not as yet experience thought; instead of thought there unfolded within his soul a symbolic image. The observation of the evolution of mankind leads back to a time in which thought-like experiences had not yet come into being but in which the symbolic picture rose in the soul of man when he contemplated the events of the world. Thought life is born in man at a definite time. It causes the extinction of the previous form of consciousness in which the world is experienced in pictures.

For the thought habits of our time it seems acceptable to imagine that man in archaic times had observed natural elements—wind and weather, the growth of seeds, the course of the stars—and then poetically *invented* spiritual beings as the active creators of these events. It is, however, far from the contemporary mode of thinking to recognize the possibility that man in older times experienced those pictures as he later experienced thought, that is, as an inner reality of his soul life.

One will gradually come to recognize that in the course of the evolution of mankind a transformation of the human organization has taken place. There was a time when the subtle organs of human nature, which make possible the development of an independent thought life, had not yet been formed. In this time man had, instead, organs, that represented for him what he experienced in the world of pictures.

As this gradually comes to be understood, a new light will fall on the significance of mythology on the one hand, and that of poetic production and thought life on the other. When the independent inner thought experience began, it brought the picture-consciousness to extinction. Thought emerged as the tool of truth. This is only one branch of what survived of the old picture-consciousness that had found its expression in the ancient myth. In another branch the extinguished picture-consciousness continued to live, if only as a pale shadow of its former existence, in the creations of fantasy and poetic imagination. Poetic fantasy and the intellectual view of the world are the two children of the one mother, the old picture-consciousness that must not be confused with the consciousness of poetic imagination.

The essential process that is to be understood is the transformation of the more delicate organization of man. It causes the beginning of thought life. In art and poetry thought as such naturally does not have an effect. Here the picture continues to exert its influence, but it has now a different relation to the human soul from the one it had when it also served in a cognitive function. As *thought* itself, the new form of consciousness appears only in the newly emerging philosophy. The other branches of human life are correspondingly transformed in a different way when thought begins to rule in the field of human knowledge.

The progress in human evolution that is characterized by this process is connected with the fact that man from the beginning of thought experience had to feel *himself* in a much more pronounced way than before, as a separate entity, as a "soul." In *myth* the picture was experienced in such a way that one felt it to be in the external world as a reality. One experienced this reality at the same time, and one was united with it. With *thought,* as well as with the poetic *picture,* man felt himself separated from nature. Engaged in thought experience, man felt himself as an entity that could not experience nature with the same intimacy as he felt when at one with thought. More and more, the definite feeling of the contrast of nature and soul came into being.

In the civilizations of the different peoples this transition from the old picture-consciousness to the consciousness of thought experience took place at different times. In Greece we can intimately observe this transition if we focus our attention on the personality of Pherekydes of Syros. He lived in a world in which picture-consciousness and thought experience still had an equal share. His three principal ideas—Zeus, Chronos and Chthon—can only be understood in such a way that the soul, in experiencing them, feels itself as belonging to the events of the external world. We are dealing here with three inwardly experienced pictures and we find access to them only when we do not allow ourselves to be distracted by anything that the thought habits of our time are likely to imagine as their meaning.

Chronos is not time as we think of it today. Chronos is a being that in contemporary language can be called "spiritual" if one keeps in mind that one does not thereby exhaust its meaning. Chronos is alive and its activity is the devouring, the consumption of the life of another being, Chthon. Chronos rules in nature; Chronos rules in man; in nature and man Chronos consumes Chthon. It is of no importance whether one considers the consumption of Chthon through Chronos as inwardly experienced or as external events; for in both realms the same process goes on. Zeus is connected with these two beings. In the meaning of Pherekydes one must no more think of Zeus as a deity in the sense of our present day conception of mythology, than as of mere "space" in its present sense, although he is the being through whom the events that go on between Chronos and Chthon are transformed into spatial, extended form.

The cooperation of Chronos, Chthon and Zeus is felt directly as a picture content in the sense of Pherekydes, just as much as one is aware of the idea that one is eating; but it is also experienced as something in the external world, like the conception of the colors blue or red. This experience can be imagined in the following way. We turn our attention to fire as it consumes its fuel. Chronos lives in the activity of fire, of warmth. Whoever regards fire in its *activity* and keeps himself under the effect, not of independent thought but of image content, looks at Chronos. In the activity of fire, not in the sensually perceived fire, he experiences *time* simultaneously. Another conception of time does not exist before the birth of thought. What is called "time" in our present age is an idea that has been developed only in the age of intellectual world conception.

If we turn our attention to water, not as it is as water but as it changes into air or vapor, or to clouds that are in the process of dissolving, we experience as an image content the force of Zeus, the spatially active "spreader." One could also say, the force of centrifugal extension. If we look on water as it becomes solid, or on the solid as it changes into fluid, we are watching Chthon. Chthon is something that later in the age of thought-ruled world conception becomes "matter," the stuff "things are made of"; Zeus has become "ether" or "space," Chronos changes into "time."

In the view of Pherekydes the world is constituted through the cooperation of these three principles. Through the combination of their action the material world of sense perception—fire, air, water and earth—come into being on the one hand, and on the other, a certain number of invisible supersensible spirit beings who animate the four material worlds. Zeus, Chronos and Chthon could be referred to as "spirit, soul and matter," but their significance is only approximated by these terms. It is only through the fusion of these three original beings that the more material realms of the world of fire, air, water and earth, and the more soul-like and spirit-like (supersensible) beings come into existence. Using expressions of later world conceptions, one can call Zeus, space-ether; Chronos, time-creator; Chthon, matter-producer—the three "mothers of the world's origin." We can still catch a glimpse of them in Goethe's *Faust*, in the scene of the second part where Faust sets out on his journey to the "mothers."

As these three primordial entities appear in Pherekydes, they remind us of conceptions of predecessors of this personality, the so-called *Orphics*. They represent a mode of conception that still lives completely in the old form of picture consciousness. In them we also find three original beings: Zeus, Chronos and Chaos. Compared to these "primeval mothers," those of Pherekydes are somewhat less picture-like. This is so because Pherekydes attempts to seize, through the exertion of thought, what his Orphic predecessors still held completely as image-experience. For this reason we can say that he appears as a personality in whom the "birth of thought life" takes place. This is expressed not so much in the more thought-like conception of the Orphic ideas of Pherekydes, as in a certain dominating mood of his soul, which we later find again in several of his philosophizing successors in Greece. For Pherekydes feels that he is forced to see the origin of things in the "good" (Arizon). He could not combine this concept with the "world of mythological deities" of ancient times. The beings of this world had soul qualities that were not in agreement with this concept. Into his three "original causes" Pherekydes could only think the concept of the "good," the perfect.

Connected with this circumstance is the fact that the birth of thought life brought with it a shattering of the foundations of the inner feelings of the soul. This inner experience should not be overlooked in a consideration of the time when the intellectual world conception began. One could not have felt this beginning as progress if one had not believed that with thought one took possession of something that was more perfect than the old form of image experience. Of course, at this stage of thought development, this feeling was not clearly expressed. But what one now, in retrospect, can clearly state with regard to the ancient Greek thinkers was then merely felt. They felt that the pictures that were experienced by our immediate ancestors did not lead to the highest, most perfect, original causes. In these pictures only the less perfect causes were revealed; we must raise our thoughts to still higher causes from which the content of those pictures is merely derived.

Through progress into thought life, the world was now conceived as divided into a more natural and a more spiritual sphere. In this more spiritual sphere, which was only now felt as such, one had to conceive what was formerly experienced in the form of pictures. To this was added the conception of a higher principle, something thought of as superior to the older, spiritual world and to nature. It was to this sublime element that thought wanted to penetrate, and it is in this region that Pherekydes meant to find his three "Primordial Mothers." A look at the world as it appears illustrates what kind of conceptions took hold of a personality like Pherekydes. Man finds a harmony in his surroundings that lies at the bottom of all phenomena and is manifested in the motions of the stars, in the course of the seasons with their blessings of thriving plant-life, etc. In this beneficial course of things, harmful, destructive powers intervene, as expressed in the pernicious effects of the weather, earthquakes, etc. In observing all this one can be lead to a realization of a dualism in the ruling powers, but the human soul must assume an underlying unity. It naturally feels that, in the last analysis, the ravaging hail, the destructive earthquake, must spring from the same source as the beneficial cycle of the seasons. In this fashion man looks through good and evil and sees behind it an original good. The same good force rules in the earthquake as in the blessed rain of spring. In the scorching, devastating heat of the sun the same element is at work that ripens the seed. The "good Mothers of all origin" are, then, in the pernicious events also. When man experiences this feeling, a powerful world riddle emerges before his soul. To find the solution, Pherekydes turns toward his Ophioneus. As Pherekydes leans on the old picture conception, Ophioneus appears to him as a kind of "world serpent." It is in reality a spirit being, which, like all other beings of the world, belongs to the children of Chronos, Zeus and Chthon, but that has later so changed that its effects are directed against those of the "good mother of origin." Thus, the world is divided into three parts. The first part consists of the "Mothers," which are presented as good, as perfect; the second part contains the beneficial world events; the third part, the destructive or the only imperfect world processes that, as Ophioneus, are intertwined in the beneficial effects.

For Pherekydes, Ophioneus is not merely a symbolic idea for the detrimental destructive world forces. Pherekydes stands with his conceptive imagination at the borderline between picture and thought. He does not think that there are devastating powers that he conceives in the pictures of Ophioneus, nor does such a thought process develop in him as an activity of fantasy. Rather, he looks on the detrimental forces, and immediately Ophioneus stands before his soul as the red color stands before our souls when we look at a rose.

Whoever sees the world only as it presents itself to image perception does not, at first, distinguish in his thought between the events of the "good mothers" and those of Ophioneus. At the borderline of a thought-formed world conception, the necessity of this distinction is felt, for only at this stage of progress does the soul feel itself to be a separate, independent entity. It feels the necessity to ask what its origin is. It must find its origin in the depths of the world where Chronos, Zeus and Chthon had not as yet found their antagonists. But the soul also feels that it cannot know anything of its own origin at first, because it sees itself in the midst of a world in which the "Mothers" work in conjunction with Ophioneus. It feels itself in a world in which the perfect and the imperfect are joined together. Ophioneus is twisted into the soul's own being.

We can feel what went on in the souls of individual personalities of the sixth century B.C. if we allow the feelings described here to make a sufficient impression on us. With the ancient mythical deities such souls felt themselves woven into the imperfect world. The deities belonged to the same imperfect world as they did themselves.

The spiritual brotherhood, which was founded by Pythagoras of Samos between the years 549 and 500 B.C. in Kroton in Magna Graecia, grew out of such a mood. Pythagoras intended to lead his followers back to the experience of the "Primordial Mothers" in which the origin of their souls was to be seen. It can be said in this respect that he and his disciples meant to serve "other gods" than those of the people. With this fact something was given that must appear as a break between spirits like Pythagoras and the people, who were satisfied with their gods. Pythagoras considered these gods as belonging to the realm of the imperfect. In this difference we also find the reason for the "secret" that is often referred to in connection with Pythagoras and that was not to be betrayed to the uninitiated. It consisted in the fact that Pythagoras had to attribute to the human soul an origin different from that of the gods of the popular religion. In the last analysis, the numerous attacks that Pythagoras experienced must be traced to this "secret." How was he to explain to others than those who carefully prepared themselves for such a knowledge that, in a certain sense, they, "as souls," could consider themselves as standing even higher than the gods of the popular religion? In what other form than in a brotherhood with a strictly regulated mode of life could the souls become aware of their lofty origin and still find themselves deeply bound up with imperfection? It was just through this feeling of deficiency that the effort was to be made to arrange life in such a way that through the process of self-perfection it would be led back to its origin. That legends and myths were likely to be formed about such aspirations of Pythagoras is comprehensible. It is also understandable that scarcely anything has come down to us historically about the true significance of this personality. Whoever observes the legends and mythical traditions of antiquity about Pythagoras in an all-encompassing picture will nevertheless recognize in it the characterization that was just given.

In the picture of Pythagoras, present-day thinking also feels the idea of the so-called 'transmigration of souls' as a disturbing factor. It is even felt to be naïve that Pythagoras is reported to have said that he knew that he had already been on earth in an earlier time as another human being. It may be recalled that that great representative of modern enlightenment, Lessing, in his *Education of the Human Race,* renewed this idea of man's repeated lives on earth out of a mode of thinking that was entirely different from that of Pythagoras. Lessing could conceive of the progress of the human race only in such a way that the human souls participated repeatedly in the life of the successive great phases of history. A soul brought into its life in a later time as a potential ability what it had gained from experience in an earlier era. Lessing found it natural that the soul had often been on earth in an earthly body, and that it would often return in the future. In this way, it struggles from life to life toward the perfection that it finds possible to obtain. He pointed out that the idea of repeated lives on earth ought not to be considered incredible because it existed in ancient times, and "because it occurred to the human mind before academic sophistry had distracted and weakened it."

The idea of reincarnation is present in Pythagoras; but it would be erroneous to believe that he—along with Pherekydes, who is mentioned as his teacher in antiquity—had yielded to this idea because he had by means of a logical conclusion arrived at the thought that the path of development indicated above could only be reached in repeated earthly lives. To attribute such an intellectual mode of thinking to Pythagoras would be to misjudge him. We are told of his extensive journeys. We hear that he met together with wise men who had preserved traditions of oldest human insight. When we observe the oldest human conceptions that have come down to us through posterity, we arrive at the view that the idea of repeated lives on Earth was widespread in remote antiquity. Pythagoras took up the thread from the oldest teachings of humanity. The mythical teachings in picture form appeared to him as deteriorated conceptions that had their origin in older and superior insights. These picture doctrines were to change in his time into a thought-formed world conception, but this intellectual world conception appeared to him as only a part of the soul's life. This part had to be developed to greater depths. It could then lead the soul to its origins. By penetrating in this direction, however, the soul discovers in its inner experience the repeated lives on earth as a *soul perception*. It does not reach its origins unless it finds its way through the repeated terrestrial lives. As a wanderer walking to a distant place naturally passes through other places on his path, so the soul on its path to the "mothers" passes the preceding lives through which it has gone during its descent from its former existence in perfection, to its present life in imperfection. If one considers everything that is pertinent in this problem, the inference is inescapable that the view of repeated earth lives is to be attributed to Pythagoras in this sense as his inner perception, not as something that was arrived at through a process of conceptual conclusion.

Now the view that is spoken of as especially characteristic of the followers of Pythagoras is that all things are based on numbers. When this statement is made, one must consider that the school of Pythagoras was continued into later times after his death. Philolaus, Archytas and others are mentioned as later Pythagoreans. It was about them especially that one in antiquity knew they "considered things as numbers." We can assume that this view goes back to Pythagoras even if historical documentation does not appear possible. We shall, however, have to suppose that this view was deeply and organically rooted in his whole mode of conception, and that it took on a more superficial form with his successors.

Let us think of Pythagoras as standing before the beginning of intellectual world conception. He saw how thought took its origin in the soul that had, starting from the "mothers," descended through its successive lives to its state of imperfection; Because he felt this he could not mean to ascend to the origins through mere thought. He had to seek the highest knowledge in a sphere in which thought was not yet at home. There he found a life of the soul that was beyond thought life. As the soul experiences proportional numbers in the sound of music, so Pythagoras developed a soul life in which he knew himself as living in a connection with the world that can be intellectually expressed in terms of numbers. But for what is thus experienced, these numbers have no other significance than the physicist's proportional tone numbers have for the experience of music.

For Pythagoras the mythical gods must be replaced by thought. At the same time, he develops an appropriate deepening of the soul life; the soul, which through thought has separated itself from the world, finds itself *at one* with the world again. It experiences itself as *not* separated from the world. This does not take place in a region in which the world-participating experience turns into a mythical picture, but in a region in which the soul reverberates with the invisible, sensually imperceptible cosmic harmonies. It brings into awareness, not its own thought intentions, but what cosmic powers exert as their will, thus allowing it to become conception in the soul of man.

In Pherekydes and Pythagoras the process of how thought-experienced world conception originates in the human soul is revealed. Working themselves free from the older forms of conception, these men arrive at an inwardly independent conception of the "soul" distinct from external "nature." What is clearly apparent in these two personalities—the process in which the soul wrests its way out of the old picture conceptions—takes place more in the *undercurrents* of the souls of the other thinkers with whom it is customary to begin the account of the development of Greek philosophy. The thinkers who are ordinarily mentioned first are *Thales* of Miletos (640–550 B.C.), *Anaximander* (born 610 B.C.), *Anaximenes* (flourished 600 B.C.) and *Heraclitus* (born 500 B.C. at Ephesus).

Whoever acknowledges the preceding arguments to be justified will also find a presentation of these men admissible that must differ from the usual historical accounts of philosophy. Such accounts are, after all, always based on the unexpressed presupposition that these men had arrived at their traditionally reported statements through an imperfect observation of nature. Thus the statement is made that the fundamental and original being of all things was to be found in "water," according to Thales;

in the "infinite," according to Anaximander; in "air," according to Anaximenes; in "fire," in the opinion of Heraclitus.

What is not considered in this treatment is the fact that these men are still really living in the process of the genesis of intellectual world conception. To be sure, they feel the independence of the human soul in a higher degree than Pherekydes, but they have not yet completed the strict separation of the life of the soul from the process of nature. One will, for instance, most certainly construct an erroneous picture of Thales's way of thinking if it is imagined that he, as a merchant, mathematician and astronomer, thought about natural events and then, in an imperfect yet similar way to that of a modern scientist, had summed up his results in the sentence, "Everything originates from water." To be a mathematician or an astronomer, etc., in those ancient times meant to deal in a practical way with the things of these professions, much in the way a craftsman makes use of technical skills rather than intellectual and scientific knowledge.

What must be presumed for a man like Thales is that he still experienced the external processes of nature as similar to inner soul processes. What presented itself to him like a natural event, as did the process and nature of "water" (the fluid, mudlike, earth-formative element), he experienced in a way that was similar to what he felt within himself in soul and body. He then experienced in himself and outside in nature the effect of water, although to a lesser degree than man of earlier times did. Both effects were for him the manifestation of *one* power. It may be pointed out that at a still later age the external effects in nature were thought of as being akin to the inner processes in a way that did not provide for a "soul" in the present sense as distinct from the body. Even in the time of intellectual world conception, the idea of the temperaments still preserves this point of view as a reminiscence of earlier times.

One called the melancholic temperament, the earthy; the phlegmatic, the watery; the sanguinic, the airy; the choleric, the fiery. These are not merely allegorical expressions. One did not feel a completely separated soul element, but experienced in oneself a soul-body entity as a unity. In this unity was felt the stream of forces that go, for instance, through a phlegmatic soul, to be like the forces in external nature that are experienced in the effects of water. One saw these external water effects to be the same as what the soul experienced in a phlegmatic mood. The thought habits of today must attempt an empathy with the old modes of conception if they want to penetrate into the soul life of earlier times.

In this way one will find in the world conception of Thales an expression of what his soul life, which was akin to the phlegmatic temperament, caused him to experience inwardly. He experienced in himself what appeared to him to be the world mystery of water. The allusion to the phlegmatic temperament of a person is likely to be associated with a derogatory meaning of the term. Justified as this may be in many cases, it is nevertheless also true that the phlegmatic temperament, when it is combined with an energetic, objective imagination, makes a sage out of a man because of its calmness, collectedness and freedom from passion. Such a disposition in Thales probably caused him to be celebrated by the Greeks as one of their wise men.

For Anaximenes, the world picture formed itself in another way. He experienced in himself the sanguine temperament. A word of his has been handed down to us that immediately shows how he felt the air element as an expression of the world mystery. "As our soul, which is a breath, holds us together, so air and breath envelop the universe."

The world conception of Heraclitus will, in an unbiased contemplation, be felt directly as a manifestation of his choleric inner life. A member of one of the most noble families of Ephesus, he became a violent antagonist of the democratic party because he had arrived at certain views, the truth of which was apparent to him in his immediate inner experience. The views of those around him, compared with his own, seemed to him to prove directly in a most natural way, the foolishness of his environment. Thus, he got into such conflicts that he left his native city and led a solitary life at the Temple of Artemis. Consider these few of his sayings that have come down to us. "It would be good if the Ephesians hanged themselves as soon as they grew up and surrendered their city to those under age." Or the one about men, "Fools in their lack of understanding, even if they hear the truth, are like the deaf: of them does the saying bear witness that they are absent when present."

The feeling that is expressed in such a choleric temperament finds itself akin to the consuming activity of fire. It does not live in the restful calm of "being." It feels itself as one with eternal "becoming." Such a soul feels stationary existence to be an absurdity. "Everything flows," is, therefore, a famous saying of Heraclitus. It is only apparently so if somewhere an unchanging being seems to be given. We are lending expression to a feeling of Heraclitus if we say, "The rock seems to represent an absolute unchanging state of being, but this is only appearance; it is inwardly in the wildest commotion; all its parts act upon one another." The mode of thinking of Heraclitus is usually characterized by his saying, "One cannot twice enter the same stream, for the second time the water is not the same." A disciple of Heraclitus, Cratylus, goes still further by saying that one could not even enter the same stream once. Thus it is with all things.

While we look at what is apparently unchanging, it has already turned into something else in the general stream of existence.

We do not consider a world conception in its full significance if we accept only its thought content. Its essential element lies in the mood it communicates to the soul, that is, in the vital force that grows out of it. One must realize how Heraclitus feels himself with his own soul in the stream of becoming. The world soul pulsates in his own human soul and communicates to it of its own life as long as the human soul knows itself as living in it. Out of such a feeling of union with the world soul, the thought originates in Heraclitus, "Whatever lives has death in itself through the stream of becoming that is running through everything, but death again has life in itself. Life and death are in our living and dying. Everything has everything else in itself; only thus can eternal becoming flow through everything." "The ocean is the purest and impurest water, drinkable and wholesome to fishes, to men undrinkable and pernicious." "Life and death are the same, waking and sleeping, young and old; the first changes into the second and again into the first." "Good and evil are one." "The straight path and the crooked . . . are one."

Anaximander is freer from the inner life, more surrendered to the element of thought itself. He sees the origin of things in a kind of world ether, an indefinite formless basic entity that has no limits. Take the Zeus of Pherekydes, deprive him of every image content that he still possesses and you have the original principle of Anaximander: Zeus turned into thought. A personality appears in Anaximander in whom thought life is borne out of the mood of soul that still has, in the preceding thinkers, the color of temperament. Such a personality feels united as a soul with the life of thought, and thereby is not so intimately interwoven with nature as the soul that does not yet experience thought as an independent element. It feels itself connected with a world order that lies *above* the events of nature. When Anaximander says that men lived first as fishes in the moist element and then developed through land animal forms, he means that the spirit germ, which man recognizes through thinking as his true being, has gone through the other forms only as through preliminary stages, with the aim of giving itself eventually the shape that has been appropriate for him from the beginning.

The thinkers mentioned so far are succeeded historically by *Xenophanes* of Kolophon (born 570 B.C.); *Parmenides* (460 B.C., living as a teacher in Athens), younger and inwardly related to Xenophanes; *Zenon* of Elea (who reached his peak around 500 B.C.); *Melissos* of Samos (about 450 B.C.).

The thought element is already alive to such a degree in these thinkers that they demand a world conception in which the life of thought is fully satisfied; they recognize truth only in this form. How must the world ground be constituted so that it can be fully absorbed within thinking? This is their question.

Xenophanes finds that the popular gods cannot stand the test of thought; therefore, he rejects them. His god must be capable of being *thought*. What the senses perceive is changeable, is burdened with qualities not appropriate to thought, whose function it is to seek what is permanent. Therefore, God is the unchangeable, eternal unity of all things to be seized in thought.

Parmenides sees the Untrue, the Deceiving, in sense-perceived, external nature. He sees what alone is true in the Unity, the Imperishable that is seized by thought. Zeno tries to come to terms with, and do justice to, the thought experience by pointing out the contradictions that result from a world view that sees truth in the change of things, in the process of becoming, in the multiplicity that is shown by the external world. One of the contradictions pointed out by Zeno is that the fastest runner (Achilles) could not catch up with a turtle, for no matter how slowly it moved, the moment Achilles arrived at the point it had just occupied, it would have moved on a little. Through such contradictions Zeno intimates how a conceptual imagination that leans on the external world is caught in self-contradiction. He points to the difficulty such thought meets when it attempts to find the truth.

One will recognize the significance of this world conception, which is called the "eleatic view" (Parmenides and Zeno are from Elea), if one considers that those who hold this view have advanced with the development of thought experience to the point of having transformed it into a special art, the so-called dialectic. In the "art of thought" the soul learns to feel itself in its self-dependence and its inward self-sufficiency. With this step, the reality of the soul is felt to be what it is through its own being. It experiences itself through the fact that it no longer, as in earlier times, follows the general world experience with its life, but unfolds independent thought experience within itself. This experience is rooted in itself and through it, it can feel itself planted into a pure spiritual ground of the world. At first, this feeling is not expressed as a distinctly formulated thought but, in the esteem it enjoyed, it can be sensed vividly as a feeling in this age. According to a Dialogue of Plato, the young Socrates is told by Parmenides that he should learn the "art of thought" from Zeno; otherwise, truth would be unattainable for him. This "art of thought" was felt to be a necessity for the human soul intending to approach the spiritual fundamental grounds of existence.

Whoever does not see how, in the progress of human development toward the stage of thought experience, real experiences—the picture experiences—came to an end with the beginning of this thought life, will not see the special quality of the Greek thinkers from the sixth to the fourth pre-Christian centuries in the light in which they must appear in this presentation. Thought formed a wall around the human soul, so to speak. The soul had formerly felt as if it were within the phenomena of nature. What it experienced in these natural phenomena, like the activities of its own body, presents itself to the soul in the form of images that appeared in vivid reality. Through the power of thought this entire panorama was now extinguished. Where previously images saturated in content prevailed, thought now expanded through the external world. The soul could experience itself in the surroundings of space and time only if it united itself with thought.

One senses such a mood of soul in *Anaxagoras* of Clazomenae in Asia Minor (born 500 B.C.). He found himself deeply bound up in his soul with thought life. His thought life encompassed what is extended in space and time. Expanded like this, it appears as the *nous,* the world reason. It penetrates the whole of nature as an entity. Nature, however, presents itself as composed only of little basic entities. The events of nature that result from the combined actions of these fundamental entities are what the senses perceive after the texture of imagery has vanished from nature. These fundamental entities are called *homoiomeries.* The soul experiences in thought the connection with the world reason (the nous) inside its wall. Through the windows of the senses it watches what the world reason causes to come into being through the action of the homoiomeries on each other.

Empedocles (born 490 B.C. in Agrigent) was a personality in whose soul the old and the new modes of conception clash as in a violent antagonism. He still feels something of the old mode of being in which the soul was more closely interwoven with external existence. Hatred and love, antipathy and sympathy live in the human soul. They also live outside the wall that encloses it. The life of the soul is thus homogeneously extended beyond its boundaries and it appears in forces that separate and connect the elements of external nature—air, fire, water and earth—thereby causing what the senses perceive in the outer world.

Empedocles is, as it were, confronted with nature, which appears to the senses to be deprived of life and soul, and he develops a soul mood that revolts against this extirpation of nature's animation. His soul cannot believe that nature really is what thought wants to make of it. Least of all can it admit that it should stand in such a relation to nature as it appears according to the intellectual world conception. We must imagine what goes on in a soul that senses such a discord in all its harshness, suffering from it. We shall then be capable of entering into the experience of how, in this soul of Empedocles, the old mode of conception is resurrected as the power of intimate feeling but is unwilling to raise this fact into full consciousness. It thus seeks a form of existence in a shade of experience hovering between thought and picture that is reechoed in the sayings of Empedocles. These lose their strangeness if they are understood in this way. The following aphorism is attributed to him. "Farewell. A mortal no longer, but an immortal god I wander about . . . and as soon as I come into the flourishing cities I am worshipped by men and women. They follow me by the thousands, seeking the path of their salvation with me, some expecting prophecies, others, curative charms for many diseases."

In such a way, a soul that is haunted by an old form of consciousness through which it feels its own existence as that of a banished god who is cast out of another form of existence into the soul-deprived world of the senses, is dazed. He therefore feels the earth to be an "unaccustomed place" into which he is cast as in punishment. There are certainly other sentiments also to be found in the soul of Empedocles because significant flashes of wisdom shine in his aphorisms. His feeling with respect to the "birth of the intellectual world conception" is characterized, however, by the thought mood mentioned above.

The thinkers who are called the atomists regarded what nature had become for the soul of man through the birth of thought in a different way. The most important among them is *Democritus* (born 460 B.C. in Abdera). *Leucippus* is a kind of forerunner to him.

With Democritus, the homoiomeries of Anaxagoras have become, to a considerable degree, more material. In Anaxagoras, one can still compare the entities of the basic parts with living germs. With Democritus, they become dead indivisible particles of matter, which in their different combinations make up the things of the outer world. They mix freely as they move to and fro; thus, the events of nature come to pass. The world reason (nous) of Anaxagoras, which has the world processes grow out of the combined action of the homoiomeries like a spiritual (incorporeal) consciousness, with Democritus, turns into the unconscious law of nature *(ananke)*. The soul is ready to recognize only what it can grasp as the result of simple thought combinations. Nature is now completely deprived of life and soul; thought has paled as a soul experience into the inner shadow of inanimate nature. In this way, with Democritus, the intellectual *prototype* of all more or less materialistically colored world conceptions of later times has made its appearance.

The atom world of Democritus represents an external world, a nature in which no trace of soul life can be found. The thought experiences in the soul, through which the soul has become aware of itself, are mere shadow experiences in Democritus. Thus, a part of the fate of thought experiences is characterized. They bring the human soul to the consciousness of its own being, but they fill it at the same time with uncertainty about itself. The soul experiences itself in itself through thought, but it can at the same time feel that it lost its anchorage in the independent spiritual world power that used to lend it security and inner stability. This emancipation of the soul was felt by the group of men in Greek intellectual life known as "Sophists." The most important among them is *Protagoras* of Abdera (480–410 B.C.). Also to be noted besides him are Gorgias, Critias, Hippias, Thrasymachus and Prodicus.

The sophists are often presented as men who superficially played with their thinking. Much has been contributed to this opinion by the manner in which Aristophanes, the playwright of comedies, treated them, but there are many things that can lead to a better appreciation of the sophists. It is noteworthy that even Socrates, who to a certain limited extent thought of himself as a pupil of Prodicus, is said to have described him as a man who had done much for the refinement of the speech and thinking of his disciples.

Protagoras's view is expressed in the famous statement, "Man is the measure of all things, of those that are, that they are; of those that are not, that they are not." In the sentiment underlying this statement the thought experience feels itself sovereign. It does not sense any connection with an objective world power. If Parmenides is of the opinion that the senses supply man with a world of deception, one could go further and add, "Why should not thinking, although one experiences it, also deceive?" Protagoras, however, would reply to this, "Why should it be man's concern if the world outside him is not as he perceives and thinks it? Does he imagine it for anyone else but himself? No matter how it may be for another being, this should be of no concern to man. The contents of his mind are only to serve him; with their aid he is to find his way through the world. Once he achieves complete clarity about himself, he cannot wish for any thought contents about the world except those that serve him." Protagoras means to be able to build on thinking. For this purpose he intends to have it rest exclusively on its own sovereign power.

With this step, however, Protagoras places himself in contradiction to the spirit that lives in the depths of Greek life. This spirit is distinctly perceptible in the Greek character. It manifests itself in the inscription, "Know Thyself," at the temple of Delphi. This ancient oracle wisdom speaks as if it contained the challenge for the progress of world conceptions that advances from the conception in images to the form of consciousness in which the secrets of the world are seized through thought. Through this challenge man is directed to his own soul. He is told that he can hear the language in his soul through which the world expresses its essence. He is thereby also directed toward something that produces uncertainties and insecurities for itself in its experience. The leading spirits of Greek civilization were to conquer the dangers of this self-supporting soul life. Thus, they were to develop thought in the soul into a world conception.

In the course of this development the sophists navigated in dangerous straits. In them the Greek spirit places itself at an abyss; it means to produce the strength of equilibrium through its own power. One should, as has been pointed out, consider the gravity and boldness of this attempt, rather than lightly condemn it even though condemnation is certainly justified for many of the sophists.

This attempt of the sophists takes place at a natural turning point of Greek life. Protagoras lived from 480 to 410 B.C. The Peloponnesian War, which occurred at this turning point of Greek civilization, lasted from 431 to 404 B.C. Before this war the individual member of Greek society had been firmly enclosed by his social connections. Commonwealth and tradition provided the measuring stick for his actions and thinking. The individual person had value and significance only as a member of the total structure. Under such circumstances the question, "What is the value of the individual human being?" could not be asked. The sophists, however, do ask this question, and in so doing introduce the era of Greek Enlightenment. Fundamentally, it is the question of how man arranges his life after he has become aware of his awakened thought life.

From Pherekydes (or Thales) to the sophists, one can observe how emaciated thought in Greece, which had already been born before these men, gradually finds its place in the stream of philosophical development. The effect thought has when it is placed in the service of world conception becomes apparent in them. The birth of thought, however, is to be observed in the entire Greek life. One could show much the same kind of development in the fields of art, poetry, public life, the various crafts and trades, and one would see everywhere how human activity changes under the influence of the form of human organization that introduces thought into the world conception. It is not correct to say that philosophy "discovers" thought. It comes into existence through the fact that the newly born thought life is used for the construction of a world picture that formerly had been formed out of experiences of a different kind.

While the sophists led the spirit of Greece, expressed in the motto, "Know Thyself," to the edge of a dangerous cliff, Socrates, who was born in Athens about 470 and was condemned to death through poison in 399 B.C., expressed this spirit with a high degree of perfection.

Historically, the picture of Socrates has come down to us through two channels of tradition. In one, we have the figure that his great disciple, Plato (427–347 B.C.), has drawn of him. Plato presents his philosophy in dialogue form, and Socrates appears in these dialogues as a teacher. He is shown as the "sage" who leads the persons around him through intellectual guidance to high stages of insight. A second picture has been drawn by Xenophon in his *Memorabilia of Socrates*. At first sight it seems as if Plato had idealized the character of Socrates and as if Xenophon had portrayed him more directly as he had been. But a more intimate inspection would likely show that both Plato and Xenophon each drew a picture of Socrates as they saw him from a special point of view. One is justified, therefore, in considering the question as to how these pictures supplement and illuminate each other.

The first thing that must appear significant here is that Socrates' philosophy has come down to posterity entirely as an expression of his personality, of the fundamental character of his soul life. Both Plato and Xenophon present Socrates in such a way that in him his personal opinion speaks everywhere. This personality carries in itself the awareness that, whoever expresses his personal opinion out of the true ground of the soul, expresses something that is more than just human opinion, something that is a manifestation of the purposes of the world order through human thinking. By those who think they know him, Socrates is taken as the living proof for the conviction that truth is revealed in the human soul through thinking if, as was the case with Socrates, this soul is grounded in its own substance. Looking on Socrates, Plato does not teach a doctrine that is asserted by contemplative thought, but the thought has a rightly developed human being speak, who then observes what he produces as truth. Thus, the manner in which Plato behaves toward Socrates becomes an expression for what man is in his relation to the world. What Plato has advanced about Socrates is significant and also the way in which he, in his activity as a writer, has placed Socrates in the world of Greek spiritual life.

With the birth of thought man was directed toward his "soul." The question now arises as to what this soul says when it begins to speak, expressing what the world forces have laid into it. Through the attitude Plato takes with respect to Socrates, the resulting answer is that in the human soul the reason of the world speaks what it intends to reveal to man. The foundation is laid with this step for the *confidence* expressed in the revelations of the human soul insofar as it develops *thought* in itself. The figure of Socrates appears in the sign of this confidence.

In ancient times the Greek consulted the oracles in the most important questions of life. He asked for prophecy, the revelation of the will and the opinion of the spiritual powers. Such an arrangement is in accord with the soul experience in images. Through the image man feels himself bound to the powers holding sway over the world. The oracle, then, is the institution by means of which somebody who is especially gifted in that direction finds his way to the spiritual powers better than other people. As long as one did not experience one's soul as separated from the outer world, the feeling was natural that this external world was able to express more through a special institution than through everyday experience. The picture spoke from without. Why should the outer world not be capable of speaking distinctly at a special place? Thought speaks to the inner soul. With thought, therefore, the soul is left *to its own resources;* it cannot feel united with another soul as with the revelations of a priestly oracle. To thought, one had to lend one's own soul. One felt of thought that it was a common possession of all men.

World reason shines into thought life without especially established institutions. Socrates felt that the force lives in the thinking soul that used to be sought in the *oracles*. He experienced the "daimonion" in himself, the spiritual force that leads the soul. Thought has brought the soul to the consciousness of itself. With his conception of the daimonion speaking in him that, always leading him, told him what to do, Socrates meant to say, "The soul that has found its way to the thought life is justified to feel as if it communicated in itself with the world reason. It is an expression of the high valuation of what the soul possesses in its thought experience."

"Virtue," under the influence of this view, is placed in a special light. Because Socrates values thought, he must presuppose that true virtue in human life reveals itself in the life of thought. True virtue must be found in thought life because it is from thought life that man derives his value. "Virtue is teachable." In this way is Socrates' conception most frequently expressed. It is teachable because whoever really seizes thought life must be in its possession. What Xenophon says about Socrates is significant in this respect. Socrates teaches a disciple about virtue and the following dialogue develops.

Socrates:

Do you believe there is a doctrine and science of justice, just as there is a doctrine of grammar?

The disciple:

Yes, I do.

Socrates:

Whom do you consider now as better versed in grammar, the one who intentionally writes and reads incorrectly, or the one who does so without intention?

The disciple:

I should think the one who does it intentionally, for if he meant to, he could also do it correctly.

Socrates:

Does it not seem to you that the one who intentionally writes incorrectly knows how to write, but the other one does not?

The disciple:
Without doubt.

Socrates:

Who now understands more of justice, he who intentionally lies or cheats, or he who does so inadvertently?

Socrates attempts to make clear to the disciple that what matters is to have the right thoughts about virtue. So also, what Socrates says about virtue aims at the establishment of *confidence* in a soul that knows itself through thought experience. The right thoughts about virtue are to be trusted more than all other motivations. Virtue makes man more valuable when he experiences it in thought.

Thus, what the pre-Socratic age strove for becomes manifest in Socrates, that is, the appreciation of what humanity has been given through the awakened thought life. Socrates' method of teaching is under the influence of this conception. He approaches man with the presupposition that thought in life is in him; it only needs to be awakened. It is for this reason that he arranges his questions in such a way that the questioned person is stimulated to awaken his own thought life. This is the substance of the Socratic method.

Plato, who was born in Athens in 427 B.C., felt, as a disciple of Socrates, that his master had helped him to consolidate his confidence in the life of thought. What the entire previous development tended to bring into appearance reaches a climax in Plato. This is the conception that in thought life the world spirit reveals itself. The awareness of this conception sheds, to begin with, its light over all of Plato's soul life. Nothing that man knows through the senses or otherwise has any value as long as the soul has not exposed it to the light of thought. Philosophy becomes for Plato the science of *ideas* as the world of true being, and the *idea* is the manifestation of the world spirit through the revelation of thought. The light of the world spirit shines into the soul of man and reveals itself there in the form of *ideas*; the human soul, in seizing the idea, unites itself with the force of the world spirit. The world that is spread in space and time is like the mass of the ocean water in which the stars are reflected, but what is real is only reflected as idea. Thus, for Plato, the whole world changes into ideas that act upon each other. Their effect in the world is produced through the fact that the ideas are reflected in *hyle*, the original matter. What we see as the many individual things and events comes to pass through this reflection. We need not extend knowledge to *hyle*, the original matter, however, for in it is no truth. We reach truth only if we strip the world picture of everything that is not idea. For Plato, the human soul is living in the idea, but this life is so constituted that the soul is not a manifestation of its life in the ideas in all its utterances. Insofar as it is submerged in the life of ideas, it appears as the "rational soul" (thought-bearing soul), and as such, the soul appears to itself when it becomes aware of itself in thought perception.

It must also manifest itself in such a way that it appears as the "non-rational soul" (not-thought-bearing soul), As such, it again appears in a twofold way as courage-developing, and as appetitive soul. Thus, Plato seems to distinguish three members or parts in the human soul: The rational soul, the courage-like (or will-exertive) soul and the appetitive soul. We shall, however, describe the spirit of his conceptional approach better if we express it in a different way. According to its nature, the soul is a member of the world of ideas, but it acts in such a way that it adds an activity to its life in reason through its courage life and its appetitive life. In this threefold mode of utterance it appears as earthbound soul. It descends as a rational soul through physical birth into a terrestrial existence, and with death again enters the world of ideas. Insofar as it is rational soul, it is *immortal*; for as such it shares with its life the eternal existence of the world of ideas.

Plato's doctrine of the soul emerges as a significant fact in the age of thought perception. The awakened thought directed man's attention toward the soul. A perception of the soul develops in Plato that is entirely the result of thought perception. Thought in Plato has become bold enough not only to point toward the soul but to express what the soul is, as it were, to describe it. What thought has to say about the soul gives it the force to know itself *in the eternal*. Indeed, thought in the soul even sheds light on the nature of the temporal by expanding its own being beyond this temporal existence. The soul perceives thought. As the soul appears in its terrestrial life, it could not produce in itself the pure form of thought. Where does the thought experience come from if it cannot be developed in the life on earth? It represents a *reminiscence* of a pre-terrestrial, purely spiritual state of being. Thought has seized the soul in such a way that it is not satisfied by the soul's terrestrial form of existence. It has been revealed to the soul in an earlier state of being (preexistence) in the spirit world (world of ideas) and the soul recalls it during its terrestrial existence through the reminiscence of the life it has spent in the spirit.

What Plato has to say about the moral life follows from this soul conception. The soul is moral if it so arranges life that it exerts itself to the largest possible measure as rational soul. *Wisdom* is the virtue that stems from the rational soul; it ennobles human life. *Fortitude* is the virtue of the will-exertive soul; *Temperance* is that of the appetitive soul. These virtues come to pass when the rational soul becomes the ruler over the other manifestations of the soul. When all three virtues harmoniously act together, there emerges what Plato calls, *Justice,* the direction toward the Good, *Dikaiosyne.*

Plato's disciple, *Aristotle* (born 384 B.C. in Stageira, Thracia, died 321 B.C.), together with his teacher, represents a climax in Greek thinking. With him the process of the absorption of thought life into the world conception has been completed and come to rest. Thought takes its rightful possession of its function to comprehend, out of its own resources, the being and events of the world. Plato still uses his conceptual imagination to bring thought to its rightful authority and to lead it into the world of ideas. With Aristotle, this authority has become a matter of course. It is now a question of confirming it everywhere in the various fields of knowledge. Aristotle understands how to use thought as a tool that penetrates into the essence of things. For Plato, it had been the task to overcome the thing or being of the external world. When it has been overcome, the soul carries in itself the idea of which the external being had only been overshadowed, but which had been foreign to it, hovering over it in a spiritual world of truth. Aristotle intends to submerge into the beings and events, and what the soul finds in this submersion, it accepts as the essence of the thing itself. The soul feels as if it had only lifted this essence out of the thing and as if it had brought this essence for its own consumption into the thought form in order to be able to carry it in itself as a reminder of the thing. To Aristotle's mind, the ideas are in the things and events. They are the side of the things through which these things have a foundation of their own in the underlying material, matter (*hyle*).

Plato, like Aristotle, lets his conception of the soul shed its light on his entire world conception. In both thinkers we describe the fundamental constitution of their philosophy as a whole if we succeed in determining the basic characteristics of their soul conceptions. To be sure, for both of them many detailed studies would have to be considered that cannot be attempted in this sketch. But the direction their mode of conception took is, for both, indicated in their soul conceptions.

Plato is concerned with what lives in the soul and, as such, shares in the spirit world. What is important for Aristotle is the question of how the soul presents itself for man in his own knowledge. As it does with other things, the soul must also submerge into itself in order to find what constitutes its own essence. The idea, which, according to Aristotle, man finds in a thing outside his soul, is the essence of the thing, but the soul has brought this essence into the form of an idea in order to have it for itself. The idea does not have its reality in the cognitive soul but in the external thing in connection with its material (*hyle*). If the soul submerges into itself, however, it finds the idea as such in reality. The soul in this sense is idea, but active idea, an entity exerting action, and it behaves also in the life of man as such an active entity. In the process of germination of man it lays hold upon material existence.

While idea and matter constitute an inseparable unity in an external thing, this is not the case with the human soul and its body. Here the independent human soul seizes upon the corporeal part, renders the idea ineffective that has been active in the body before and inserts itself in its place. In Aristotle's view, a soul-like principle is active already in the bodily element with which the human soul unites itself, for he sees also in the bodies of the plants and of animals, soul-like entities of a subordinate kind at work. A body that carries in itself the soul elements of the plant and animal is, as it were, fructified by the human soul. Thus, for the terrestrial man, a body-soul entity is linked up with a spirit-soul entity. The spirit-soul entity suppresses the *independent* activity of the body-soul element during the earth life of man and uses the body-soul entity as an instrument. Five soul manifestations come into being through this process. These, in Aristotle, appear as five members of the soul: The plant-like soul (threptikon), the sentient soul (aisthetikon), the desire-developing soul (orektikon), the will-exerting soul (kinetikon) and the spirit-soul (dianoetikon). Man is spiritual soul through what belongs to the spiritual world and what, in the process of germination, links itself up with the body-soul entity. The other members of the soul come into being as the spiritual soul unfolds itself in the body and thereby leads its Earth life.

With Aristotle's focus on a spiritual soul the perspective toward a spiritual world in general is naturally given. The world picture of Aristotle stands before our contemplative eye in such a way that we see below the life of things and events, thus presenting matter *and* idea; the higher we lift our eye, the more we see vanish whatever bears a material character. Pure spiritual essence appears, representing itself to man as idea, that is, the sphere of the world in which deity as pure spirituality that moves everything has its being. The spiritual soul of man belongs to this world sphere; before it is united with a body-soul entity, it does not exist as an individual being but only as a part of the world spirit. Through this connection it acquires its individual existence separated from the world spirit and continues to live after the separation from the body as a spiritual being. Thus, the individual soul entity has its beginning with the human earthly life and then lives on as immortal. A preexistence of the soul before earth life is assumed by Plato but not by Aristotle. The denial of the soul's preexistence is as natural to Aristotle, who has the idea exist in the thing, as the opposite view is natural to Plato, who conceives of the idea as hovering over the thing. Aristotle finds the idea in the thing, and the soul acquires in its body what it is to be in the spirit world as an individuality.

Aristotle is the thinker who has brought thought to the point where it unfolds to a world conception through its contact with the essence of the world. The age before Aristotle led to the experience of thought; Aristotle seizes the thoughts and applies them to whatever he finds in the world. The natural way, peculiar to Aristotle, in which he lives in thought as a matter of course, leads him also to investigate logic, the laws of thought itself. Such a science could only come into being after the awakened thought had reached a stage of great maturity and of such a harmonious relationship to the things of the outer world as we find it in Aristotle.

Compared with Aristotle, the other thinkers of antiquity who appear as his contemporaries or as his successors seem to be of much less significance. They give the impression that their abilities lack a certain energy that prevents them from attaining the stage of insight Aristotle had reached. One gets the feeling that they disagree with him because they are stating opinions about things they do not understand as well as he. One is inclined to explain their views by pointing to the deficiency that led them to utter opinions that have already been disproved essentially in Aristotle's work.

To begin with, one can receive such an impression from the *Stoics* and the *Epicureans*. *Zeno of Kition* (342–270 B.C.), *Kleanthes* (born 200 B.C.), *Chrysippus* (282– 209 B.C.), and others belong to the Stoics, whose name was derived from the Hall of Columns in Athens, the Stoa. They accept what appears reasonable to them in earlier world conceptions; but they are mainly concerned with finding out what man's position is in the world by contemplation of it. They want to base on this, their decision as to how to arrange life in such a way that it is in agreement with the world order, and also in such a way that man can unfold his life in this world order according to his own nature. According to them, man dulls his natural being through desire, passion and covetousness. Through equanimity and freedom from desire, he feels best what he is meant to be and what he can be. The ideal man is the "sage" who does not hamper the process of the inner development of the human being by any vice.

As the thinkers before Aristotle were striving to obtain the knowledge that, after him, becomes accessible to man through the ability to perceive thoughts in the full consciousness of his soul, with the Stoics, reflection concentrates on the question as to what man is to do in order to express his nature as a human being in the best way.

Epicurus (born 324 B.C., died 270 B.C.) developed in his own way the elements that had already been latent in the earlier atomistic thinkers. He builds a view of life on this foundation that can be considered to be an answer to the question: As the human soul emerges as the blossom of world processes, how is it to live in order to shape its separate existence, its self-dependence in accordance with thinking guided by reason? Epicurus could answer this question only by a method that considered life only between birth and death, for nothing else can, with perfect intellectual honesty, be derived from the atomistic world conception. The fact of pain must appear to such a conception as a peculiar enigma of life. For pain is one of those facts that drive the soul out of the consciousness of its unity with the things of the world. One can consider the motion of the stars and the fall of rain to be like the motion of one's own hand, as was done in the world conception of more remote antiquity. That is to say, one can feel in both kinds of events the same uniform spirit-soul reality. The fact that events can produce pain in man but cannot do so in the external world, however, drives the soul to the recognition of its own special nature. A doctrine of virtues, which, like the one of Epicurus, endeavors to live in harmony with world reason, can, as may easily be conceived, appreciate an ideal of life that leads to the avoidance of pain and displeasure. Thus, everything that does away with displeasure becomes the highest Epicurean life value.

This view of life found numerous followers in later antiquity, especially among Roman gentlemen of cultural aspiration. The Roman poet, T. Lucretius Carus (95–52 B.C.), has expressed it in perfect artistic form in his poem, *De Rerum Natura.*

The process of perceiving thoughts leads the soul to the recognition of its own being; but it can also occur that the soul feels powerless to deepen its thought experience sufficiently to find a connection with the grounds of the world through this experience. The soul then finds itself torn loose from these grounds through its own thinking. It feels that thinking contains its own being; but it does not find a way to recognize in its thought life anything but its own statement. The soul can then only surrender to a complete renunciation of any kind of true knowledge. *Pyrrho* (360–270 B.C.) and his followers, whose philosophical belief is called skepticism, were in such a situation. Skepticism, the philosophy of doubt, attributes no other power to the thought experience than the formation of human opinions about the world. Whether or not these opinions have any significance for the world outside man is a question about which it is unwilling to make a decision. [A true skeptic is agnostic on a subject. Doubt denotes an opinion for which a burden of proof is needed. Skepticism should be neutral – e.Ed]

In a certain sense, one can see a well-rounded picture in the series of Greek thinkers. One will have to admit, of course, that such an attempt to connect the views of the individual thinkers only too easily brings out irrelevant aspects of secondary significance. What remains most important is still the contemplation of the individual personalities and the impressions one can gain concerning the fact of how, in these personalities, the general human element is brought to manifestation in special cases. One can observe a process in this line of Greek thinkers that can be called the birth, growth and life of thought: in the pre-Socratic thinkers, the prelude; in Socrates, Plato and Aristotle, the culmination; after them, a decline and a kind of dissolution of thought life.

Whoever contemplates this development can arrive at the question as to whether thought life really has the power to give everything to the soul toward which it has led it by bringing it to the complete consciousness of itself. For the unbiased observer, Greek thought life has an element that makes it appear "perfect" in the best sense of the word. It is as if the energy of thought in the Greek thinkers had worked out everything that it contains in itself. Whoever judges differently will notice on closer inspection that somewhere in his judgment an error is involved. Later world conceptions have produced accomplishments through other forces of the soul. Of the later thoughts as such, it can always be shown that with respect to their real thought content they can already be found in some earlier Greek thinker. *What* can be thought and how one can doubt about thinking and knowledge, all enters the field of consciousness in Greek civilization, and in the manifestation of thought the soul takes possession of its own being.

Has Greek thought life, however, shown the soul that it has the power to supply it with everything that it has stimulated in it? The philosophical current called Neo-Platonism, which in a way forms an aftermath of Greek thought life, was confronted with this question. *Plotinus* (205–270 A.D.) was its chief representative. *Philo*, who lived at the beginning of the Christian era in Alexandria, could be considered a forerunner of this movement. He does not base his effort to construct a world conception on the creative energy of thought. Rather, he *applies* thought in order to understand the revelation of the *Old Testament*. He interprets what is told in this document as fact in an intellectual, allegorical manner. For him, the accounts of the *Old Testament* turn into symbols for soul events to which he attempts to gain access intellectually.

Plotinus does not regard thought experience as something that embraces the soul in its full life. Behind thought life another life of the soul must lie, a soul life that would be concealed rather than revealed by the action of thought. The soul must overcome the life in thought, must extinguish it in itself and only after this extinction can it arrive at a form of experience that unites it with the origin of the world. Thought leads the soul to itself; now it must seize something in itself that will again lead it out of the realm into which thought has brought it. What Plotinus strives for is an *illumination* that begins in the soul after it has left the realm to which it has been carried by thought. In this way he expects to rise up to a world being that does not enter into thought life. World reason, therefore, toward which Plato and Aristotle strive, is not, according to Plotinus, the last reality at which the soul arrives. It is rather the outgrowth of a still higher reality that lies beyond all thinking. From this reality beyond all thought, which cannot be compared with anything that could be a possible object of thought, all world processes emanate.

Thought, as it could manifest itself in Greek spiritual life, has, as it were, gone through a complete revolution and thereby all possible relationships of man to thought seem to be exhausted. Plotinus looks for sources other than those given in thought revelation. He leaves the continuing evolution of thought life and enters the realm of mysticism. It is not intended to give a description of the development of mysticism here, but only the development of thought life and what has its origin in this process is to be outlined. There are, however, at various points in the spiritual development of mankind connections between intellectual world conceptions and mysticism. We find such a point of contact in Plotinus. His soul life is not ruled only by thinking. He has a mystical experience that presents an inner awareness without the presence of thoughts in his soul. In this experience he finds his soul united with the world foundation. His way of presenting the connection of the world with its ground, however, is to be expressed in thoughts. The reality beyond thought is the most perfect; what proceeds from it is less perfect. In this way, the process continues down into the visible world, the most imperfect. Man finds himself in this world of imperfection. Through the act of perfecting his soul, he is to cast off what the world in which he finds himself can give him, and is thus to find a path of development through which he becomes a being that is of one accord with the perfect origin.

We see a personality in Plotinus who feels the impossibility to continue Greek thought life. He cannot find anything that would grow as a further branch of world conception out of thought itself. If one looks for the sense in which the evolution of philosophy proceeds, one is justified in saying that the formation of picture conception has turned into that of thought conceptions. In a similar way, the production of thought conception must change again into something else, but the evolution of the world conception is not ready for this in the age of Plotinus. He therefore abandons thought and searches outside thought experience. Greek thoughts, however, fructified by his mystical experiences, develop into the evolutionary ideas that present the world process as a sequence of stages proceeding in a descending order, from a highest most perfect being to imperfect beings. In the thinking of Plotinus, Greek thoughts continue to have their effect. They do not develop as an organic growth of the original forces, however, but are taken over into the mystical consciousness. They do not undergo a transformation through their own energies but through nonintellectual forces.

Ammonius Sakkas (175–242), *Porphyrius* (232–304), *Iamblichus* (who lived in the fourth century A.D.), *Proclus* (410–485), and others are followers and expounders of this philosophy.

In a way similar to that of Plotinus and his successors, Greek thinking in its more Platonic shade continued under the influence of a nonintellectual element. Greek thought in its Pythagorean nuance is treated by *Nigidius Figulus, Apollonius of Tyana, Moderatus of Gades,* and others.

Note:

1. This book, which is to give a picture of the world and life conceptions of the nineteenth century is, in its second edition, supplemented by a brief account of the preceding philosophies insofar as they are based on an *intellectual* conception of the world. I have done this because I feel that the ideas of the last century are better shown in their inner significance if they are not taken by themselves, but if the highlights of thought of the preceding ages fall on them. In such an "introduction" not all the "documentary materials" can be given that must form the basis of this short sketch. If I should have the opportunity to develop the sketch into an independent book, it would become clear that the appropriate basis really exists. I also have no doubt that others who want to see in this sketch a suggestion for new viewpoints will find the documentary evidence in the historical sources that have been traditionally handed down to us.

Δ

In summary of some of the ideas put forward in the preceding chapter; There are four distinctly discernible epochs in the evolution of the philosophical struggle of mankind that presented themselves to the philosopher's view. He had to recognize the difference of these epochs as distinct as the difference of species in the realm of nature. This observation led him to acknowledge in the realm of the history of man's philosophical development the existence of objective spiritual impulses following a definite law of evolution of their own, independent of the individual men in whom they are observed. The achievements of these men as philosophers thus appear as the manifestation of these impulses that direct the course of events under the surface of external history.

It can be shown that in the evolutionary course of the philosophical struggle of mankind, periods are distinguishable, each of which lasts between seven and eight centuries. In each of these epochs there is a distinctly different impulse at work, as if it were under the surface of external history, sending its rays into the human personalities and thus causing the evolution of man's mode of philosophizing while taking its own definite course of development.

The first epoch of the development of philosophical views begins in Greek antiquity. It can be distinctly traced back as far as Pherekydes of Syros and Thales of Miletos and it comes to a close in the age of beginning Christianity. The spiritual aspiration of mankind in this age shows an essentially different character from that of earlier times. It is the age of awakening thought life. Prior to this age, the human soul lived in imaginative (symbolic) thought pictures that expressed its relation to the world and existence.

A new period begins with the dawn of the Christian era. The human soul can now no longer experience thought as a perception from the outer world. It now feels thought as the product of its own (inner) being. An impulse much more powerful than the stream of thought life now radiates into the soul from the deeper currents of the spiritual creative process. It is only now that self-consciousness awakes in mankind in a form adequate to the true nature of this self-consciousness. What men had experienced in this respect before that time had only been harbingers and anticipatory phenomena of what one should in its deepest meaning call inwardly experienced self-consciousness.

It is to be hoped that a future history of spiritual evolution will call this time the 'Age of Awakening Self-Consciousness.' Only now does man become in the true sense of the word aware of the whole scope of his soul life as 'Ego.' The full weight of this fact is more instinctively felt than distinctly known by the philosophical spirits of that time. All philosophical aspirations of that epoch retain this general character up to the time of Scotus Erigena. The philosophers of this period are completely submerged in religious conceptions with their philosophical thinking. Through this type of thought formation, the human soul, finding itself in an awakened self-consciousness entirely left to its own resources, strives to gain the consciousness of its submergence in the life of the world organism. Thought becomes a mere means to express the conviction regarding the relation of man's soul to the world that one has gained from religious sources. Steeped in this view, nourished by religious conceptions, thought life grows like the seed of a plant in the soul of the earth, until it breaks forth into the light.

From Pherekydes (or Thales) to the Sophists, one can observe how emaciated thought in Greece, which had already been born before these men, gradually finds its place in the stream of philosophical development. The effect thought has when it is placed in the service of world conception becomes apparent in them. The birth of thought, however, is to be observed in the entire Greek life. One could show much the same kind of development in the fields of art, poetry, public life, the various crafts and trades, and one would see everywhere how human activity changes under the influence of the form of human organization that introduces thought into the world conception. It is not correct to say that philosophy 'discovers' thought. It comes into existence through the fact that the newly born thought life is used for the construction of a world picture that formerly had been formed out of experiences of a different kind.

From the beginning of the Christian Era to Scotus Erigena, the experience of thought continues to be effective in such a way that its form is determined by the presupposition of a spiritual world, namely, the world of religious revelation. From the eighth to the sixteenth century, thought experience wrests itself free from the inner self-consciousness but allows, besides its own germinating power, the other power of consciousness, revelation, to continue in its existence. From the sixteenth century on, it is the picture of nature that eliminates the experience of thought itself; henceforth, the self-consciousness attempts to produce, out of its own energies, the resources through which it is possible to form a world conception with the help of thought. It is with this task that Descartes finds himself confronted. It is the task of the thinkers of the new period of world conception.

Goethe's *Faust* and The Mothers

Steiner gave wisdom teachings that revealed the most comprehensive cosmology of the Divine Hierarchy, and thus had to reveal the three aspects of Sophia—Mother/Daughter/Holy Sophia (Anthroposophia). Now is the time for clear thinkers, enriched by Spiritual Science, to study and embrace Sophia in all Her forms and finally clarify the true nature of the elemental kingdoms and their relationship with The Mothers.

Johann Wolfgang von Goethe understood the realm of The Mothers better than most. He describes this mysterious and powerful realm with reverence, fear, and trepidation. He knows that the aspirant must descend into the bowls of earth and meet The Mothers as part of any spiritual initiation. Goethe has Faust conversing with Mephistopheles about this realm in *Faust*, Part II. Act I. Scene V.

> *A Gloomy Gallery*
> **Mephistopheles**
> Unwillingly! There's a greater mystery, I say,
> Goddesses, enthroned on high, and solitary.
> No space round them, not even time: only
> To speak of them embarrasses me.
> They are The Mothers!
>
> **Faust (Terrified)**
> Mothers!
>
> **Mephistopheles**
> Are you afraid?

Faust
The Mothers! Mothers! It sounds so strange!

Mephistopheles
As, it is. Goddesses, unknown, as you see,
To you Mortals, not named by us willingly.
You must dig in the Depths to reach them:
It's your own fault that we need them.

Faust
Where is the path?

Mephistopheles
No path! Into the un-enterable,
Never to be entered: One path to the un-askable,
Never to be asked. Are you ready?
No locks, no bolts to manipulate,
You'll drift about in solitary space.
Can you conceive the waste and solitary?

Faust
I think you might spare the speeches then:
They always smell of the witches' kitchen,
Of a long-forgotten time, to me.
Have I not trafficked with the world?
Learned the void, the void unfurled? -
When I spoke with reason, as I descried,
Contradiction, doubly loud, replied:
Have I not fled, from hateful trickery,
Into the wild, into the solitary,
And, not to lose all, and live alone,
Surrendered to the Devil's own?

Mephistopheles
And if you'd swum through every ocean,
And seen the boundless space all round

You'd still have seen wave on wave in motion,
Though you might have been afraid to drown.
You'd have seen something. Seen, within
The green still seas, the leaping dolphin:
Seen clouds go by, Sun, Moon, and star -
You'll see none in the endless void, afar,
Hear not a single footstep fall,
Find no firm place to rest at all.

Faust
You speak as chief of all Mystagogues, who
Deceive their neophytes, the loyal and true:
Only reversed. You send me to the Void,
So, I'll increase the power and skill employed:
To use me, like a cat, that's your desire:
Just to claw your chestnuts from the fire.
The same as ever! I'll find what I'll discover:
In your Nothingness, I hope, the All I will recover.

Mephistopheles
I'll praise you, before you separate from me,
That you know the Devil, I can truly see:
Here take this key.

Faust
That tiny thing!

Mephistopheles
Grasp it, it has a worth you're undervaluing.

Faust
It's growing in my hand, it shines and glows!

Mephistopheles
What one possesses in it, would you now know?
The key will sniff the place out, from all others.

Follow it down: it leads you to The Mothers.

Faust
The Mothers! That always strikes me like a blow!
What is that word that, once heard, scares me so?

Mephistopheles
Are you so limited one new word disturbs you?
Will you only hear what you're accustomed to?
Don't be troubled, whatever strange sound rings,
You've already long been used to marvelous things.

Faust
Yes, there's no good for me in lethargy.
A shudder's the truest sign of humanity:
Though the world is such we may not feel it,
Once seized by it, we feel Immensity deeply.

Mephistopheles
Then, descend! I might as easily say rise!
It's all the same. Escape from what exists,
Into the boundless realm where all Form lies!
Delight in what's no longer on the list:
Where turmoil rolls along all cloudily:
Then, far from your body, swing the key!

Faust (Inspired)
Good! I feel new strength, firmly grasped,
My heart expands, on now to the great task.

Mephistopheles
Sight of a glowing tripod will tell you, finally,
You're in the last deep, deepest there might be.
By its light you'll see The Mothers,
Some sit about, as they wish, the others,
Stand and move. Formation, Transformation,

Eternal minds in eternal recreation.
Images of all creatures float, portrayed:
They'll not see you: they only see a shade.
Be of good heart, the danger there is great,
Go to the tripod: don't hesitate,
And touch it with the key!
(Faust assumes a commanding attitude with the key.)

Mephistopheles (Watching him)
That's right!
It will close itself, and follow as a servant might:
Exalted by your good luck, you'll calmly rise,
And be back with it, before you've blinked your eyes.
And, once you've brought it here all right,
Call the Hero and Heroine from the night,
The first man who has ever achieved it:
It's done, and you're the one who did it.
By magic process then you'll surely find,
The incense' vapor will become divine.

Faust
And now: what?

Mephistopheles
Strain with all your being: downward.
Stamp to descend, stamp again to go upward.
(Faust stamps and sinks out of sight.)
If he might only gain some good from that key!
I'm curious as to whether he'll return to me.

Scene VII: The Hall of the Knights, Dimly Lit

Faust (Sublimely)
In your name, Mothers, you enthroned
In boundlessness, set eternally alone,

And yet together. All the Forms of Life
Float round your heads, active, not alive.
Whatever was, in all its glow and gleam,
Moves there still since it must always be.
And you assign it, with omnipotent might,
To day's pavilion or the vault of night.
Life holds some fast on its sweet track,
Others the bold magician must bring back:
Filled with faith, and richly generous,
He shows, what each desires, the Marvelous.

Faust
What rape! Am I nothing in this place!
Is this key no longer in my hand!
It led me through terror, waste, and wave,
Through solitude, to where, set firm, I stand.
Here's a foothold! Here's reality,
Where spirit dare with spirits disagree,
And prepare itself for its great, dual mastery.
She was so far: how could she closer shine!
I'll rescue her, and she'll be doubly mine.
The risk! The Mothers! They must grant her!
Who knows her once, can never live without her.

Goethe has given us a poetic initiation into the mysteries of The Mothers that is not for the meek or faint-hearted. It is a process of initiation to witness Old Saturn, Old Sun, and Old Moon Beings, forces, and secrets from the past. Truly, like Faust, our hearts would quake to stand before the creators of the mineral, plant, and animal kingdoms. The Mothers created and still sustain these kingdoms and their elementary effects on the human beings physical, etheric, and astral bodies.

Let's hear what Steiner has to say further about Goethe's insight and the initiatory meeting of The Mothers in *Faust*.

Isis and Madonna, **Rudolf Steiner, Berlin, April 29, 1909, GA 57**

"Today our attention is to be drawn to a secret truth of this kind which for centuries has endeavored to find expression in art; it is true this has always found its scientific formulation in certain narrow circles, but for a wider public it will only become a matter of popular knowledge in the future through spiritual science. Goethe himself was able in his soul to approach this truth from very many angles. In one of my lectures here on Goethe I pointed to the significant moment in his life that was an instance of this kind of experience. In the second of the lectures on Faust I told you how Goethe on reading the Roman writer Plutarch came across the remarkable story of Nikias, who wanted to make subject again to the Romans a certain town in Sicily belonging to the Carthaginians, and on that account was being pursued. In his flight he feigned insanity, and by his strange cry: "The Mothers, The Mothers are pursuing me!" it was recognized that this insanity was of no ordinary kind. For in that region there existed a so-called 'Temple of The Mothers,' set up in connection with ancient Mysteries; hence it was known what was signified by the expression 'The Mothers.' When Goethe was able to let the full significance of the expression 'The Mothers' sink into his soul, he realized that if he wanted to reach the highest point of awe-inspiring beauty in one of the scenes in the second part of his *Faust*, he could not express this better than by sending Faust himself to The Mothers."

"Now what does this journey to The Mothers signify for Faust? We have made brief mention of this in the lecture referred to. Mephistopheles himself cannot enter the realm where The Mothers are enthroned although he gives Faust the key. Mephistopheles is the spirit of materialism, the spirit contained in the forces and powers of man's material existence. To him the realm of The Mothers is the realm of nothingness. Faust, the spiritual human being, with his bent towards the spirit is able to answer: "In thy nothingness I hope to find the All." Then follows the highly remarkable and significant description of the realm of The Mothers, and we are told how they weave and live in a sphere out of which the forms of the visible world are fashioned; how man, if he would penetrate to The Mothers, must rise above all that lives in space and time. Formation, transformation, this is the essence of their realm. They are mysterious Goddesses holding sway in a spiritual realm behind the reality of the senses. Faust must penetrate to them if he is to obtain knowledge of all that transcends the sensory and physical. Only by widening his soul to this realm of The Mothers can Faust worthily unite in Helen the eternal with the temporal. In that lecture on *Faust* it was possible to indicate that Goethe fully understood how in this realm of The Mothers one has to do with a sphere into which man is able to penetrate when he awakens slumbering spiritual forces in his soul. This is for him the great moment in which are revealed to him the spiritual beings and facts which are always around us, but which with the eyes of the senses we see as little as the blind man sees color and light. It is the moment when the spiritual eyes and ears are opened to a world lying behind the physical world. Entrance into this realm is portrayed by the journey to The Mothers."

"In these lectures it was repeatedly indicated that when man practices certain inner exercises on his soul, certain minutely prescribed methods for sinking deeply into the world of his conceptions, feelings and will, then his spiritual eyes and ears actually become open and new realms are unfolded around him. It was also shown that whoever enters this realm is confused by all the impressions that work upon him. Whereas in the physical world we perceive objects in sharp outline from which we take our bearings, in the spiritual world we have a confused feeling of inter-weaving, hovering form, just as Goethe describes it in the second part of Faust. But it is out of this realm of The Mothers that there is born all that is given to our senses, just as in the mountains metal is born out of the mother-ore. And because this mysterious realm, the Mother-realm of everything earthly and physical, the realm containing, so to say, the divine substance of all things—because this mysterious realm is resounding in Goethe, the expression "The Mothers" works with such fascination and awesome beauty. Thus, when he read in Plutarch that someone cried "The Mothers, The Mothers," he recognized that this was not a mad vision into an insane and unreal world, but a vision into a world of spiritual reality. The Mother problem of the world stood before Goethe while he was reading Plutarch, and in the way he did with much else he inserted this Mother problem as a mystery into the second part of his *Faust*."

"Now anyone wishing to enter this realm of The Mothers, the realm of the spiritual world, has had at all times to undertake, besides other exercises that may be found in *Knowledge of the Higher Worlds,* what has invariably been called preparatory purification, catharsis of the soul. He must so prepare himself that his soul, out of which the higher spiritual forces are to be derived is free of all urge and passion for the ordinary world of the senses.

"What has remained to man from that realm of soul and spirit, to man who did not withdraw like Osiris from the physical sense world but entered into it? What has remained to him? It is his soul, his being of spirit and soul that will always draw him onwards to the original source of spirit and soul—to Osiris. This is the human soul dwelling within us, Isis, in a certain sense the *eternal feminine who draws us onward* to the realm out of which we are born."

"Isis, when she is purified and has laid aside all that she has received from the physical, is impregnated from the spiritual world and gives birth to Horus, the higher man, who is to be victorious over the lower human being. Thus, we see Isis as the representative of the human soul, as that in us which as the divine spiritual is born of the universal Father and has remained within us, seeking Osiris and only finding him through initiation or death. By conjuring this Osiris and Isis saga in a picture before our soul we are looking into the realm that lies behind the physical world of the senses, into a time when man was still among The Mothers, the primordial grounds of existence, when Isis was not yet enclosed in the physical body but still united in the golden age with her spouse Osiris."

"Then there is revealed to us the most beautiful flower of mankind, the highest human ideal, which is born out of the human body impregnated by the eternal world-Spirit. Hence how could it be other than the most sublime ideal, the highest peak of humanity, the Christ Himself—for He is the ideal of what they represent—Who would naturally enter the realm of The Mothers. In Goethe's *Faust* we meet with three Mothers seated on golden tripods—three Mothers. The human soul has passed through its evolution during the ages when it was not as yet in a human body. What we today have as human conception and human birth appears to us only as final emblem and symbol of the earlier form of the same thing. In the physical Mother we see the ultimate physical form of a spiritual Mother who is behind her; and we see the impregnation of this spiritual Mother taking place not in the way happening on earth today but out of the Cosmos itself, just as in higher knowledge our souls are fructified from out the Cosmos. We look back to ever more spiritual forms of fructification and reproduction."

"Therefore, in the true sense of spiritual science we do not speak only of one Mother but of The Mothers, realizing that what we have today as the physical Mother is the last development of the soul-spiritual figure out of the spiritual realm. Crux Ansata. There are in fact images of Isis representing not one Mother but Mothers, three Mothers. In front we have a figure, Isis with the Horus child at her breast, resembling the oldest representations of the Madonna. But behind this figure in certain Egyptian representations, we have another figure, an Isis, bearing on her head the two familiar cow horns and the wings of the hawk, offering the 'crux ansata' to the child. We see that what is physical, human, in the foremost figure is here more spiritualized. Behind there is yet a third figure, bearing a lion's head and representing the third stage of the human soul. This is how these three Isis figures appear, one behind the other. It is an actual fact that our human soul bears in it three natures—a will nature, found in the inmost depths of the being, a feeling nature, and a wisdom nature. These are the three soul Mothers; we meet them in the three figures of the Egyptian Isis."

"That behind the physical Mother we have the superphysical Mother, the spiritual Mother, the Isis of spiritual antiquity, with the hawk's wings, the cow horns, with the globe of the world between them on the head of Isis—this is profound symbolism. Those who understand something of the ancient so-called theory of numbers have always said—and this corresponds with a deep truth—that the sacred number three represents the divine masculine in the Cosmos. This sacred number three is pictorially expressed by the globe of the world and two cow horns which are, if you like, a kind of image of the Madonna's crescent, but actually represents the fruitful working of the forces of nature."

"The globe represents the creative activity of the Cosmos. I should have to speak for hours were I to give a picture of the masculine element in the world. Thus, behind the physical Isis stands her representative the superphysical Isis, who is not impregnated by one of her own kind but by the divine masculine living and weaving throughout the world. The process of fructification is still portrayed as being akin to the process of cognition. The consciousness that the process of cognition is a kind of fructification was still living in ancient times. You may read in the *Bible*: "Adam knew his wife and she brought forth ..." What today we receive as spiritual gives birth to the spiritual in the soul; it is something that represents a last remnant of the ancient mode of fructification. What comes to expression here shows us how today we are fructified by the spirit of the world receiving this spirit into the human soul as spirit of the world in order to acquire human knowledge, human feeling, human will."

"This is what is represented in Isis. She is fructified by the divine male element, so that the head is fructified; and it is not material substance that is offered the child, as in the case of the physical Isis, but the 'crux ansata' which is the sign of life. Whereas here from the physical Isis physical substance of life is offered, there is offered the spirit of life in its symbol. Behind the physical Mother of life there appears the spiritual Mother of life; behind her again the primal force of all life, represented with the life force, just as the will dwells behind everything in the still spiritual, far distant past. Here we have the three Mothers, and also the way in which out of the Cosmos these three Mothers impart vitalizing force to the Sun. Here we have what is not an artistic expression, nevertheless a symbolic expression of a profound cosmic truth. What lasted throughout the Egyptian evolution as the Isis symbol was received in more recent times and transformed in accordance with the progress made by humanity as a result of the appearance of Christ Jesus on earth; for in Christ Jesus, we have the great prototype of everything that the human soul is destined to bring forth out of itself. The human soul in its fructification out of the spirit of the world is given tangible form in the Madonna. In the Madonna we meet, as it were, with Isis reborn and in an appropriate way enhanced, transfigured."

"What could be portrayed in pictures at the beginning of the lecture now comes before our souls as bound up with the evolution of humanity, streaming forth from hoary antiquity, artistically transfigured and given new form in the modern pictures presented throughout the world to the human souls thirsting for art. Here we see how in very truth art, as in Goethe's words, becomes the exponent of truth. We see how in reality when our gaze falls on the Madonna, when this gaze is permeated with deep feeling, the soul partakes in certain knowledge of the mighty riddle of the world. We realize that in such surrender our soul, seeking in itself for the eternal feminine, is yearning for the divine Father-Spirit born out of the Cosmos, to Whom as the Sun we give birth in our own soul. What we are as man, and how as man we are related to the Universe, this is what meets us in the pictures of the Madonna. That is why the pictures of the Madonna are such holy things, apart altogether from any religious stream, from any religious dogma. Hence, we can feel it as something born out of the Cosmos when the hazy masses of cloud form themselves into the heads of Angels, and out of the whole the representative of the human soul comes into being. The Madonna also includes what can be born out of the human soul, the true higher man slumbering in every human being, all that is best in man, what as spirit flows and weaves through the world. Goethe too felt this when he gave final form to his *Faust* when he had led him on through the different stages up to higher knowledge and the higher life. This is why he makes Faust go to The Mothers and why the name 'Mothers' sounds to Faust so awe-inspiring and so beautiful, instilling in him a feeling for the wisdom echoing down from ancient times. Thus, Goethe felt that he must send Faust to The Mothers, that only there could Faust seek and find the eternal through which Euphorion can come into being. Because the human soul appeared to him to be represented by the Madonna, Goethe gave expression to the riddle of the soul in the words of the Chorus Mysticus: "The eternal feminine draws us upwards."

"Whatever modern times may have to say, this is the reason why Raphael, in his wonderful picture of the Madonna, succeeded so well in leading us back to the realms to which the old figures of Isis belong. From what is spiritual, from what can no longer be expressed in a human figure because it would be too material, from that Isis whose force can be represented symbolically only by the lion's head, we descend to the human Isis who transmits her force to Horus through physical substance. Raphael unconsciously expressed this in his Sistine Madonna. But spiritual science will lead man consciously back to the spiritual realm out of which he has descended. Two lectures that I shall be giving here will furnish examples of how man has descended out of spiritual heights and will ascend again to this higher existence. Both lectures, that of 1st May and that of 6th May, 1909, will show us in a strictly scientific sense how these Madonna pictures and representations of Isis are indeed dearly and definitely artistic exponents of the very deepest secrets of Nature and of the spirit, and how in reality they are just a transcription of Plato's sublime words: "Once man was a spiritual being; he descended to earth only because he was robbed of his spiritual wings, and was enveloped in a physical body. He will struggle out of this physical body again and re-ascend to the world of spirit and soul." This was proclaimed by the philosopher Plato. Pictures of the Madonna proclaim the same, for in the most beautiful sense they are what Goethe wished to express in the words: "Art is the worthiest exponent of the recognized mysteries of the world." Man need not fear that art will become abstract or wholly allegorical if it is once again compelled, I repeat compelled, to recognize the higher spiritual realities; nor need he fear that it will become stiff and lifeless when it finds itself unable to continue using outer, crude physical models."

Spiritual Scientific Notes on Goethe's Faust, **Volume II, Rudolf Steiner, Lecture IV,** *Faust and the 'Mothers,'* **Dornach, November 2, 1917, GA 273**

"Now I have often spoken here before about the importance of the 'Mothers scene' in the second part of Goethe's *Faust*; this scene, however, is of such a nature that one can repeatedly return to it because through its significant content, apart from the aesthetic value of the way in which it is introduced into the poem, it really contains a kind of culminating point of all that is spiritual in present day life. And if this 'Mothers scene' is allowed to work upon us, we shall well be able to say that it contains a very great deal of all that Goethe is wishing to indicate. It comes indeed out of Goethe's immediate soul experiences just as on the other it throws light on the significant, deep knowledge that we are obliged to recognize in him if we are to have any notion at all of what is meant by this scene where Faust is offered by Mephistopheles the possibility of descending to The Mothers. If we notice how, on Faust's reappearing and coming forth from The Mothers, the Astrologer refers to him as 'priest,' and that Faust henceforward refers to himself as 'priest,' we have to realize that there is something of deep import in this conversion of what Faust has been before into the priest. He has descended to The Mothers: he has gone through some kind of transformation. Leaving aside what one otherwise knows of the matter and what has been said by us in the course of years, we need reflect only upon how the Greek poets, in speaking of the Mysteries, refer to those who were initiated as having learnt to know the three World-Mothers—Rhea, Demeter, and Proserpina. These three Mothers, their being, what they essentially are—all this was said to be learned through direct perception by those initiated into the Mysteries in Greece."

"When we dwell upon the significant manner in which Goethe speaks in this scene, and also upon what takes place in the next, we shall no longer be in any doubt that in reality Faust has been led into regions, into kingdoms, that Goethe thought to be like that kingdom of The Mothers into which the initiate into the Greek Mysteries was led. By this we are shown how full of import Goethe's meaning is.

"And now remind yourselves of how the moment Mephistopheles mentions the word 'Mothers' Faust shudders, saying what is so full of meaning: "Mothers, Mothers! How strange that sounds!" And this is all introduced by Mephistopheles' words "It is with reluctance that I disclose the higher mystery." Thus, it is really a matter here of something hidden, a mystery, that Goethe, in this half secret way, found necessary to impart to the world in connection with the development of his Faust.

"In his connection with Faust, Mephistopheles, in his capacity as an ahrimanic force, belongs to our world of the senses, but as a supersensible being. He has been transplanted.

He has no power over the worlds into which Faust is now to be transplanted. They really do not exist for him. Faust has to pass over into a different state of consciousness that perceives, beneath the foundation of our world of the senses, the never-ceasing weaving and living, surging and becoming, from which our sense-world is drawn. And Faust is to become acquainted with the forces that are there below."

"The 'Mothers' is a name not without significance for entering this world. Think of the connection of the word 'Mothers' with everything that is growing, becoming. In the attributes of The Mothers is the union of what is physical and material with what is not. Picture to yourselves the coming into physical existence of the human creature, his incarnation. You must picture a certain process that takes place through the interworking of the Cosmos with the mother-principle, before the union of the male and female is consummated. The man who is about to become physical prepares himself beforehand in the female element. And we must now make a picture of this preparation that is confined to what goes on up to the moment when impregnation takes place—all therefore that takes place before impregnation. One has a quite wrong and materialistically biased notion if one imagines that there lie already formed in the woman all the forces that lead to the physical human embryo. That is not so. A working of the cosmic forces of the spheres takes place; into the woman work cosmic forces. The human embryo is always a result of cosmic activity. What is described in materialistic natural science as the germ-cell is in a certain measure produced out of the mother alone, but it is a counterpart of the great cosmic germ-cell."

"Let us hold this picture in mind—this becoming of the human germ-cell before impregnation and let us ask ourselves what the Greeks looked for in their three mothers, Rhea, Demeter, and Proserpina. In these three Mothers they saw a picture of those forces that, working down out of the Cosmos, prepare the human cell. These forces, however, do not come from the part of the Cosmos that belongs to the physical but to the supersensible. The Mothers Demeter, Rhea, and Proserpina belong to the supersensible world. No wonder then that Faust has the feeling that an unknown kingdom is making its presence felt when the word 'Mothers' is spoken."

"I ask you to think over this and then to remember that it is all this that Goethe wants to indicate. In this scene of *Faust* he wishes to point out to the world that there is a spiritual kingdom, and that here he is showing the way in which man can relate himself to it. This is how things are connected."

"Since the beginning of the Fifth Post-Atlantean Epoch the knowledge of these things has to a great extent been lost. I have told you that Goethe applied the knowledge he had personally received through great spiritual vision. The whole connection with The Mothers had entered into Goethe's soul when he read Plutarch. For Plutarch, the Roman storyteller whom Goethe read, speaks of The Mothers; and the following particular scene in Plutarch seems to have made a deep impression on Goethe.

"The Romans were at war with Carthage. Nicias is in favor of the Romans and wishes to seize the town of Engyon from the Carthaginians; he is therefore to be given over to the Carthaginians. So, he feigns madness and runs through the streets crying "The Mothers—The Mothers are pursuing me!" From this you may see that in the time of which Plutarch writes this relation of The Mothers is brought into connection not with the normal understanding of the senses, but with a condition of man when this normal understanding is not present. It is beyond all doubt that what Goethe read in Plutarch stirred him to bring to expression in his *Faust* this idea of The Mothers."

"We also find mention in Plutarch of how the world has a triangular form. Now naturally these words 'the world has a triangular form' must not be taken in a heavy literal sense, for the spatial is but a symbol of what has neither time nor space. Since we live in space, spatial images must be used for what is nevertheless beyond image, time, or space."

"Thus, Plutarch gives the picture of a triangular world. This the whole world. According to Plutarch, in the center of this triangle that is the world, the field of truth is found. Now out of this whole world Plutarch differentiates 183 worlds; 183 worlds, so he says, are in the whole circumference, they move around, and in the middle is this resting field of truth. This resting field of truth Plutarch describes as being separated by time from the surrounding 183 worlds—sixty on each of the three sides of the triangle and one at each angle makes 183. When, therefore, you take this imagination of Plutarch's, you have a world considered as consisting of three parts and in the cloud formation around it the 183 worlds welling and surging. That is at the same time the imagination for the 'Mothers.' The number 183 is given by Plutarch."

"Moreover, when we take our Earth upon which we are still evolving, and about which we cannot speak as of something completed, and when we look from this Earth to Saturn, Sun and Moon, there we find The Mothers that figure in another form in the Greek Mysteries under names Proserpina, Demeter, and Rhea. For all the forces that are in Old Saturn, Old Sun and Old Moon are still working—working on into our own time. And those forces that are physical are but the shadow, the image, of what is spiritual. Everything physical is a mere picture of the spiritual."

"We now ask whether these forces thus related to the Moon have a real existence anywhere. The Greeks looked upon them as mysterious, as very full of mystery. And our modern destiny is connected with the fact that these forces no longer retain their character as mysteries but have been made available for all. If we only concentrate on this one thing, on these forces that are connected with the Moon—then we have one of The Mothers. What is this one Mother? We shall best approach the answer to this question in the following way."

"What is there under the Earth ruling as the being of electricity is Moon-impulse that has been left behind. It definitely does not belong to the earth. It is impulse remaining over from the Moon and was spoken of as such by the Greeks. And the Greeks still had knowledge of the relation between this force, distributed throughout the whole earth, and the reproductive forces. And there is this relation with the forces of growth and of increase. This was one of The Mothers."

"Now you can imagine that all these premonitions of mighty connections did not arise before Faust merely as theories, but he felt himself obliged to seek out—to enter right into these impulses. Knowledge of this force was, first of all, given to those being initiated into the Greek Mysteries, this force together with the two other Mothers. The Greeks held all that was connected with electricity in secret in the Mysteries. And herein is where lies the decadence of the future of the Earth—of which I have already spoken from another point-of-view—that these forces will be made public. One of these forces has already become so during the Fifth Post-Atlantean Period—electricity. The others will be known about in the decadence of the Sixth and Seventh Periods."

"All this, even in the decadent new secret societies, is still among the things about which their conservative members will not speak. Goethe quite rightly judged it fit to give out knowledge of these things in the only way possible for him in that age. At the same time, however, you have one of the passages from which you can see how the great poet Goethe did not simply write as other poets write, but that each word of his bore its special impress and had its appointed place."

"Take for example the relation of The Mothers to electricity. Goethe belongs to those who treat such things out of a thoroughly expert knowledge."

"Do you now see what one possesses in it?
The key will ferret out the proper place.
Follow it up, it leads you to The Mothers."

Faust

"To the 'Mothers.' That strikes me always like a shock!"

"As if he had received an electric shock. This is written with intention—not haphazardly. In this scene nothing in connection with the matter in question is haphazard. Meeting The Mothers is tantamount to meeting the sub-natural forces beneath the earth."

The New Isis Myth

Rudolf Steiner provides a poetic description of the Being Anthroposophia in a moral imagination he calls *The New Isis Myth*. It is a perplexing and challenging 'new myth' for the aspirant of spiritual science to contemplate over and over again. No matter how many times one reads this myth, its archetypes keep unfolding new and hidden aspects of the being Steiner calls the New Isis. This New Isis—Anthroposophia—is found by 'looking under' the statue Steiner called The Representative of Mankind, which depicts Christ holding Lucifer and Ahriman at bay. This statue is somewhat like a new St. Michael and the Dragon archetype.

The *New Isis Myth* will be experienced differently by those who come to look at the Representative of Mankind. Some will not notice that Isis Sophia has come to birth and that later She herself will give birth to a child. What is certain though, is that we each must look for this New Isis and lift the veil that is shrouding her from being seen by all.

***Ancient Myths, their Meaning and Connection with Evolution,* Rudolf Steiner, Lecture III, *How Can Osiris Be Awakened to New Life?* January 6, 1918, GA 180**

"A statue was intended to be the central point of the Building [First Goetheanum]. This statue presented a Group of beings: the Representative of Man, then—Luciferic and Ahrimanic figures. People looked at the statue and did not know in the age of scientific profundity in the land Philisterium that the Statue, in fact, was only the veil for an invisible statue. But the invisible statue was not noticed by people, for it was the new Isis, the Isis of a new age.

"Some few persons of the land of scientific profundity had once heard of this remarkable connection between what was visible and what, as Isis-image, was concealed behind what was open and evident. And then in their profound allegorical-symbolical manner of speech they had put forward the assertion that this combination of the Representative of Man with "Lucifer and Ahriman signified Isis. With this word 'signified,' however, they not only ruined the artistic intention from which the whole thing was supposed to proceed—for an artistic creation does not merely signify something but is something—but they completely misunderstood all that underlay it. For it was not in the least the point that the figures signified something, but that they already were what they appeared to be. And behind the figures was not an abstract new Isis, but an actual, real new Isis. The figures 'signified' nothing at all, but they were in fact, in themselves, that which they made themselves out to be. But they possessed the peculiarity that behind them there was the real being, the new Isis.

"Some few who in special circumstances, in special moments, had nevertheless seen this new Isis, found that she is asleep. And so one can say: the real deeper-lying statue that conceals itself behind the external statue is the sleeping new Isis, a sleeping figure—visible—but seen by few. Many persons then turned in special moments to the inscription, which is plainly there at the spot where the statue stands in preparation, but which also has been read by few. And yet the inscription stands clearly there, just as clearly as the inscription once stood on the veiled form at Sais. In fact, the inscription stands there:

"I am Mankind, I am the Past, the Present and the Future. Every mortal should lift my veil."

"Another figure, as a visitor, once approached the sleeping figure of the new Isis, and then again and again. And the sleeping Isis considered this visitor her special benefactor and loved him. And one day she believed in a particular illusion, just as the visitor believed one day in a particular illusion: the new Isis had an offspring—and she considered the visitor whom she looked on as her benefactor, to be the father. He regarded himself as the father, but he was not. The spirit-visitor, who was none other than the new Typhon, believed that he could acquire a special increase of his power in the world if he took possession of this new Isis. So, the new Isis had an offspring, but she did not know its nature, she knew nothing of the being of this new offspring. And she moved it about, she dragged it far off into other lands, because she believed that she must do so. She trailed the new offspring about, and since she had trailed and dragged it through various regions of the world it fell to pieces into fourteen parts through the very power of the world.

"Thus, the new Isis had carried her offspring into the world and the world had dismembered it in fourteen pieces. When the spirit-visitor, the new Typhon, had come to know of this, he gathered together the fourteen pieces, and with all the knowledge of natural scientific profundity he again made a being, a single whole, out of the fourteen pieces. But in this being there were only mechanical laws, the law of the machine. Thus, a being had arisen with the appearance of life, but with the laws of the machine. And since this being had arisen out of fourteen pieces, it could reproduce itself again, fourteen-fold. And Typhon could give a reflection of his own being to each piece, so that each of the fourteen offspring of the new Isis had a countenance that resembled the new Typhon.

"And Isis had to follow all this strange affair, half-divining it; half-divining she could see the whole miraculous change that had come to her offspring. She knew that she had herself dragged it about, that she had herself brought all this to pass. But there came a day when in its true, its genuine form she could accept it again from a group of spirits who were elemental spirits of nature, could receive it from nature elementals.

"As she received her true offspring which only through an illusion had been stamped into the offspring of Typhon, there dawned upon her a remarkable clairvoyant vision: she suddenly noticed that she still had the cow-horns of ancient Egypt, in spite of having become a new Isis.

"And lo and behold, when she had thus become clairvoyant, the power of her clairvoyance summoned—some say Typhon himself, some say, Mercury. And he was obliged through the power of the clairvoyance of the new Isis to set a crown on her head in the place where once the old Isis had had the crown which Horus had seized from her, that is to say, on the spot where she developed the cow-horns. But this crown was merely of paper—covered with all sorts of writings of a profoundly scientific nature—still it was of paper. And she now had two crowns on her head, the cow-horns and the paper crown embellished with all the wisdom of scientific profundity.

"Through the strength of her clairvoyance there one day arose in her the deep meaning, as far as the age could reach, of that which is described in *St. John's Gospel* as the Logos. There arose in her the Johannine significance of the Mystery of Golgotha. Through this strength the power of the cow-horns grasped the paper crown and changed it into an actual golden crown of genuine substance."

America's Wooden Doll of Anthroposophy

The Life of Man on Earth, Facts Concerning Christianity, Rudolf Steiner, Lecture III, *Life on Earth, Race, Color*, March 3, 1923, Dornach, GA 349

"It is very remarkable: In Europe, over here, what we call Anthroposophy can be developed. It must be developed out of the Spirit—*that does not come at all out of racial characteristics*. It must be developed out of the Spirit. And the men who are unwilling to approach the Spirit will plunge Europe into disaster. The Americans do not yet need it, especially those who travel over there. For they can still maintain themselves on racial characteristics. We in Europe develop Anthroposophy out of the Spirit. Over there they develop something that is a kind of wooden doll of Anthroposophy. Everything becomes materialistic."

"But for one who is not a fanatic, there is something similar in American culture to what is anthroposophical science in Europe. Only, everything there is wooden, it is not yet alive. We can make it alive in Europe out of the Spirit: those over there take it out of instinct. The time will one day come when this American "wooden man"—which actually everyone is still—when he will begin to speak. Then he will have something to say very similar to European Anthroposophy. One can say that we in Europe develop Anthroposophy in a spiritual way; the American develops it in a natural way. Therefore, when I explain anthroposophical matters, I can so often point out: '*Well, this is how it is anthroposophically, and that is the American caricature of it.*'"

The Mysteries of Sophia

Who is Sophia? Is She the Holy Spirit or the wisdom aspect of Christ? Is She an amorphous primal soup, a duality of heavenly and earthly, the breath that weaves in between the Male Trinity? Is She a group of syzygies that have united with the Male Trinity?

Even after Rudolf Steiner's indications on Isis, Isis-Sophia, and Anthroposophia, we find many anthroposophical writers expressing completely different opinions of who this multifaceted being is. Rudolf Steiner said repeatedly that a detailed biography of the being of Isis-Sophia - TheoSophia - PhiloSophia - Natura - AnthropoSophia could be written. Yet it would seem, at first glance, that Steiner personally said little about Her in a biographical manner. In his book *Riddles of Philosophy* Steiner describes the evolution of philosophy and indicates that She is a being who has grown alongside human intellectual and spiritual development since 2100 BC. He even describes Anthroposophia as a 42-year-old human being (without a physical body) who passes through the individual each time a step in spiritual development is taken. Steiner said that She was 'in the room' during the laying of the foundation stone of the first Goetheanum and also during the Christmas Conference.

Who is this being of Sophia and how is a spiritual scientist supposed to sort through the many and varied opinions about her existence? Can we uncover Steiner's mysterious indications, and find the *Biography of Sophia*? One of the most accepted versions of Sophia is that She, in some enigmatic way, is the Holy Spirit. As such, She can be found in sacred literature to be one of the creative (or receptive) principles present at the moment of creation. Solving the mystery of how an un-manifest God (no one has ever seen God the Father) manifests the created Cosmos is bewildering. Often, Sophia (Wisdom) is there at creation as a 'reflection,' 'mirror,' or 'epiphany' of the Father God. But at the moment of creation, She is marginalized or demoted from Her primal position as Creatrix to one that is a 'creature' of the Creator. She takes on the role of one who has been created, not one who creates.

Rudolf Steiner tells us that Anthroposophia was working actively during the life, death, and resurrection of Jesus Christ, imprinting these spiritual advancements permanently into the etheric realm of Shambhala. Anthroposophia was age twenty-one during the Mystery of Golgotha and She continued to grow alongside humans as they developed; including Mary, Jesus, St. John, and others whose consciousness was spiritually advancing at that time.

Anthroposophia (the Earthly Sophia, Isis-Sophia) nor the Heavenly Sophia (the Wisdom Being of the Kyriotetes/the Daughter, Heavenly Sophia) cannot be the Holy Spirit because they have entirely different biographies. And yet, there is something in Anthroposophia that was advanced when the tongues of flame descended at Pentecost and brought the Holy Spirit to the disciples of Christ. Indeed, Anthroposophia and the Holy Spirit work closely together and can be confused as the same being. But they are not. Let's continue following Her biography.

Anthroposophia works in the realm of the Angels by helping the development of Moral Imagination, just as the Holy Spirit does. The difference is that Anthroposophia prepares the soul to advance from Sentient-Soul to Intellectual-Soul to Consciousness-Soul, at which point, Moral Imagination is developed. The three purified soul bodies combine to become the Virgin Sophia, the purified Consciousness-Soul which can develop into the Spiritual Soul. Then the Holy Spirit, called the Spirit-Self, can pour into the Virgin Soul that which it has been prepared to receive.

Anthroposophia works to prepare the Virgin Sophia to enter the realm of the Angels where Moral Imagination lives with the Holy Spirit, the Spirit-Self. This merging is described in great detail by Steiner who tells us that the higher part of the Consciousness-Soul, the Spiritual Soul, gleans from the world the eternal thoughts that stand behind sense impressions. The Earthly ego that is derived from the combination of all the eternal (timeless) thoughts that the Virgin Sophia has gleaned from the world of 'illusion' is given over to the higher self, the Spirit-Self to develop the higher ego. Humans have three egos, the Earthly ego is transformed into the Higher ego that is found in the realm of the Spirit-Self. This is the personal Higher ego. Sophia is the midwife of this process of ascension. Sophia helps us connect to our personal guardian Angel who leads us to the Holy Spirit of Christ. In the far future, humanity will have evolved into the realm of the Angels where Moral Imagination lives as archetypal thought-forms that continuously create. In those future ages, Sophia will walk amongst all people and converse with them whenever Wisdom is present in thinking (Moral Imagination). Interacting with Sophia will, in all cases, lead to the Wisdom of Christ's Love and deeper understanding of His cosmic nature.

Through understanding and embodying the Wisdom (Sophia) of Christ we become able to redeem the Tree of Knowledge of Good and Evil. Eating the fruit of that tree brought knowledge of death to the Garden of Eden; but now, we should eat the fruit to awaken and become gods who know the eternal, who are aware of their immortality and the Christ-power that overcomes death for all times.

When we reflect upon the biography of the Being of Wisdom from the ranks of the Kyriotetes, we have a complex account of cosmic deeds that go back to the Old Sun incarnation of the Earth when Archangels were in their human stage and working with the donations of the Beings of Wisdom. This Being of Cosmic Wisdom (Heavenly Sophia) used the combined efforts of the Kyriotetes during the Old Sun Planetary Condition of the Earth to create an atmosphere of light in which the Archangels found their life. The leader of the Beings of Wisdom (Heavenly Sophia) works especially through the Archangel Michael, who is the Sun Archangel and the one called the 'countenance of Christ.' In the realm of the Archangels (Life-Spirit) the cosmic leader of the Beings of Wisdom (Heavenly Sophia) works through the Archangel Michael, especially in our current age which is ruled by Michael who has risen to the rank of an Archai—Spirit of Time. Christ Himself works in the realm of the Life-Spirit and brings forth the Waters of Life that flow out from New Jerusalem and the Tree of Life. Both the Heavenly Sophia (Cosmic Being of Wisdom) and Christ (Cosmic Being of Love) are united in the realm of Life-Spirit as Sophia Christos. They join together in the alchemical 'mysterious conjunction' that appears as the wedding of the Virgin Sophia to the Lamb of God—humanity to Christ. It is the development of this Cosmic Wisdom (Sophia) of Christ that Rudolf Steiner indicated was the goal of the Consciousness-Soul era—to attain the 'Sophia of Christ.'

It is seldom spoken that the Cosmic Being of Wisdom (Sophia), just like Christ (as the second person in the Divine Trinity), came down through the ranks of the spiritual hierarchies below Her until She manifested as an over-lighting Angel on the Earth. Christ used the body of Jesus of Nazareth (the 'Sister Soul of Adam,' 'the Paradisiacal Adam,' the 'Adam Kadmon'), a pure body that had never physically incarnated before, as a vessel for three years starting from the Baptism in the River Jordan until His death. Christ accomplished His cosmic deeds on Earth as the "Son" of the Father God, the second person in the Holy Trinity. Christ used the combined forces of the Elohim (on the Sun) as a vessel for His descent from the spiritual realm of the Elohim through the realms of the Archai, Archangels, Angels, and human. As Christ descended through each of these three ranks, he performed deeds to help humanity develop the basic foundation necessary for free, individualized thinking. These deeds are called by Rudolf Steiner, the 'Pre-Earthly Deeds of Christ' that he spoke about on numerous occasions. The gifts Christ gave humanity through these Pre-Earthly

Deeds are referred to as: standing upright, speaking, and thinking. Steiner characterizes these three deeds also as balancing the forces of the zodiac, the planets, and the Earth. He also says these deeds could be characterized as harmonizing the heart and the six major organs, as well as the soul capacities of thinking, feeling, and willing.

The leader of the Beings of Wisdom (Kyriotetes) also descended through the ranks of the spiritual hierarchies below the Kyriotetes. This being, the Heavenly Sophia, descended through the Beings of Wisdom (Kyriotetes), Beings of Movement (Dynamis), and the Beings of Form (Elohim), who all reside on the Sun and planets, and later through the ranks of the Archai, Archangels, and Angels and into the realm of the human being by over-lighting the one called the 'Mother of Jesus.' The over-lighting of Mary of Jerusalem (later called Sophia or Mary Sophia) was so profound that through it she redeemed the 'fall into matter' by uniting the cosmic wisdom brought down from on high and the wisdom given to Her by Jesus before His baptism (as described by Steiner in his *Fifth Gospel*). One can say that Mary of Jerusalem as depicted in the *Gospel of Matthew*, who was Eve in a past life, redeemed the expulsion from the Garden of Eden by uniting with her higher self that was brought to her by the Cosmic Being of Wisdom (Heavenly Sophia). Mary of Jerusalem was the vessel not only for the Cosmic Being of Wisdom from the Kyriotetes and the wisdom of Jesus of Nazareth, but also for the 'Sister Soul of Eve' (the Paradisiacal Eve, the Eve Kadmon) who, like the 'Sister Soul of Adam' (Adam Kadmon) had remained in paradise until she incarnated for the first time as Mary of Nazareth (*Gospel of Luke*). The two Mary's (from Nazareth and Jerusalem) joined together as one soul and later the Heavenly Sophia over-lighted the combined Marys (Mary Sophia) as she accompanied Jesus Christ throughout His ministry.

Through Steiner's teachings we learn there were two Mary's (Nazareth and Jerusalem) and two Jesus boys (Nazareth and Jerusalem). Just before the baptism of Jesus (of Nazareth) in the River Jordan by John the Baptist, Jesus made a soul wrenching confession and spiritual transmission to his stepmother Mary Sophia. After this profound conversation, the now-deceased Mary (of Nazareth) united with Mary (of Jerusalem) through the intercession of the Cosmic Being of Wisdom (Heavenly Sophia). This union of the Cosmic Being of Wisdom (Kyriotetes) and the 'Paradisiacal Eve' in the body of Mary of Jerusalem (the original Eve) completed the full cycle of the return to the divine for Eve/Mary Sophia and pointed to the future when humanity will be able to unite with both Sophia (Spirit-Self) and their Christened Self (Life-Spirit). Then, the Cosmic Being of Wisdom (Heavenly Sophia) will become 'physically present' as an intimate counselor of the spirit who leads us to the understanding of the Cosmic Wisdom (Sophia) of Christ which is found in the realm of the Life-Spirit (Sophia Christos). The marriage in New Jerusalem is between our higher ego (Spirit-Self) and the being of Christ as our own Christened Self (Life-Spirit). It is the marriage of the Virgin Sophia to the Lamb of God which causes New Jerusalem to descend and the Tree of Life to bring forth fruit as the Waters of Life spring from the base of the tree in four directions. This description is also the universal archetype of the union of the Cosmic Beings who work through the ranks of the Kyriotetes and the Elohim, Sophia and Christ.

The wedding of Christ and Sophia is described in Steiner's indications concerning the Pre-Earthly Deeds of Christ that were accompanied and helped into 'birth' by Sophia (Kyriotetes) on the Sun. Sophia helped Christ donate to the creation of the human being from the Sun where the archetypal form of the human being was being created. The 'Sister Souls' of Adam and Eve, who are called the Adam Kadmon and Eve Kadmon, after Hebrew tradition, stayed on the Sun (paradise) in the 'Mother-Lodge of Humanity' until the completed form of the human being was thoroughly prepared to become a 'free thinker' during the time of the incarnations of Mary of Nazareth and Jesus of Nazareth (Paradisiacal Twins). Sophia and Christ were bringing down to humanity what was needed for human intellectual and spiritual development while the paradisiacal twins of Adam Kadmon and Eve Kadmon remained protected from the Earthly forces of the 'fall.' Sophia and Christ worked together from the Sun through the realms of the Archai, Archangels, and Angels to create humanity's form and to ensure that the realms of Sprit-Self, Life-Spirit and Spirit-Human were created and sustained. These realms are beyond time and space and directly relate to the redemption of the astral (Spirit-Self), etheric (Life-Spirit) and physical bodies (Spirit-Human) of human beings. These realms, like the physical, etheric, and astral bodies that were created by Christ's and Sophia's efforts, are now raised back up into the realms of Angels, Archangels, and Archai from whence they initially came. This is a true wedding of the redeemed physical, astral, etheric bodies with their three spiritual egos in the spiritual world.

Since we call Christ the Son of the Father God, perhaps we might call the Cosmic Being of Wisdom (Heavenly Sophia), who used the combined Kyriotetes as a vessel that descended into the being of Mary of Jerusalem, the Daughter of The Mothers who works together with Christ in the realm of Life-Spirit where Moral Inspirations live. We can see three distinctly different beings in Sophia: The Mothers, Sophia the Daughter (Heavenly Sophia, Leader of the Kyriotetes), and Anthroposophia. Christ comes from the Father while Sophia comes from The Mothers, or the primal Mother.

The Being Anthroposophia evolved over time along with human consciousness. We can call Anthroposophia, the Holy Sophia because She evolves together with the Holy Spirit in the realm of Angels (Spirit-Self) helping humans like guardian Angels. One could say that just as the Cosmic Being of Wisdom (Sophia the Daughter) and Cosmic Being of Love (Christ the Son) work together in a close union in the realm of Life-Spirit (Moral Inspiration—Archangelic realm). Anthroposophia (Holy Sophia) the Holy Spirit work together in the realm of the Spirit-Self (Moral Imagination—Angelic realm).

We can easily see the activities of two different beings in the 'heavenly' and 'earthly' Sophia that create two separate biographies.

We have heard that both biographies are linked inextricably with two of the three beings in the Male Trinity. The Heavenly Sophia and the Earthly Sophia tend to mirror the work of Christ and the Holy Spirit. Both Sophias seem to be empowered with a force beyond their rank in the spiritual hierarchies. Christ came from the Holy Trinity and used the seven Elohim as a vessel. The Heavenly Sophia used the combined efforts of the Kyriotetes as a vessel. Since Christ came from a Holy Trinity, the Cosmic Sophia must have come from somewhere before She used the Kyriotetes as a vessel. Almost all religions and mythologies say creation came from, or was donated by, a Great Goddess or Mother of All. This aspect of mythology, theology, and ancient beliefs is almost universal. Then why, one might ask, did Rudolf Steiner not clearly point out the third person in the Divine Feminine Trinity—the Primal Mother—The Mothers? If he had, he would have been the first to insinuate a Divine Feminine Trinity since the time of the *Zohar*.

Steiner actually did describe the biographies of The Mothers, Sophia, and Anthroposophia. But first, let's be clear that the mysteries of Sophia were still a secret in Steiner's day. He indicated that the Sophia mysteries would not be revealed fully until the Sixth Age of Civilization, which he called the Russian/Slavic age, a period that does not happen for at least another thousand years. Steiner was not free to speak directly about these mysteries of Sophia; but he did say repeatedly that what we needed in our time is the Wisdom of, the Sophia of, the Christ. He described two of the three aspects of the divine feminine trinity in greater detail than anyone else before him, and therefore, did go as far as any other spiritual researcher had gone in revealing Sophia's true nature and her biography. He described Anthroposophia's biography in great detail in *The Riddle of Philosophy*. Steiner's entire work was a revelation of Sophia the 'Wisdom of Christ.' One could even say that Steiner's spiritual science was the Moral Inspiration of Sophia, Anthroposophia, which truly brought forward the Sophia of Christ.

You might now be wondering: If Sophia mirrors the Godhead, who is a trinity, then why wouldn't Sophia also be a trinity?

This question certainly resounded in the author for many years until the discovery of a few Steiner quotes that began to shed light on the mystery of Sophia that he kept somewhat veiled in his time. In answering some questions at the end of a lecture to the workmen, Steiner remarked that the combined efforts of the hierarchy together sound forth as the word, 'suffering.' When asked if there was another word that could be used, he remarked: "Yes, they sound forth the name of the Great Goddess, the Mother of All." This then, is The Mothers, or the first person in the Divine Feminine Trinity of Mother, the Daughter, and the Holy Sophia (Anthroposophia).

Steiner also says that the ancients knew the previous incarnations of the Earth (Old Saturn, Old Sun, Old Moon) as the 'Mothers.' the three elementary kingdoms. Goethe spoke of this tradition quite accurately in *Faust* with chilling descriptions of the 'Realm of The Mothers' and the fear it instills in anyone who dares to approach them. Steiner indicated that these 'Mothers' were beings who have woven our realm together through all of the efforts, sacrifices, and donations of the nine hierarchies during Old Saturn, Old Sun, and Old Moon. We owe the past to the gifts of The Mothers, and they are the basis for the ancient ubiquitous belief in the Great Mother, the triple goddess of birth, death, and rebirth. There is no end to the enumeration of the many triple goddesses or triune feminine forces found in myths and ancient beliefs. The primacy of the Feminine Trinity is prominent in all religions and the later male extrapolations are derived from these original feminine deities. That is why the two Trinities of Male and Female are so compatible, and incomplete without the missing half.

Finding The Mothers, the threefold Mother, in Anthroposophy is not hard at all when the blinders are removed. Steiner tells us that The Mothers were, at one time, three but later became one. They were the Three Sisters (Three Marys) known as the Maters Dolorosa (Sorrowful Mothers) who became the Mater Gloriosa (Mothers of Glory). It was historical necessity that the Three Mothers become the One Mother. This is reflected in the thought that the initial 'Mother of Creation' reflected or mirrored the Godhead, was a trinity of birth, death, and rebirth. Thus, the original Mother was seen as three because She would become three through the deeds of Her Daughter and the Holy Sophia (Anthroposophia), thereby creating a trinity which perfectly reflects the Male Trinity. The Mothers birthed creation up until the time that the Kyriotetes (Sophia) and the Elohim (Christ) entered into the development of the human being and made the donations that helped The Mothers (Old Saturn, Old Sun, Old Moon) develop the human being as a free thinker. Then, in 2100 BC, Anthroposophia (Holy Sophia) incarnated and completed the manifestation of the Divine Feminine Trinity. Each member of the Divine Feminine Trinity shares their power, wisdom, and love with the other two members.

The feminine qualities involved in the creation, destruction, and rebirth of the Cosmos and humanity have been marginalized. A religious patriarchy has kept Isis-Sophia hidden and powerless. Just think about the word Isis today in contemporary world matters and think about how every aspect of the feminine has been eradicated in these cultures. Even the human female is kept hidden from public view, with all but her eyes looking out from under heavy garments, while the male force dominates its religion, culture, and geopolitics. This is not the Isis-Sophia of hope, wisdom, and love, but a perversion of Isis; one of fear, doubt, and hatred. Indeed, what we see is the total and complete eradication of the feminine, heavenly and earthly, in all respects.

The Divine Feminine Trinity comes to life by looking at each of the separate biographies of Sophia and embracing the lost divine feminine in our lives, religions, and cultures. Let the confusion and speculation fall aside as a grand picture of what the Divine Feminine Trinity has suffered for the evolution of humanity. A true cosmic romance of the deepest love and union comes before our eyes when we look at the golden footprints of Sophia. There is no end to the majesty of human development that can arise when we unite the two trinities of male and female as creation becomes complete and the mysteries of the past, present, and future come into focus. We need the birth of a new Isis-Sophia as the divine feminine nature is redeemed and reinstated to a position of respect, honor, and reverence. We need to seek the Sophia mysteries as the 'eternal feminine calls us upward and onward.'

In our time, we need to create or resurrect devotion to Wisdom (Sophia) so that we align with the spiritual forces coming from the Second Coming of Christ, the descent of the Holy Spirit, and the intervention of the Father God. Sophia and Christ are united as Sophia-Christos. The Holy Spirit and the Holy Sophia also work together very closely. The Father God is made whole through uniting with The Mothers of Creation, the primal creative substance of suffering, sacrifice, and wisdom.

The following selections reveal what Rudolf Steiner has indicated about the primal significance of the feminine nature over the course of human development. The student of Anthroposophy is encouraged to study these selections from the original Steiner sources to construct his or her own Biographies of Sophia.

Rudolf Steiner on the Significance of the Feminine

Cosmic Memory: The Story of Atlantis and Lemuria, **Rudolf Steiner, Lecture VI,** *The Division of the Sexes,* **1904, GA 11**

"All who strive for a true understanding of human development must be aware that the first strides in imagining, in the creation of inner images, were made by women. They are the ones who first thought, imagined and remembered, and that is a pre-requisite for the formation of memory. Memory, in turn, made possible the development of habits, and habits laid the foundation for a legal code, a kind of framework of custom and morality. It was man who knew and dealt with the forces of nature, but in was woman who first interpreted them. The inner rhythms of nature sounded from the lips of 'wise' women. People gathered around them, feeling the chanted phrases to be the communications of higher powers. Gatherings such as these were the first religious services."

"In relationship to the grand evolution of humanity, the female nature is primary and was the original source of procreation in the far distant past of the Polarian and Hyperborean ages. Parthenogenesis is implied in the development of the human fetus in utero and clearly described by Steiner in his *Occult Science an Outline*. Generation without the polarity of male and female was the original means of human propagation. Humans were not divided into two sexes until the Moon separated itself from the Earth."

The Temple Legend, Rudolf Steiner, Lecture XVIII, *Freemasonry and Human Evolution* II, Berlin, October 23, 1905, GA 93

"Now we want to clarify how that came about. It came about thus: in the beginning, before there was a separate male and female sex, there was a twofold sexuality within each single individual. We must now ask: What was it that could become fertilized, and what was it that did the fertilizing, in the one single individual? In ancient Greek mythology Zeus is portrayed with ample female breasts. A truth expresses itself therein, which was known in the old mysteries and which we also learn from the records, that the sex - if I may call it that - which immediately preceded our own, outwardly and physically resembled not the male but the female gender. So that, before the outward separation, we have thus both sexes in one individual that outwardly - in physical expression and in all perceptions and being - was female. Therefore, at the beginning of the human race, we have to do with a bisexual individual tending towards the female. Only later did the male sex follow. Now we must be clear that in this individual, which had both sexes in it, a fertilizing agent, or male seed, was also present. Woman contained man within her. When we have grasped the fact that the woman had the male principle within her, then we can conceive, with our ordinary scientific concepts, that reproduction was ensured. We want to bear in mind that at this time this happened via the woman."

"Now came the time when things had to go their separate ways. What character did the fertilizing principle in the woman then have, which on the physical plane would fertilize the female nature? What worked in the female body as a seed, was the male; and that was the spiritual, the wisdom. Woman contributed the substance; the spirit gave it form. Any structuring of the physical plane is a realization of wisdom. Wisdom worked in the female. Now the two differentiated themselves, in that the two things which had previously worked as one now appeared as two separated poles. What was previously united in a single human organ, divided itself, whereby a duality in human development originated. This duality came about thus: first, the fertility - the ability of the female egg to fertilize itself - within the one individual, ceased to function. The female egg lost the possibility of becoming fertilized from its own body. So, we are now dealing with a female which has become infertile and, above everything, the spiritual. The division of the two sexes came about through the separation of the physical organs, and the other sex was now endowed with the possibility of fertilization. Two individuals appeared, one with physical femininity and the other with physical masculinity. With the man, wisdom has a female character, with the woman, it has a male character."

"The separation is a very definite event that one can follow; we will now have to be satisfied, however, with just indications. We are dealing, then, with male-tinged wisdom in the woman and female-tinged wisdom in the man. This female-tinged wisdom is passive, suited to receiving, listening, watching - to taking in from the surroundings. The male-tinged wisdom, the active wisdom, is suited to being productive. Thus, we have a two- fold wisdom; the female wisdom that is active and that naturally will also be transferred to the men. So that there may indeed be plenty of men who take over the female wisdom, the race propagates itself below on the physical plane; and above, we are dealing with an active intuition stemming from women, and with a passive cognition, decidedly male in character.

"This figures in the old mystery teaching as the antithesis between the Sons of Abel, or Sons of God, and the Sons of Cain, or Sons of Man. Abel represents the female, active intuition. Therefore, he is unable to take hold of anything from the outside world which needs to be worked upon. He takes up the divine, which streams through him, that flows into his intuitiveness. The 'Herdsman' symbolizes that. He tends and nurtures life, while intuition nurtures the divine life of wisdom. Cain has the male wisdom that receives the outward. This wisdom espouses the Earth in order to till it; the material is outside himself. He is an agriculturalist."

"Now there is a very interesting and important legend in which these truths are symbolically expressed for the Freemasons. That is the Temple Legend. And the reason for it is as follows: The *Bible* itself, the *Old Testament*, derives from the female, the intuitive wisdom, and bears its stamp. The *Old Testament* is female wisdom. Male wisdom was not able to attain to intuition. It confined itself to building and work. It took stones and constructed buildings. It took metals and made implements. The Temple Legend puts it thus: One of the Elohim impregnated Eve and Cain was born. Afterwards, another of the Elohim, Jehovah, also known as Adonai, created Adam. And Adam begat Abel by Eve. This legend counterposed the wisdom of Cain and the Biblical wisdom, so that, by the beginning of the fourth Post-Atlantean epoch, we have two opposing currents: the *Bible*, representing womanly wisdom, and the Temple wisdom as its opposing male counterpart. Already, in pre-Christian times, what the male wisdom wanted stood in opposition to the female wisdom."

Spiritual Science and Medicine, Rudolf Steiner, Lecture XIX, April 8, 1920, GA 312

"It is the task of the male to keep the female world as healthy as possible for it is through women that influences from beyond the Earth will then be drawn into the sphere of Earthly processes. Woman has the inclination to unite herself ever more and more with extra-terrestrial processes. She tends increasingly to be drawn up into heavenly worlds. It is little wonder that the secrets of the divine feminine have been hidden by males in every way possible. The female had to be diminished and dethroned so that the agenda of male supremacy could come to full birth. The power, wisdom and practices of the feminine divine were kept faithfully by women through rituals, symbols and old wives' tales. Isis-Sophia had to be shrouded in order to keep from being destroyed altogether. Her golden footprints were still left for those with 'eyes to see,' Her secrets went underground into the mystery religions where the secrets of The Mothers and the Beings of Wisdom were held sacred. Those who still had the remnants of clairvoyance were able to sense the truth beneath the confused teachings about the Triple Goddess. They were pulled upward towards the eternal feminine that calls Her children back home. Women have a capacity of spirit naturally."

The Enigma of the Being Anthroposophia

The indication below, and many like it, have puzzled Anthroposophists as they tried to create and maintain a relationship with Anthroposophia, a being they are told is so important and yet they cannot comprehend. On one hand, Steiner tells his students to focus on this being and on the other hand tells them that the mysteries of Sophia will only be revealed in the future. This has led to much speculation that seems to go nowhere. Just as soon as a writer thinks he understands Sophia, a new dimension of Her opens and all previous limitations of Sophia are extinguished. Pretty soon, we don't know the difference between Christ and Sophia, Anthroposophia and the Holy Spirit, or Archangel Michael and Sophia. It seems that their areas of influence overlap and that they must either work together or perhaps are the same being. The importance Steiner places on the Archangel [Archai] Michael must be balanced with Anthroposophia but doesn't seem logical until one realizes that the Archangel Michael is a 'Son of Sophia,' one of the highest emissaries of Sophia. Michael is also the emissary of Christ. The confusion mounts until the simple answer is spelled out by Steiner without any dogma concerning the Mysteries of Sophia. The answers are found in Steiner's work, but the formulation of a specific concept of the Divine Feminine Trinity was not clearly spelled out.

Rudolf Steiner tells us in *Supersensible Man* (Lecture V, November 18, 1923, GA 231):

"When we are in a position to assimilate anthroposophical knowledge not only through reading and listening, but when we are more and more able to experience the content of anthroposophy in our heart, in our feelings, then it is as if living, cosmic beings enter our souls. Then, anthroposophy will appear to us increasingly as a living being. And we will become aware that something is knocking at the threshold of our heart saying, 'Let me in, because I am you yourself; I am your true nature, your very humanity.'"

Through Steiner's injunctions to "Let me in, because I am you yourself; I am your true nature, your very humanity," the student is told to develop a relationship with a spiritual being who knows us better than we know ourselves. Anthroposophia is to become our counselor and the objective reflection of our own personal self-development. The interaction with this being will take the student to the next steps of self-knowledge. Anthroposophia will midwife the soul until the Virgin Sophia can be born in our Spiritual Soul (higher part of the Consciousness-Soul) as a place for the spirit to dwell.

Steiner continues to describe the importance of Anthroposophia in the selections below.

The Anthroposophic Movement, Rudolf Steiner, Lecture VII, *The Consolidation of the Anthroposophical Movement*, June 16, 1923, GA 258

"A feeling, a kind of sense, that Anthroposophia—quite apart from the existence of anthroposophist—must be looked upon as an independent living being; as one, so to speak, who goes about amongst us and to whom we are responsible at every moment of our lives. It was said in this lecture to the theologians in so many words: Anthroposophia is actually an invisible person, going about amongst visible people, and to whom, so long as they are only few in number, they owe the very greatest responsibility, - one who must really be treated as an invisible human being, actually living amongst us, whose opinion must be sought on every single thing we do in life. Whenever, therefore, so long as there is only a little band of anthroposophists, anything is formed in the way of human associations—friendships, or fellowships, or any sort of clique—it becomes all the more necessary that this invisible being should be asked, and that everything should be such that it can be justified before this invisible being. Of course, this will be, in the same measure, ever less and less the case, the more widespread Anthroposophy becomes. But so long as it is only the possession of a little band, it remains absolutely necessary that everything that is done should be done, so to speak, in consultation with this human being 'Anthroposophia.' It is one of the essential life conditions that Anthroposophia should be regarded as a living being."

The Being of Anthroposophy, Rudolf Steiner, Berlin, February 3, 1919, GA 145

"What, therefore, must be developed? It must unfold that, once again, as a matter of course, a 'Sophia' becomes present. But we must learn to relate this Sophia to the Consciousness-Soul, bring her down directly to human beings. This is happening during the age of the Consciousness-Soul. And thereby Sophia becomes the being who directly enlightens human beings. After Sophia has entered human beings, she must take their being with her and present it to them outwardly, objectively. Thus, Sophia will be drawn into the human soul and arrive at the point of being so inwardly connected with it that a love poem as beautiful as Dante wrote may be written about her."

"Sophia will become objective again, but she will take with her what humanity is, and objectively present herself in this form. Thus, she will present herself not only as Sophia, but as Anthroposophia—as the Sophia who, after passing through the human soul, through the very being of the human being, henceforth bears that being within her, and in this form, she will confront enlightened human beings as the objective being Sophia who once stood before the Greeks."

"Such is the progression of human evolutionary history in relation to the spiritual questions we have been considering. Here I must leave the matter to all those who wish to examine in even greater detail, following the destiny of Sophia, Philosophia, and Anthroposophia, how we may show how humanity develops progressively through those parts of the soul we call the Intellectual-Soul, the Consciousness-Soul, and the spirit-self. People will learn how profoundly what anthroposophy gives us is based in our whole being. What we receive through anthroposophy is our very own being."

"This once floated toward us in the form of a celestial goddess with whom we were able to enter into a relationship. This divine being lived on as Sophia and Philosophia, and now we can once again bring her out of ourselves and place her before us as the fruit of true anthroposophical self-knowledge. We can wait patiently until the world is willing to test the depth of the foundations of what we have to say, right down to the smallest details. It is the essence of anthroposophy that its own being consists of the being of the human, and its effectiveness, its reality, consists in that we receive from anthroposophy what we ourselves are and what we must place before ourselves, because we must practice self-knowledge."

"Sophia must become present again. But we must learn to relate this Sophia to the Consciousness-Soul, bring her down directly to human beings. And thereby Sophia becomes the being who directly enlightens human beings. After Sophia has entered human beings, she must take their being with her and present it to them outwardly, objectively. Thus, Sophia will be drawn into the soul and become inwardly connected. Thus, she will present herself not only as Sophia, but as Anthroposophia—as the Sophia who, after passing through the human soul, through the very being of the human being, henceforth bears that being within her. And in this form, she will confront enlightened human beings as the objective being Sophia who once stood before the Greeks."

"What we receive through Anthroposophy is the essence of ourselves, which in former times descended to man in order to manifest itself as a celestial goddess with whom he was able to find a personal relationship, who lived as the Sophia, as Philo-Sophia, and to whom he will give birth again out of himself, placing her before him as the fruit of true self- knowledge in Anthroposophy. For the being of anthroposophy is such that its own being consists in that which constitutes the essence of man's being; and the nature of its influence is that man receives in Anthroposophy what he himself is and that he must place this before him, because he must practice self-knowledge."

"The mysteries of Sophia are spoken of by Rudolf Steiner in ways that no one fully understands. The nature of Anthroposophia as a human being is referred to again and again. What he insinuates is that the 'human' being of Anthroposophia is essentially the collective consciousness of humanity as it develops over the course of history. This is what makes Anthroposophia so 'human' in every way except for having a physical body. Anthroposophia seems to 'defy' space and time as She is present to every human who is progressing on his and her personal spiritual path. She works with each individual and is personally present for each person. She is intimately concerned with our personal advancement and takes our hand and shows us the way. These characteristics are inexplicable to the rational mind, and yet Steiner focuses on his students becoming aware of all aspects of the workings of this being."

The Riddles of Philosophy, Rudolf Steiner, *The World Conception of the Greek Thinkers,* GA 18

"Anthroposophia is in herself an invisible human being who goes amongst visible human beings towards whom we have the greatest conceivable responsibility who must indeed be regarded as an invisible human being, as someone with a real existence, who should be consulted in all life's individual actions, to whom we are responsible in everything that happens is to be viewed in consultation with the human being Anthroposophia as a living being So that is what is necessary: true seriousness in our following of that invisible human being to whom I have just spoken."

Perception of the Nature of Thought, Rudolf Steiner, Dornach, January 10, 1915, GA 161

"Thus, we are living today in the midst of the Consciousness-Soul epoch, looking towards the dawn of the age of the Spirit-Self; and we know that something is separating itself off from man, something which will, however, carry through the times that are to come what man has won as the fruit of passing through the Consciousness-Soul age. What is it that has to be developed?

What must be developed is without doubt the presence once again amongst mankind of a 'Sophia.' But man has learnt to relate this 'Sophia' to his Consciousness-Soul, to bring her into direct relationship with human beings. This has taken place during the Consciousness-Soul epoch, and the Sophia has thereby become the being who explains man as such. Once she has entered into man, she must take his being with her and place it objectively before him from without. Thus the Sophia enters into the human soul and separates it again, but she will take with her man's essential being and place it objectively before him—now not merely as the 'Sophia' but as Anthroposophia, as the Sophia who, after passing through the human soul, through man's being, henceforth bears this being of man within her and thus appears before an enlightened human being as once the Sophia stood as an objective being before the Greece."

Towards the end of Steiner's life, he often referred to Anthroposophia as the living being who fills Anthroposophy with the Wisdom (Sophia) of Christ. He even equates Anthroposophia with the Spirits of Wisdom, who we now know as the Daughter. Anthroposophia seems to have the power and characteristics of the Beings of Wisdom (Kyriotetes). In one way of looking at it, you could say that the Cosmic Being of Wisdom fills Anthroposophia just as Christ fills the Holy Spirit. Again, this points in the direction of the Divine Feminine Trinity and the co-equal power shared by the two sets of three members of each Trinity.

The Christmas Conference, Rudolf Steiner, Lecture IV, *The Laying of the Foundation Stone*, GA 260

"And if you hear this resounding in your own hearts, my dear friends, then what you will establish here will be a true union of human beings on behalf of Anthroposophia, and will carry the spirit which prevails in radiant thought-light around our dodecahedral stone of love out into the world, where it may shed light and warmth on the progress of human souls and the progress of the world."

Perception of Nature of Thought, Rudolf Steiner, Dornach, January 10, 1915, GA 161

"If we go back to the perception of thoughts which prevailed in the time of the old Greek philosophers then we must say: Philosophic thought in ancient Greece—in spite of the fact that it was the age of the intellectual or mind-soul in ancient Greece—was still a perceptive thinking, was still deeply influenced by the sentient soul, in fact by the sentient, the astral, body. It still clung to the external. The thinking of Thales, of the first philosopher was still influenced by the etheric body. They created their Water—Air—Fire—Philosophies out of their temperament, and the temperament lives in the etheric body. One can therefore say that the philosophy of the sentient body goes into the philosophy of the etheric body. Then we come into the Christian period. The Christ- Impulse penetrates into the sentient soul. Philosophy is experienced inwardly but in connection with what one can feel and believe; the influences of the sentient soul are present. In the third period, that of scholasticism, the intellectual or mind-soul is the essential element of philosophical development. Now the development of philosophy follows a different course from that of human evolution in general. And for the first time since the 16th century we now have philosophy coinciding with the general evolution of mankind, for we have the free thoughts ruling in the consciousness soul.—Consciousness soul! The magnificent example of how free thought prevails from the abstraction of existence up to the highest spirituality, how a thought-organism, leaving aside the world entirely, rules purely in itself, that is the philosophy of Hegel—the thought that lives solely in the consciousness.

"If you follow this scheme it is actually the part that I could not show in my book for the public, though it lies in it. And if you read the descriptions given of the separate epochs you will, if you are proper Anthroposophists, very clearly connect them with what I have written here (see diagram). There is thus a development corresponding to that of man himself: from the etheric body to the sentient body, to the sentient soul, to the intellectual soul, to the consciousness soul. We follow a path like the path of man's evolution, but differently regulated. It is not the path of human evolution, it is different. *Beings* are evolving and they make use of human forces in the sentient soul, in the intellectual soul etc. Through man and his works pass other beings with other laws than those of human development.

"You see—these are activities of the Sun-laws!

"Here we need not ascend to such super-sensible regions as when we investigate human destiny. It is in the philosophical development of mankind that we have an example of what remains from the Sun-laws.

"Such Angeloi evolve. And while men believe that they themselves philosophize, Sun-laws work in them—inasmuch as men bear within them what the Old Sun-evolution laid down in their physical and etheric bodies. And the laws of the Sun-existence, working from epoch to epoch, cause philosophy to become precisely what it is. Because they are Sun-laws, the Christ, the Being of the Sun, could also enter them during the second period. Preparation is made in the first period and then the Christ, the Sun-Being, becomes active in the second period.

"You see how everything is linked together. But inasmuch as the Christ, the Sun-Being, enters in, He comes into connection with an evolution which is not the human evolution, not man's earthly evolution, but actually Sun-evolution within Earth existence.

"Sun-evolution within Earth existence! Just think what we have actually reached in these reflections. We are considering the course of philosophical development, philosophical thought since the time of ancient Greece, and when we consider how this has evolved from philosopher to philosopher we say to ourselves: there are active within not earthly laws, but Sun laws! The laws which at that time held sway between the Spirits of Wisdom and the Archangels come to light again on earth in the philosophical search for wisdom. Read in the book *Occult Science* how the Spirits of Wisdom enter during the Sun-evolution. Now during earthly evolution they enter again not into what is new but into what has remained from the Sun-evolution. And man develops his philosophy not knowing that in this development the Spirits of Wisdom are pulsing through his soul. The Old Sun existence lives in the evolution of philosophy; it really and truly lives within something that has stayed behind, something that is connected with the Old Sun-evolution."

With the being of Anthroposophia we find a clear and detailed biography of one of the three aspects of the Divine Feminine Trinity. Through developing a relationship with the being Anthroposophia, the wisdom of Christ unfolds revealing the cosmic workings of the Son (Elohim) and the Daughter (Kyriotetes). The evolving spiritual scientist needs the Holy Spirit to reveal the nature of the Cosmic Christ through the being of Anthroposophia in the realm of the Spirit-Self (Manas). Likewise, through the Sophia (Beings of Wisdom) the nature of the Son of God the Father becomes revealed through the Archangel Michael in the realm of the Life-Spirit (Budhi). Then, through the Mother, the Father God is revealed by the Archai in the realm of Spirit-Man (Atman). Anthroposophia has the task of bringing us to the understanding of the other members of both the Male and Female Trinities. Through Anthroposophia, we begin to communicate with the higher realms, discern wisdom, and come to know the beings who inhabit those realms.

The Triple Goddess

We have seen through the work of Rudolf Steiner that a Divine Feminine Trinity is implied in his teachings and that Anthroposophia is the guide to help us understand these profound mysteries of the future. Two contemporary students of Steiner's, Valentin Tomberg, and Robert Powell, write about a Divine Feminine Trinity and attribute the source to Cabalistic lore concerning the Tree of Life. Neither author develops the concept much and does not align his ideas with Steiner's teachings. But they were right that Jewish mysticism teaches that there is a feminine divine principle that is a trinity. Jewish Mysticism and the Kabbalah suggest that there is a Feminine Divine Trinity that works together in concert with a Male Divine Trinity.

Shekinah (Sophia or Wisdom) is called the 'Soul of God,' the 'Mother or Origin.' and the 'Motherly Space.' There is an inner glory, and that is the Shekinah and the Holy Ghost together. Shekinah is threefold as 'Queen,' 'Daughter,' and 'Bride of God.'

The Jewish Feminine Trinity is hidden in mysticism. Every aspect of human nature and the Cosmos seem to be parceled into a trinity. The trinity is found in the human body with thought, air in speech passing through the larynx, and the wedding of thought and speech to spirit. Everywhere in the human constitution are trinities: thinking, feeling, willing—waking, sleeping, and dreaming—body, soul, and spirit. It is only natural, since we are created in the image of the Divine Trinity, that we also find these trinities in ourselves and the world.

On the Mysteries of Ancient and Modern Times, Rudolf Steiner, Dornach, December 26, 1917, GA 180

"These three, the inspiring Spirit, the Virgin Mother, and the Logos or the Word—must of course be maintained; they must be sought for through Spiritual Science also. I did endeavor to point out these things during my recent lectures, when I described the transition from the old Mysteries to the new. I said that Antiquity only got so far with its Mysteries that it was able to revere in Pallas Athene, the Virgin Wisdom. Pallas Athene is indeed a virgin figure; but within the ancient epoch this Virgin Wisdom did not give birth to the Logos. This is precisely the characteristic feature of ancient Greece, for example: it stops short at the Virgin Wisdom, whereas the new Age passes on to the Son of the Virgin Wisdom—to the Logos, which is there on the physical plane through that which represents it: the human word, human speech, or language. For human speech may truly be regarded from the point of view of its connection with Wisdom. In the Earthly life of man, Wisdom lives itself out through human thought. The air that is breathed out through our larynx, configured through our larynx and its movements, is wedded to the Wisdom that dwells in our thoughts; and the content we have to express is the inspiring Spirit. Every time you speak—no matter how profane the impulse of your speaking is—you have expressed Earthly representation of the Trinity. The thought in your head, and the configured air that passes through your larynx—these two are wedded and united under the influence of the Spirit (that is to say, when you are voicing things of the sense-world, united by the percept itself). It is indeed the Earthly expression of the Trinity.

And the Divine, the spiritual Trinity, must stand behind it—the all-embracing Wisdom which becomes Teaching for mankind, and which expresses the Universal content. Anthroposophical Spiritual Science cannot admit or confess its faith in any Earthly constitution; for an Earthly constitution, whatever it might claim, would be unfolding mere claims of power. Anthroposophical Spiritual Science takes the Virgin cosmic Word in real earnest."

"If we think in the sense of anthroposophical Spiritual Science, then, in this content of all that is brought forward by this Science, we see not a mere sum of abstractions or abstract ideas but a living entity that fills us and infills us; For it can even fill us in our soul with active impulse. Thus, it becomes the Word, the Teaching, not in a mere scholastic sense. For spiritual-scientific Wisdom grows to be of service in social life. The Word itself becomes of social service, and the content which it expresses brought down from super-sensible worlds into the world of sense, so to be the underlying basis of our impulses of action is the inspiring Spirit. Thus, I would say: We look for Pallas Athene, the Virgin Wisdom, the Virgin Wisdom of the Cosmos; but we also look for the Son who is born of her, who finds expression in this: that in all the things we do and will in the social life, the Virgin Wisdom is working with us, giving us that which becomes the guiding impulse of our willing and our doing. Then we express the Spirit—the Holy Spirit, the Supersensible—in our sense-perceptible actions on the physical plane."

"In the realm of the soul there are three soul forces that work on the Sentient-Soul, Intellectual-Soul, and Consciousness-Soul. Each of these forces is represented by one of the 'three Marys' under the cross of Christ. Each one of the Marys represents a stage of spiritual development that relates to one of the three aspects of the soul. The Sentient-Soul is represented by Mary

Magdalen, the Intellectual-Soul is represented by Mary the wife of Cleopas, and the Consciousness-Soul is represented by the Mother of Jesus."

Gospel of John, Rudolf Steiner, Basle, Lecture V, November 20, 1907, GA 100

"Let us now consider another scene in this Gospel. In (*John* 19:25), we read: "Now there stood by the cross of Jesus, His mother, and His mother's sister, Mary the wife of Cleophas, and Mary Magdalene." If we wish to understand this *Gospel*, it is necessary to know who these three women are. We do not usually give two sisters the same name; neither was it the custom in former times. The passage we have quoted proves that, according to *St. John's Gospel*, the mother of Jesus was not called Mary. If we search through the whole of this *Gospel* we nowhere find it said that the mother of Jesus was called Mary. In the scene of the Marriage of Cana, for example, Chapter 2, we only read, "the mother of Jesus was there." In these words, something important is indicated, something we only understand when we know how the writer of this *Gospel* uses his words. What does the expression 'the mother of Jesus' mean? We have seen that man consists of physical, etheric, and astral bodies. We must not consider the transition of the astral body to the Spirit-Self so simply. The Ego transforms the astral body very slowly and gradually into Sentient-Soul, Intellectual-Soul, and Consciousness-Soul. The Ego goes on working and only when it has developed the Consciousness-Soul is it able so to purify it that Spirit-Self can arise in it."

"The Spirit Human will only be developed in the distant future, and Life-Spirit is also only germinal in most people of the present day. The development of the Spirit-Self has only just begun; it is closely united with the spiritual soul (somewhat like a sword in its sheath). The Sentient-Soul is similarly united with the astral body. The human being thus consists of nine parts or principles; but as the Spirit-Self and the spiritual soul, and the Sentient-Soul and the astral body are so closely united, we often speak of seven parts. Spirit-Self is the same as the 'Holy Spirit,' who according to Esoteric Christianity, is the guiding Being in the astral world. According to the same teaching, Life-Spirit is called the Word or the Son; and Spirit Human is the 'Father Spirit' or the 'Father.' Those human beings who had brought the Spirit-Self to birth within them, were called Children of God; in such men "the light shone into the Darkness and they received the light." Outwardly they were, men of flesh and blood, but they bore a higher man within them; the Spirit-Self had been born within them out of the Spiritual Soul. The "mother" of such a spiritualized man is not a bodily mother, she lies within him; she is the purified and spiritualized Consciousness-Soul; she is the principle who gives birth to the higher man. This spiritual birth, a birth in the highest sense, is described in *St. John's Gospel*. The Spirit-Self or the Holy Spirit pours into the most highly purified Spiritual [Consciousness] Soul. This is referred to in the words, "I saw the Spirit descending from heaven like a dove, and it abode upon him." (*John* 1:32).

"As the Spiritual [Consciousness] Soul is the principle in which the Spirit-Self develops, this principle is called the 'Mother of Christ,' or, in the occult schools, the 'Virgin Sophia.' Through the fertilization of the Virgin Sophia the Christ could be born in Jesus of Nazareth. In the occult school of Dionysius, the Intellectual-Soul was called 'Mary,' and the Sentient-Soul 'Mary Magdalene.'"

"Mary Magdalene represents the process of cleansing the astral body to develop new organs of supersensible perception.

That is why the spiritual scientist must understand and move through this stage of spiritual development. Conquering the desires of the astral body is a necessary stage of renunciation and purification.

Reflections of Consciousness, Super-consciousness and Sub-consciousness, Rudolf Steiner, Munich, February 25, 1912, GA 143

"Let us suppose that someone desires most intensely to be the reincarnated Mary Magdalene, (I once mentioned that I have already met twenty-four reincarnated Magdalenes in my life); let us assume that someone desires most intensely to be Mary Magdalene. But let us also assume that this person does not confess this wish to himself (we need not confess our wishes to ourselves—this is unnecessary). Well—someone may read the story of Mary Magdalene and may like it immensely. In his sub-consciousness the desire to be Mary Magdalene may now immediately arise. He is aware of nothing in his usual consciousness except that he likes this character. The person in question has a liking for this character. He is aware of this in his upper consciousness. But in his subconscious lives the burning desire to be himself this Mary Magdalene—yet he knows nothing about this. He does not bother about this. He is guided by the facts of his usual consciousness; he can go through the world without being compelled at all to become aware of this erroneous fact in his consciousness—the intense wish to be Mary Magdalene. But let us suppose that such a person has attained, in some way or other, a kind of occult training. This would enable him to descend into his sub-consciousness—but he would not become aware of the fact, 'in me lives the desire to be Mary Magdalene'—he would not become aware of this in the same way that he becomes aware of a headache. If he were to notice this desire to be Mary Magdalene then he would be sensible and assume toward this desire the same attitude as toward a pain—namely, he would try to get rid of it. But through an irregular descent into sub-consciousness, this does not take place, because his desire acquires the form of something which is outside his own personality, and to the man in question it appears as the vision: 'You are Mary Magdalene.' This fact stands before him, is projected outside his own being. Moreover, a human being at this stage of development is no longer able to control such a fact through his Ego. This lack of control cannot arise when we undergo a regular, sound, and absolutely careful training; for then the Ego accompanies all experiences in every sphere. But as soon as the Ego no longer accompanies all our experiences, the fact described above can arise in the form of an objective outer happening."

"The observer believes that he can remember the events connected with Mary Magdalene and feels himself identified with this Mary Magdalene. This is unquestionably possible. I emphasize this possibility, because it shows you that only careful training and the conscientiousness with which we penetrate into occultism, can rescue us from falling into error. If we know that we must first see before us an entire world, that we must see around us facts, not something which we apply to our own selves, but something that is in us, and yet appears like the picture of a whole world—if we know that we do well to consider what we first see before us is the projection of our own inner life—then we possess a good shield against the errors which can beset us along this path. The best thing of all is to consider at first everything that rises out of our inner being as if it were an exterior fact. In most cases these facts arise out of our desires, vanities, and ambition—in a few words, out of all the qualities connected with human selfishness."

Why Sophia is Not the Holy Spirit

Much confusion surrounds the idea of Sophia's place in relationship to the Male Trinity. She is often confused with the Holy Spirit (third person in the Male Trinity) in an attempt to make Her the female aspect of the Trinity. She is called the feminine side of Jesus (second person in the Trinity). She is also called Wisdom, who was present at creation like the Father God (first person in the Trinity). She is also pictured as the developing human consciousness—Anthroposophia. Sophia is parceled out in every combination and arrangement except the obvious, a Divine Feminine Trinity.

Let's examine a few remarks of Rudolf Steiner's concerning the question of why Sophia is often conflated with the Holy Spirit.

The Mystery of Golgotha, Rudolf Steiner, Cologne, December 2, 1906, GA 97

"The same event which took place upon Golgotha took place in the ancient Mysteries. Under the Cross stood the Disciple 'whom the Lord loved,' the Disciple who had rested upon his bosom and had been raised to his heart. Also, the women are there under the Cross: the Mother of Jesus, his mother's sister Mary, and Mary Magdalene. John does not say that the mother of Jesus was called 'Mary,' but that this was the name of his mother's sister. His mother's name was Sophia."

"John baptizes Jesus in the river Jordan. A dove descends from heaven. At this moment a spiritual act of conception takes place. But who is the mother of Jesus who conceives at this moment."

Why Sophia is Not the Holy Spirit

"The Chela, Jesus of Nazareth, at this moment divests himself of his Ego, his highly developed Manas (Spirit-Self) is fructified, and the Budhi (Life-Spirit) enters into it. The highly developed Manas that received the Budhi is Wisdom—Sophia, the Mother who is fructified by the Father of Jesus. Maria, which is the same as Maya, has the general meaning of 'Mother name.' The *Gospel* records: "The Angel came in unto her and said: Hail thou that art highly favored—behold thou shalt conceive in thy womb and bring forth a son—the Holy Ghost shall come upon thee and the power of the Highest shall overshadow thee." The Holy Ghost is Jesus' father: the descending dove fructifies the Sophia that lives in Jesus."

"The *Gospel* should therefore be read as follows: "Under the Cross stood the mother of Jesus, Sophia." To this mother Jesus says: "Woman, behold thy son." He himself had transferred the Sophia that lived within him to the Disciple John; he transformed him into a son of Sophia and said: "Behold, thy mother. Henceforth you should recognize the divine wisdom as your mother and dedicate yourself to her alone." John had recorded this divine wisdom; Sophia is embodied in the *Gospel of St. John*. Jesus had given him this wisdom, and he was authorized by Christ to transmit it to the world."

"The Consciousness-Soul (Spiritual Soul) is the home of the Virgin Sophia both microcosmically and macrocosmically. The Holy Spirit is truly separate and different than Sophia, Anthroposophia or the Mother of All."

There is one remark that numerous authors have quoted as proof that Steiner believed the Holy Spirit is female and perhaps Sophia. But this quotation is incomplete and comes from 'notes' in a letter to one of Steiner's students in the early days when he was still with the Theosophical Society. With careful reading, you can see that Steiner does not say Sophia is the Holy Spirit.

Brief Band II: 1890-1925, Rudolf Steiner, *A Letter to Dr. Wilhelm Hübbe-Schleiden,* 1902, GA 39

"It is doubtless correct that the Christ in us is not really different from what theological dogma terms the Holy Spirit, but it seems to me that we should nevertheless make a distinction between these two concepts *in relation to something else.* The Holy Spirit and the Christ within are one and the same, but at different *stages of development.* One could also say that the 'Holy Spirit' is the (female) Mother principle of the (male) Son principal Christ. We owe the 'Christ within' to the development which proceeds in us through the 'Holy Spirit' (or Christ-creator).

"In another place we find a somewhat ambiguous remark that leads to confusion about the Holy Spirit and its feminine nature. But close examination will show that Steiner is not saying that the Holy Spirit and Sophia are one and the same.

"For originally the Holy Spirit was nothing other than the Mother of God (Isis, etc). Christianity rejected this feminine (Isis) principle and only retained the Son.

"In the Holy Spirit Christianity retained a rudiment of the feminine principle. It is for this reason that Christian dogma naturally fuses the Holy Spirit with the 'Son.' They are one and the same, and the discarded Isis principle became incomprehensible as 'Holy Spirit' on the one hand, and yet was adopted in an exoteric way again as the Virgin Mary. Isis was first dissipated into the 'Holy Spirit,' and then re-established as 'Mary' without people being aware of the connection."

The following is so central to understanding this topic that we are including the complete lecture of May 31, 1908 (presented without quotation marks) to end this section.

The Gospel of John, Rudolf Steiner, Lecture XII, *The Nature of the Virgin Sophia and of the Holy Spirit*, Hamburg, May 31, 1908, GA 103

"Yesterday we reached the point of discussing the change which takes place in the human astral body through Meditation, Concentration and other practices which are given in the various methods of initiation. We have seen that the astral body is thereby affected in such a way that it develops within itself the organs which it needs for perceiving in the higher worlds and we have said that up to this point, the principle of initiation is everywhere really the same—although the forms of its practices conform wholly to the respective cultural epochs. The principal difference appears with the occurrence of the next thing which must follow. In order that the pupil may be able actually to perceive in the higher worlds, it is necessary that the organs which have been formed out of the astral part, impress or stamp themselves upon the ether body, be impressed into the etheric element.

"The re-fashioning of the astral body indirectly through Meditation and Concentration, is called by an ancient name, 'katharsis,' or purification. Katharsis or purification has as its purpose the discarding from the astral body all that hinders it from becoming harmoniously and regularly organized, thus enabling it to acquire higher organs. It is endowed with the germ of these higher organs; it is only necessary to bring forth the forces which are present in it. We have said that the most varied methods can be employed for bringing about this katharsis. A person can go very far in this matter of katharsis if, for example, he has gone through and inwardly experienced all that is in my book, *The Philosophy of Spiritual Activity*, and feels that this book was for him a stimulation and that now he has reached the point where he can himself actually reproduce the thoughts just as they are there presented. If a person holds the same relationship to this book that a virtuoso, in playing a selection on the piano, holds to the composer of the piece, that is, he reproduces the whole thing within himself—naturally according to his ability to do so—then through the strictly built up sequence of thought of this book—for it is written in this manner—katharsis will be developed to a high degree. For the important point in such things as this book is that the thoughts are all placed in such a way that they become active. In many other books of the present, just by changing the system a little, what has been said earlier in the book can just as well be said later. In *The Philosophy of Spiritual Activity* this is not possible. Page 150 can as little be placed fifty pages earlier in the subject matter as the hind legs of a dog can be exchanged with the forelegs; for the book is a logically arranged organism and the working out of the thoughts in it has an effect similar to an inner schooling. Hence there are various methods of bringing about katharsis. If a person has not been successful in doing this after having gone through this book, he should not think that what has been said is untrue, but rather that he has not studied it properly or with sufficient energy or thoroughness.

"Something else must now be considered and that is that when this katharsis has taken place, when the astral organs have been formed in the astral body, it must all be imprinted upon the ether body. In the pre-Christian initiation, it was done in the following manner. After the pupil had undergone the suitable preparatory training, which often lasted for years, he was told: The time has now come when the astral body has developed far enough to have astral organs of perception, now these can become aware of their counterpart in the ether body. Then the pupil was subjected to a procedure which today—at least for our Cultural Period—is not only unnecessary, but is not in all seriousness feasible. He was put into a lethargic condition for three and a half days, and was treated during this time in such a way that not only the astral body left the physical and ether bodies—a thing that occurs every night in sleep—but to a certain degree the ether body also was lifted out; but care was taken that the physical body remained intact and that the pupil did not die in the meantime. The ether body was then liberated from the forces of the physical body which act upon it. It had become, as it were, elastic and plastic and when the sensory organs that had been formed in the astral body sank down into it, the ether body received an imprint from the whole astral body. When the pupil was brought again into a normal condition by the Hierophant, when the astral body and ego were again united with the physical and ether bodies—a procedure which the Hierophant well understood—then not only did he experience katharsis, but also what is called 'Illumination' or 'Photismos.' The pupil could then not only perceive in the world around him all those things that were physically perceptible, but he could employ the spiritual organs of perception, which means, he could see and perceive the spiritual. Initiation consisted essentially of these two processes, Purification or Purging, and Illumination.

"Then the course of human evolution entered upon a phase in which it gradually became impossible to draw the ether body out of the physical without a very great disturbance in all its functions; because the whole tendency of the Post-Atlantean evolution was to cause the ether body to be attached closer and closer to the physical body. It was consequently necessary to carry out other methods of initiation which proceed in such a manner that without the separating of the physical and ether bodies, the astral body, having become sufficiently developed through katharsis and able of itself to return again to the physical and etheric bodies, was able to imprint its organs on the ether body in spite of the hindrance of the physical body. What had to happen was that stronger forces had to become active in Meditation and Concentration in order that there might be the strong impulse in the astral body for overcoming the power of resistance of the physical body. In the first place there was the actual specifically Christian initiation in which it was necessary for the pupil to undergo the procedure which was described yesterday as the seven steps. When he had undergone these feelings and experiences, his astral body had been so intensely affected it formed its organs of perception plastically—perhaps only after years, but still sooner or later—and then impressed them upon the ether body, thus making of the pupil one of the Illuminati. This kind of initiation which is specifically Christian could only be described fully, if I were able to hold lectures about its particular aspects, every day for about a fortnight instead of only for a few days. But that is not the important thing. Yesterday you were given certain details of the Christian initiation. We only wish to become acquainted with its principle.

"By continually meditating upon passages of the *Gospel of St. John*, the Christian pupil is actually in a condition to reach initiation without the three and a half day continued lethargic sleep. If each day he allows the first verses of the *Gospel of St. John*, from "In the beginning was the Word" to the passage 'full of devotion and truth,' to work upon him, they become an exceedingly significant meditation. They have this force within them, for this *Gospel* is not there simply to be read and understood in its entirety with the intellect, but it must be inwardly fully experienced and felt. It is a force which comes to the help of initiation and works for it. Then will the 'Washing of the Feet,' the 'Scourging' and other inner processes be experienced as astral visions, wholly corresponding to the description in the *Gospel* itself, beginning with the 13th Chapter.

"The Rosicrucian initiation, although resting upon a Christian foundation works more with other symbolic ideas which produce katharsis, chiefly with imaginative pictures. That is another modification which had to be used, because mankind had progressed a step further in its evolution and the methods of initiation must conform to what has gradually been evolved.

"We must understand that when a person has attained this initiation, he is fundamentally quite different from the person he was before it. While formerly he was only associated with the things of the physical world, he now acquires the possibility likewise of association with the events and beings of the spiritual world. This pre-supposes that the human being acquires knowledge in a much more real sense than in that abstract, dry, prosaic sense in which we usually speak of knowledge. For a person who acquires spiritual knowledge, finds the process to be something quite different. It is a complete realization of that beautiful expression, 'Know thyself.' But the most dangerous thing in the realm of knowledge is to grasp these words erroneously and today this occurs only too frequently. Many people construe these words to mean that they should no longer look about the physical world, but should gaze into their own inner being and seek there for everything spiritual. This is a very mistaken understanding of the saying, for that is not at all what it means. We must clearly understand that true higher knowledge is also an evolution from one standpoint, which the human being has attained, to another which he had not reached previously. If a person practices self-knowledge only by brooding upon himself, he sees only what he already possesses. He thereby acquires nothing new, but only knowledge of his own lower self in the present meaning of the word. This inner nature is only one part that is necessary for knowledge. The other part that is necessary must be added. Without the two parts, there is no real knowledge. By means of his inner nature, he can develop organs through which he can gain knowledge. But just as the eye, as an external sense organ, would not perceive the sun by gazing into itself, but only by looking outward at the sun, so must the inner perceptive organs gaze outwardly, in other words, gaze into an *external spiritual* in order actually to perceive. The concept 'Knowledge' had a much deeper, a more real meaning in those ages when spiritual things were better understood than at present. Read in the Bible the words, 'Abraham knew his wife!' or this or that Patriarch 'knew his wife.' One does not need to seek very far in order to understand that by this expression fructification is meant. When one considers the words, 'Know thyself,' in the Greek, they do not mean that you stare into your own inner being, but that you fructify yourself with what streams into you from the spiritual world. 'Know thyself' means: *Fructify thyself with the content of the spiritual world!*

"Two things are needed for this namely, that the human being prepare himself through katharsis and illumination, and then that he open his inner being freely to the spiritual world. In this connection we may liken his inner nature to the female aspect, the outer spiritual to the male. The inner being must be made susceptible of receiving the higher self. When this has happened, then the higher human self streams into him from the spiritual world. One may ask: Where is this higher human self? Is it within the personal man? No, it is not there. On Old Saturn, Old Sun and Old Moon, the higher self was diffused over the entire Cosmos. At that time the Cosmic Ego was spread out over all human kind, but now men have to permit it to work upon them. They must permit this Ego to work upon their previously prepared inner natures. This means that the human inner nature, in other words, the astral body has to be cleansed, purified and ennobled and subjected to katharsis, then a person may expect that the external spirit will stream into him for his illumination. That will occur when the human being has been so well prepared that he has subjected his astral body to katharsis, thereby developing his inner organs of perception. The astral body, in any case, has progressed so far that now when it dips down into the ether and physical bodies, illumination or photismos results. What actually occurs is that the astral body imprints its organs upon the ether body, making it possible for the human being to perceive a spiritual world about him; making it possible for his inner being, the astral body, to receive what the ether body is able to offer to it, what the ether body draws out of the entire Cosmos, out of the Cosmic Ego [ICh= 'IAm'].

"This cleansed, purified astral body, which bears within it at the moment of illumination none of the impure impressions of the physical world, but only the organs of perception of the spiritual world is called in Esoteric Christianity the 'pure, chaste, wise Virgin Sophia.' By means of all that he receives during katharsis, the pupil cleanses and purifies his astral body so that it is transformed into the Virgin Sophia. And when the Virgin Sophia encounters the Cosmic Ego, the Universal Ego which causes illumination, the pupil is surrounded by light, spiritual light. This second power that approaches the Virgin Sophia, is called in Esoteric Christianity—is also so called today—the 'Holy Spirit.' Therefore according to Esoteric Christianity, it is correct to say that through his processes of initiation the Christian esotericist attains the purification and cleansing of his astral body; he makes his astral body into the Virgin Sophia and is illuminated from above—if you wish, you may call it overshadowed—by the 'Holy Spirit,' by the Cosmic, Universal Ego. And a person thus illuminated, who, in other words, according to Esoteric Christianity has received the 'Holy Spirit' into himself, speaks forthwith in a different manner. How does he speak? When he speaks about Saturn, Sun and Moon, about the different members of the human being, about the processes of cosmic evolution, he is not expressing *his* own opinion. *His* views do not at all come into consideration. When such a person speaks about Saturn, it is Saturn itself that is speaking through him. When he speaks about the Sun, the Spiritual Being of the Sun speaks through him. He is the instrument. His personal ego has been eclipsed, which means that at such moments it has become impersonal and it is the Cosmic Universal Ego that is using his ego as its instrument through which to speak. Therefore, in true esoteric teaching which proceeds from Esoteric Christianity, one should not speak of *views or opinions*; for in the highest sense of the word this is incorrect—*there are no such things*. According to Esoteric Christianity, whoever speaks with the right attitude of mind toward the world will say to himself, for instance: If I tell people that there were two horses outside, the important thing is not that one of them pleases me less than the other and that I think one is a worthless horse. The important point is that I describe the horses to the others and give the facts. In like manner, what has been observed in the spiritual worlds must be described irrespective of all personal opinions. In every spiritual-scientific system of teaching, only the series of facts must be related and this must have nothing to do with the opinions of the one who relates them.

"Thus we have acquired two concepts in their spiritual significance. We have learned to know the nature of the Virgin Sophia, which is the purified astral body, and the nature of the 'Holy Spirit,' the Cosmic Universal Ego; which is received by the Virgin Sophia and which can then speak out of this purified astral body. There is something else to be attained, a still higher stage, that is the ability to help someone else, the ability to give him the impulse to accomplish both of these. Men of our evolutionary epoch can receive the Virgin Sophia (the purified astral body) and the Holy Spirit (illumination) in the manner described; but only Christ Jesus could give to the Earth what was necessary to accomplish this. He has implanted in the spiritual part of the Earth those forces which make it possible for that to happen at all which has been described in the Christian initiation. You may ask how did this come about?

"Two things are necessary for an understanding of this. First we must make ourselves acquainted with something purely historical, that is, with the manner of giving of names which was quite different in the age in which the *Gospels* were written from the way in which it is done at present.

"Those who interpret the *Gospel* at present do not at all understand the principle of giving names at the time the *Gospels* were written and therefore they do not speak as they should. It is, in fact, exceedingly difficult to describe the principle of giving names at that time, yet we can make it comprehensible, even though we only indicate it in rough outlines. Let us suppose, in the case of someone whom we meet, that instead of holding to the name which does not at all fit him, and which has been given to him in the abstract way customary today, we were to harken to and notice his most distinguishing characteristics, were to notice the most prominent attribute of his character and were in a position to discern clairvoyantly the deeper foundations of his being, then were to give him his name in accordance with those most important qualities which we believe should be attributed to him. Were we to follow such a method of giving names, we should be doing something, at a lower more elementary stage, similar to what was done at that time by those who gave names in the manner of the writer of the *Gospel of St. John*. In order to make very clear his manner of giving names, let us consider the following:

The author of the *St. John's Gospel* regarded the physical, historic Mother of Jesus in her most prominent characteristics and asked himself,—Where shall I find a name for her which will express most perfectly her real being? Then, because she had by means of her earlier incarnations, reached those spiritual heights upon which she stood; and because she appeared in her external personality to be a counterpart, a revelation of what was called in Esoteric Christianity, the Virgin Sophia, he called the Mother of Jesus the 'Virgin Sophia'—and this is what she was always called in the esoteric places where Esoteric Christianity was taught. Exoterically he leaves her entirely *nameless* in contradistinction to those others who have chosen for her the secular name, Mary. He could not take the secular name, he had to express in the name the profound, world historic evolution. He does this by indicating that she cannot be called Mary and what is more, he places by her side her sister Mary, wife of Cleophas and calls her simply the 'Mother of Jesus.' He shows thereby that he does not wish to mention her name, that it cannot be publicly revealed. In esoteric circles, she is always called the 'Sophia.' *It was she who represented the 'Virgin Sophia' as an external historical personality.*

"If we now wish to penetrate further into the nature of Christianity and its founder, we must take under consideration yet another mystery. We should understand clearly how to make a distinction between the personality who, in Esoteric Christianity, was called 'Jesus of Nazareth' and Him who was called 'Christ Jesus'—*the Christ dwelling within Jesus of Nazareth.*

"Now what does this mean? It means that in the historical personality of Jesus of Nazareth, we have to do with a highly developed human being who had passed through many incarnations and after a cycle of high development was again reincarnated; a person who, because of this, was attracted to a mother so pure that the writer of the *Gospel* could call her the 'Virgin Sophia.' Thus we are dealing with a highly developed human being, Jesus of Nazareth, who had progressed far in his evolution in his previous incarnations and in this incarnation had entered upon a highly spiritual stage. The other evangelists were not illuminated to such a high degree as the writer of this *Gospel*. It was more the actual sense-world that was revealed to them, a world in which they saw their Master and Messiah moving about as Jesus of Nazareth. The mysterious spiritual relationships, at least those of the heights into which the writer of the *Gospel of St. John* could peer, were concealed from them. For this reason they laid special emphasis upon the fact that in Jesus of Nazareth lived the Father, who had always existed in Judaism and was transmitted down through the generations as the God of the Jews. And they expressed this when they said: 'If we trace back the ancestry of Jesus of Nazareth through generation after generation, we are able to prove that the same blood flows in Him that has flowed down through these generations.' The evangelists give the genealogical tables and precisely according to them they also show at what different stages of evolution they stand. For

Matthew, the important thing is to show that in Jesus of Nazareth we have a person in whom Father Abraham is living. The blood of Father Abraham has flowed down through the generations as far as Jesus. He thus traces the genealogical tables back to Abraham. He has a more materialistic point of view than Luke. The important thing for Luke was not alone to show that the God who lived in Abraham was present in Jesus; but that the ancestry, the line of descent, can be traced back still further, even to Adam and that Adam was a son of the very Godhead—which means that he belonged to the time when humanity had just made the transition from a spiritual to a physical state. Both Matthew and Luke wished to show that this earthly Jesus of Nazareth has His being only in what can be traced back to the divine Father-power. This was not a matter of importance for the writer of the *Gospel of St. John* who could gaze into the spiritual world. The important thing for him was not the words, 'I and Father Abraham are one'; but that at every moment of time, there exists in the human being the Eternal which was present in him before Father Abraham. This he wished to show. In the beginning was the Word which is called the 'I Am.' Before all external things and beings, *He was*. He was in the beginning. For those who wished rather to describe Jesus of Nazareth and were only able to describe him, it was a question of showing how from the beginning the blood flowed down through the generations. It was important to them to show that the same blood flowing down through the generations flowed also in Joseph, the father of Jesus.

"If we could speak quite esoterically it would naturally be necessary to speak of the idea of the so-called 'virgin birth'; but this can be discussed only in the most intimate circles. It belongs to the deepest mysteries that exist and the misunderstanding connected with this idea arises because people do not know what is meant by the 'virgin birth.' They think that it means there was no fatherhood. But it is not that; a much more profound, a more mysterious something lies at the back of it which is quite compatible with what the other disciples wish to show, that is, that Joseph is the father of Jesus. If they were to deny this, then all the trouble they take to show this to be a fact would be meaningless. They wish to show that the ancient God exists in Jesus of Nazareth. Luke especially wished to make this very clear, therefore he traces the whole ancestry back to Adam and then to God. How could he have come to this conclusion, if he really wished only to say: I am showing you that this genealogical tree exists; but Joseph, as a matter of fact, had nothing to do with it. It would be very strange if people were to take the trouble to represent Joseph as a very important personality and then were to shove him aside out of the whole affair.

"In the event of Palestine, we have not only to do with this highly developed personality, Jesus of Nazareth, who had passed through many incarnations, and had developed himself so highly that he needed such an extraordinary mother as the Virgin Sophia; but we have also to do with a second mystery. When Jesus of Nazareth was thirty years of age, he had advanced to such a stage through what he had experienced in his present incarnation that he could perform an action which it is possible for one to perform in exceptional cases. We know that the human being consists of physical, etheric and astral bodies and an ego. This fourfold human being is the human being as he lives here among us. If a person stands at a certain high stage of evolution, it is possible for him at a particular moment to draw out his ego from the three bodies and abandon them, leaving them intact and entirely uninjured. This ego then goes into the spiritual worlds and the three bodies remain behind. We meet this process at times in cosmic evolution. At some especially exalted, enraptured moment, the ego of a person departs and enters into the spirit world—under certain conditions this can be extended over a long period—and because the three bodies are so highly developed by the ego that lived in them, they are fit instruments for a still higher being who now takes possession of them. In the thirtieth year of Jesus of Nazareth, that Being whom we have called the Christ, took possession of his physical, etheric and astral bodies. This Christ Being could not incarnate in an ordinary child's body; but only in one which had first been prepared by a highly developed ego—*for this Christ-Being had never before been incarnated in a physical body.* Therefore from the thirtieth year on, we are dealing with the Christ in Jesus of Nazareth.

"What in reality took place? The fact is that the corporality of Jesus of Nazareth which he had left behind was so mature, so perfect, that the Sun Logos, the Being of the six Elohim, which we have described as the Spiritual Being of the Sun, was able to penetrate into it. It could incarnate for three years in this corporality, could become flesh. The Sun Logos Who can shine into human beings through illumination, the Sun Logos Himself, the Holy Spirit, entered. The Universal-Ego, the Cosmic Ego entered and from then on during three years, the Sun Logos spoke through the body of Jesus. The Christ speaks through the body of Jesus during these three years. This event is indicated in the *Gospel of St. John* and also in the other *Gospels* as the descent of the dove, of the Holy Spirit, upon Jesus of Nazareth. In Esoteric Christianity it is said, that at that moment the ego of Jesus of Nazareth left his body, and that from then on the Christ is in him, speaking through him in order to teach and work. This is the first event that happens, according to the *Gospel of St. John*. We now have the Christ within the astral, etheric and physical bodies of

Jesus of Nazareth. There He worked as has been described until the Mystery of Golgotha occurred. What occurred on Golgotha? Let us consider that important moment when the blood flowed from the wounds of the Crucified Savior. In order that you may understand me better, I shall compare what occurred with something else.

"Let us suppose we have here a vessel filled with water. In the water, salt is dissolved and the water becomes quite transparent. Because we have warmed the water, we have made a salt solution. Now let us cool the water. The salt precipitates and we see how the salt condenses below and forms a deposit at the bottom of the vessel. That is the process for one who sees only with physical eyes. But for a person who can see with spiritual eyes, something else is happening. While the salt is condensing below, the spirit of the salt streams up through the water, filling it. The salt can only become condensed when the spirit of the salt has departed from it and become diffused into the water. Those who understand these things know that wherever condensation takes place, a spiritualization also always occurs. What thus condenses below has its counterpart above in the spiritual, just as in the case of the salt, when it condenses and is precipitated below, its spirit streams upward and disseminates. Therefore, it was not only a physical process that took place when the blood flowed from the wounds of the Savior—but it was actually accompanied by a spiritual process; that is, the Holy Spirit which was received at the Baptism united Itself with the Earth—*that the Christ Himself flowed into the very being of the Earth*. From now on, the Earth was changed, and this is the reason for saying to you, in earlier lectures, that if a person had viewed the Earth from a distant star, he would have observed that its whole appearance was altered with the Mystery of Golgotha. The Sun Logos became a part of the Earth, formed an alliance with it and became the Spirit of the Earth. This He achieved by entering into the body of Jesus of Nazareth in his thirtieth year, and by remaining active there for three years, after which He continued to remain on the Earth. Now the important thing is that this Event must produce an effect upon the true Christian; that it must give something by which he may gradually develop the beginnings of a purified astral body in the Christian sense. There had to be something there for the Christian whereby he could make his astral body gradually more and more like a Virgin Sophia; and through it, receive into himself the Holy Spirit which was able to spread out over the entire Earth—*but which could not be received by anyone whose astral body did not resemble the Virgin Sophia.* There had to be something which possesses the power to transform the human astral body into a Virgin Sophia. What is this power? It consists in the fact of Christ Jesus entrusting to the Disciple whom He loved—in other words to the writer of the *Gospel of St. John*—the mission of describing truly and faithfully through his own illumination the events of Palestine in order that men might be affected by them. If men permit what is written in the *Gospel of St. John* to work sufficiently upon them, their astral body is in the process of becoming a Virgin Sophia and it will become receptive to the Holy Spirit. Gradually, through the strength of the impulse which emanates from this *Gospel*, it will become susceptible of feeling the true spirit and later of perceiving it. This mission, this charge, was given to the writer of the *Gospel* by Jesus Christ. You need but read the *Gospel*. The Mother of Jesus—the Virgin Sophia in the esoteric meaning of Christianity—stands at the foot of the Cross, and from the Cross the Christ says to the Disciple whom He loved: 'Henceforth, this is thy Mother and from this hour the Disciple took her unto himself.' This means: 'That force which was in My astral body and made it capable of becoming bearer of the Holy Spirit, I now give over to thee; thou shalt write down what this astral body has been able to acquire through its development.' 'And the Disciple took her unto himself,' that means he wrote the *Gospel of St. John*. And this *Gospel of St. John* is the *Gospel* in which the writer has concealed powers which develop the Virgin Sophia. At the Cross, the mission was entrusted to him of receiving that force as his *mother* and of being the true, genuine interpreter of the Messiah. This really means that if you live wholly in accordance with the *Gospel of St. John* and understand it spiritually, it has the force to lead you to Christian katharsis, it has the power to give you the Virgin Sophia. Then will the Holy Spirit, united with the Earth, grant you illumination or photismos according to the Christian meaning. And what the most intimate disciples experienced there in Palestine was so powerful that from that time on, they possessed at least the capacity of perceiving in the spiritual world. The most intimate disciples had received this capacity into themselves. Perceiving in the spirit, in the Christian sense, means that the person transforms his astral body to such a degree through the power of the Event of Palestine that what he sees need not be before him externally and physically-sensible. He possesses something by means of which he can perceive in the spirit. There were such intimate pupils. The woman who anointed the feet of Christ Jesus in Bethany had received through the Event of Palestine the powerful force needed for spiritual perception, and she is, for example, one of those who first understood that what had lived in Jesus was present after His death, that is, had been resurrected. She possessed this faculty. It may be asked: Whence came this possibility? It came through the development of her inner sense-organs. Are we told this in the *Gospel*? We are indeed; we are told that Mary Magdalene was led to the grave, that the body had disappeared and that she saw there two spiritual forms. These two spiritual forms are always to be seen when a corpse is present for a certain time after death. On the one side is to be seen the astral body, and on the other, what gradually separates from it as the etheric body, then passing over into the cosmic ether. Wholly apart from the physical body, there are two spiritual forms present which belong to the spiritual world.

> 'Then the disciples went away again unto their own home. But Mary stood without at the sepulchre weeping; and as she wept she stooped down and looked into the sepulchre, and seeth two angels in white sitting.'

> "She beheld this because she had become clairvoyant through the force and power of the Event of Palestine. And she beheld something more: she beheld the Risen Christ. Was it necessary for her to be clairvoyant, to be able to behold the Christ? If you have seen a person in physical form a few days ago, do you not think you would recognize him again if he should appear before you?

> 'And when she had thus said, she turned herself back and saw Jesus standing and knew not that it was Jesus.
> 'Jesus saith unto her, Woman why weepest thou? Whom seekest thou? She, supposing it to be the gardener...'

> "And in order that it might be told to us as exactly as possible, it was not only said once; but again at the next appearance of the Risen Christ, when Jesus appeared at the sea of Gennesareth.

> 'But when the morning was now come, Jesus stood on the shore: but the disciples knew not that it was Jesus.'

"The esoteric pupils find Him there. Those who had received the full force of the Event of Palestine could grasp the situation and see that it was the Risen Jesus who could be perceived spiritually. Although the disciples and Mary Magdalene saw Him, yet there were some among them who were less able to develop clairvoyant power. One of these was Thomas. It is said that he was not present the first time the disciples saw the Lord, and he declared he would have to lay his hands in His wounds, he would have to touch physically the body of the Risen Christ. You ask: What happened? The effort was then made to assist him to develop spiritual perception. And how was this done? Let us take the words of the *Gospel* itself:

> 'And after a week His disciples were again within, and Thomas with them: then came Jesus the doors being shut, and stood in their midst, and said, Peace be unto you.
>
> 'Then saith He to Thomas, reach hither thy fingers and behold My hands, and reach hither thy hand and thrust it into My side: and be not faithless, but believing. And thou shalt behold something if thou dost not rely upon the outer appearance, but art impregnated with inner power.'

"This inner power which should proceed from the Event of Palestine is called 'Faith.' It is no ordinary force; but an inner clairvoyant power. Permeate thyself with inner power, then thou needest no longer hold as real that only which thou seest externally; for blessed are they who are able to know what they do not see outwardly!

"Thus we see that we have to do with the full reality and truth of the Resurrection and that only those are fully able to understand it, who have first developed the inner power to perceive in the spirit world. This will make the last chapter of the *Gospel of St. John* comprehensible to you, in which again and again it is pointed out that the closest followers of Christ Jesus have reached the stage of the Virgin Sophia, because the Event of Golgotha had been consummated in their presence. But when they had to stand firm for the first time, had actually to behold a spiritual event, they were still blinded and had first to find their way. They did not know that He was the same One Who had earlier been among them. Here is something which we must grasp with the most subtle concepts; for the grossly materialistic person would say: 'Then the Resurrection is undermined!' The miracle of the Resurrection is to be taken quite literally; for He said: 'Lo, I remain with you always, even unto the end of the age, unto the end of the cosmic age.'

"He is there and will come again, although not in a form of flesh; but in a form in which those who have been sufficiently developed through the power of the *Gospel of St. John,* can actually perceive Him and possessing the power to perceive Him, they will no longer be unbelieving. The mission of the Spiritual Science Movement is to prepare those who have the will to allow themselves to be prepared, for the return of the Christ upon Earth. This is the cosmo-historical significance of Spiritual Science, to prepare mankind and to keep its eyes open for the time when the Christ will appear again actively among men in the sixth cultural epoch, in order that this may be accomplished for a great part of humanity which was indicated to us in the Marriage at Cana.

"Therefore the world-concept obtained from Spiritual Science appears like an execution of the testament of Christianity. In order to be lead to real Christianity, the men of the future will have to receive that spiritual teaching which Spiritual Science is able to give. Many people may still say today: Spiritual Science is something that really contradicts true Christianity. But those are the 'little popes' who form opinions about things of which they know nothing and who then make into a dogma: *What I do not know does not exist.*

"This intolerance will become greater and greater in the future and Christianity will experience the greatest danger just from those people who, at present, believe they can be called good Christians. The Christianity of Spiritual Science will experience serious attacks from the Christians in name; for all concepts must change if a true spiritual understanding of Christianity is to come about. Above all, the soul must become more and more conversant with and understanding of the legacy of the writer of the *Gospel of St. John*, the great school of the Virgin Sophia, the *St. John's Gospel* itself. Only Spiritual Science can lead us deeper into this *Gospel*.

"In these lectures, only examples could be given showing how Spiritual Science can introduce us into the *Gospel of St. John*; for it is impossible to explain the whole of it. We read in the *Gospel* itself:

> 'And there are also many other things which Jesus did; and I suppose that were they all written down one after the other, the world could not contain all the books that would have to be written.'

"Just as the *Gospel* itself cannot go into all the details of the Event of Palestine, so too is it impossible for even the longest course of lectures to present the full spiritual content of the *Gospel*. Therefore we must be satisfied with those indications which could be given at this time; we must content ourselves with the thought that through just such indications in the course of human evolution, the true testament of Christianity becomes executed. Let us allow all this to have such an effect upon us that we may possess the power to hold fast to the foundation which we recognize in the *Gospel of St. John*, when others come to us and say: You are giving us too complicated concepts, too many concepts which we must first make our own in order to comprehend this *Gospel*: the *Gospel* is for the simple and naïve and one dare not approach them with many concepts and thoughts. Many say this today. They perhaps refer to another saying: 'Blessed are the poor in spirit, for theirs is the kingdom of heaven.' One can merely quote such a saying as long as one does not understand it, for it really says: 'Blessed are the beggars in spirit, for they shall reach the kingdom of heaven within themselves.' This means that those who are like beggars of the spirit, who desire to receive more and more of the spirit, will find in themselves the kingdom of heaven!

"At the present time the idea is all too prevalent that everything religious is identical with all that is primitive and simple. People say: We acknowledge that Science possesses many and complicated ideas; but we do not grant the same to Faith and Religion. Faith and Religion—so say many 'Christians'—must be simple and naïve! They demand this! And many rely upon a conception which is little quoted perhaps, but which in the present is haunting the minds of men and which Voltaire, one of the great teachers of materialism, has expressed in the words:

'One who wishes to be a prophet must find believers; for what he asserts must be believed, and only what is simple, what is always repeated in its simplicity, that alone finds believers.'

"This is often so with the prophets, both true and false. They take the trouble to say something and to repeat it again and again and the people learn to believe it, because it is constantly repeated. The representative of Spiritual Science desires to be no such prophet. He does not wish to be a prophet at all. And although it may often be said: 'Yes, you not only repeat; but you are always elucidating things from other sides, you are always discussing them in other ways'; when they speak thus to him, he is guilty of no fault. A prophet wishes that people believe in *him*. Spiritual Science has no desire to lead to *belief*, but to *knowledge*. Therefore let us take Voltaire's utterance in another way. He says:—"The *simple* is *believed* and is the concern of the prophet." Spiritual Science says:—the *manifold* is *known*. Let us try to understand more and more that Spiritual Science is something that is manifold—not a *creed*, but a *path* to knowledge, and consequently it bears within it the manifold. Therefore let us not shrink from collecting a great deal in order that we may understand one of the most important Christian documents, the *Gospel of St. John*. We have attempted to assemble the most varied material which places us in the position of being able to understand more and more the profound truths of this *Gospel*; able to understand how the physical mother of Jesus was an external manifestation, an external image of the Virgin Sophia; to understand what spiritual importance the Virgin Sophia had for the pupil of the Mysteries, whom the Christ loved; again to understand how, for the other Evangelists—who view the bodily descent of Jesus as important—the physical father plays his significant part when it was a question of the external imprint of the God-idea in the blood; and further, to understand what significance the Holy Spirit had for John, the Holy Spirit through which the Christ was begotten in the body of Jesus and dwelt therein during the three years and which is symbolized for us in the descent of the Dove at the Baptism by John.

"If we understand that we must call the father of Christ Jesus the Holy Spirit who begot the Christ in the bodies of Jesus, then if we are able to comprehend a thing from all sides, we shall find it easy to understand that those disciples who were less highly initiated could not give us so profound a picture of the Events of Palestine as *the Disciple whom the Lord loved*. And if people, at present, speak of the Synoptics—which are the only authoritative *Gospels* for them—this only shows that they do not have the will to rise to an understanding of the true form of the *Gospel of St. John*. For everybody resembles the God he understands. If we try to make into a feeling, into an experience, what we can learn from Spiritual Science about the *Gospel of St. John*, we shall then find that this *Gospel* is not a text-book, *but a force which can be active within our souls*.

"If these short lectures have aroused in you the feeling that this *Gospel* contains not only what we have been discussing here; but that indirectly, through the medium of words, it contains the *force* which can develop the soul further, then what was really intended in these lectures has been rightly understood. Because in them, not only was something intended for the understanding—for the intellectual capacity of understanding—but that which takes its round-about path through this intellectual capacity of understanding should condense into feelings and inner experiences, and these feelings and experiences should be a result of the facts that have been presented here. If, in a certain sense, this has been rightly understood, we shall also comprehend what is meant when it is said that the Movement for Spiritual Science has the mission of raising Christianity into Wisdom, of rightly understanding Christianity, indirectly through Spiritual Wisdom. We shall understand that Christianity is only in the beginning of its activity, and its true mission will be fulfilled when it is understood in its true spiritual form. The more these lectures are understood in this way, the more have they been comprehended in the sense in which they were intended."

The Mother of the Divine Feminine Trinity

The following remarks of Rudolf Steiner highlight the nature of the 'Mother' aspect of the Divine Feminine Trinity. The evolution, or biography, of this being is part of the creation of the natural world. All that presents itself in the world around us are the prior donations of The Mothers, the three previous incarnations of the Earth (Old Saturn, Old Sun, and Old Moon).

Anthroposophy in the Light of Goethe's Faust, **Rudolf Steiner, Lecture X,** *The Realm of The Mothers: The Mater Gloriosa*, **Dornach, August 16, 1915, GA 272**

"The Mothers, who are also an 'Ever Feminine,' are three in number; the Mother, the Mater Gloriosa, is singular. Now these two kinds of striving—to The Mothers on the one hand, which places us in the period of evolution before the Mystery of Golgotha, and to the Mother on the other, the Mater Gloriosa, which places us in the period of evolution after the Mystery of Golgotha—don't they show us with their overwhelming poetic splendor what the Mystery of Golgotha has brought us? ... The three Mothers became the one Mother, the Mater Gloriosa, in that the human being has progressed to the point of being inwardly permeated by the 'I,' in the manner with which we are familiar…

"…And this transition from the Ever-Feminine as a *trinity* to the Ever-Feminine as a *unity* is one of the greatest, most wonderful, most beautiful of all the artistic enhancements in the second part of *Faust*."

Isis and Madonna, Rudolf Steiner, Lecture XVI, Berlin, April 29, 1909, GA 57

"Now what does this journey to the Mothers signify for Faust? We have made brief mention of this in the lecture referred to. Mephistopheles himself cannot enter the realm where the Mothers are enthroned although he gives Faust the key. Mephistopheles is the spirit of materialism, the spirit contained in the forces and powers of man's material existence. To him the realm of the Mothers is the realm of nothingness. Faust, the spiritual human being, with his bent towards the spirit is able to answer: 'In thy nothingness I hope to find the All.' Then follows the highly remarkable and significant description of the realm of the Mothers, and we are told how they weave and live in a sphere out of which the forms of the visible world are fashioned; how man, if he would penetrate to the Mothers, must rise above all that lives in space and time. Formation, transformation, this is the essence of their realm. They are mysterious Goddesses holding sway in a spiritual realm behind the reality of the senses. Faust must penetrate to them if he is to obtain knowledge of all that transcends the sensory and physical. Only by widening his soul to this realm of the Mothers can Faust worthily unite in Helen the eternal with the temporal. In that lecture on *Faust* it was possible to indicate that Goethe fully understood how in this realm of the Mothers one has to do with a sphere into which man is able to penetrate when he awakens slumbering spiritual forces in his soul. This is for him the great moment in which are revealed to him the spiritual beings and facts which are always around us, but which with the eyes of the senses we see as little as the blind man sees color and light. It is the moment when the spiritual eyes and ears are opened to a world lying behind the physical world. Entrance into this realm is portrayed by the journey to the Mothers.

"In these lectures it was repeatedly indicated that when man practices certain inner exercises on his soul, certain minutely-prescribed methods for sinking deeply into the world of his conceptions, feelings and will, then his spiritual eyes and ears actually become open and new realms are unfolded around him. It was also shown that whoever enters this realm is confused by all the impressions that work upon him. Whereas in the physical world we perceive objects in sharp outline from which we take our bearings, in the spiritual world we have a confused feeling of inter-weaving, hovering form, just as Goethe describes it in the second part of *Faust*. But it is out of this realm of the Mothers that there is born all that is given to our senses, just as in the mountains metal is born out of the mother-ore. And because this mysterious realm, the Mother-realm of everything earthly and physical, the realm containing, so to say, the divine substance of all things—because this mysterious realm is resounding in Goethe, the expression 'the Mothers' works with such fascination and awesome beauty…

"…Now anyone wishing to enter this realm of the Mothers, the realm of the spiritual world, has had at all times to undertake, besides other exercises that may be found in *Knowledge of the Higher Worlds*, what has invariably been called preparatory purification, catharsis of the soul. He must so prepare himself that his soul, out of which the higher spiritual forces are to be derived is free of all urge and passion for the ordinary world of the senses. The soul must be purified from all those things which have sensuous attraction and provide food for the senses and which hold the understanding captive in the physical body. The soul must be free, then it can awaken within itself the spiritual eye and penetrate into the spiritual realm. The so-called purified soul, the soul that has passed through catharsis and is no longer turned towards the physical world of the senses, wherever knowledge of this mystery has existed has always been called the higher being of man, that inner being of which it has been said that it does not originate in anything the outer eyes can investigate, but in sources of a higher soul and spiritual nature; it has not an earthly but a heavenly home. It was thought that the ennobled, purified soul was connected with this true origin of man, for what has been spiritual science through the ages has never been able to speak of a purely material evolution, of a perfection or imperfection in accordance with the senses. Spiritual science does not condemn as erroneous what today is called evolution, the ascent from the lowest to the most perfect physical being wandering on the face of the earth, namely, physical man. As I have often emphasized, that is fully recognized. The scientific theory of evolution and descent is fully recognized by spiritual science, but at the same time it is pointed out that the whole being we call man is not included in this evolution, which evolution only applies to the external side of man's development.

"Now when we trace man back through all the changes of time we find that the further we go back to ever more imperfect physical forms the more we meet with man's origin as a soul-spiritual-being. We have often gone back to an age of human evolution when the being we now call man had as yet no kind of physical existence and was securely sheltered within an existence of spirit and soul. Attention has repeatedly been drawn to how, in the sense of spiritual science we look upon the material form, man's physical body, as a densification of a being who was once only spirit and soul. This being of spirit and soul has been densified, as it were, to present-day man, as water is solidified into ice. This picture has often been made use of, when it is said: Let us imagine a quantity of water condensed to ice so that finally we are left with a certain amount of water together with the part that is changed into ice. Here we have an image of man's origin. In the man who was once just soul and spirit there existed as yet nothing of the physical, material bodily nature today perceptible to the eyes and tangible for the hands. Man becomes gradually ever more physical, until he comes to his present physical form. The age to which orthodox science can look back reveals indeed man in the physical form we see today. But spiritual science looks back into a primordial past when man was born out of the spiritual world and was still of a spirit and soul nature. When we contemplate the soul of man today we can say that the soul element in him is the last remnant, so to speak, of the spiritual and soul nature that once was his. We look at the inner nature of man, learning to know his spiritual and soul being, and come to realize that as he is in his inner being, so he was once long ago when he was born out of the womb of the spiritual world. This being of soul is sheathed from outside in the lower elements of the sense world, but he can be purified and cleansed, can raise himself to a perception free of the senses, thereby regaining the spirituality out of which he was born. This is the process of spiritual knowledge that passes through purification. Thus in spirit we gaze into man's being of soul, and speaking not merely in imagery but with reality say: Knowing this soul being in its truth, we perceive that the being is not of this world. In the background of this soul being we see a divine spiritual world out of which he was born...

"…Now let us try to turn what has been said into a physical picture. Let us ask ourselves: Do we not possess a physical picture of what has been described, where the spiritual world is represented by cloud formations out of which the spiritual is born in the form of angels' heads portraying the human soul? Have we not in the Virgin's figure in Raphael's Sistine Madonna a picture born out of the divine spiritual world?

"Let us go on to ask: What becomes of a man whose soul has been cleansed and purified, who has ascended to higher knowledge and has unfolded in his soul those spiritual images that give life within him to the divine, living and weaving through the world? This human being who gives birth in man to the higher man, to a man who represents a little world in the great world, who out of his purified soul brings forth the true higher man—what is he? He cannot be otherwise described than by the word clairvoyant. If we try to make a picture of the soul that gives birth to the higher man out of himself, out of the spiritual universe, we need only call to mind the picture of the *Sistine Madonna*, the Madonna with the wonderful Child in her arms.

"Thus in the *Sistine Madonna* we have a picture of the human soul born of the spiritual universe, and springing from this soul the highest that a human being can bring forth—man's own spiritual birth, what within him is a new begetting of cosmic creative activity.

"Let us try to experience in our feeling what clairvoyant consciousness does. There was once a time when the structure of the world was founded on divine spirituality; for it would be senseless to seek in the world for spirit if this spirit had not originally built the world. All that surrounds us in the world has sprung from the spirit we seek in the soul. Thus the soul has sprung from the divine Father-spirit living and weaving

The Mother of the Divine Feminine Trinity

throughout the universe, bearing the Son of wisdom Who is like unto this Father-spirit, of Whom He is a repetition.

"We understand now the way in which Goethe approached this problem in all its mystical significance when he tried to gather the whole content of *Faust* together in the 'Chorus Mysticus,' where he speaks of the human soul as the 'eternal feminine' that draws us onward to the universal spirit of the world. This was Goethe's attitude to his Madonna problem at the very end of *Faust*. From the figure which the portrayal of the Madonna has assumed, even today it is hardly possible to recognize fully what is here expressed as in a picture which is nevertheless founded on profound truth. If, however, we trace this Madonna problem back to its origin, we shall realize that in very truth the mightiest human problem, though closely veiled, confronts us in the figure of the Madonna. These Madonnas are, it is true, greatly changed from the simple figure of the catacombs in the first Christian centuries, where we find Madonnas with the Child groping for the mother's breast. From this first simple figure, having little to do with art, it is a long way to the fifteenth century, to Michaelangelo and Raphael, where after many transformations the Child and the Madonna have become in the modern sense much more in accordance with art—in accordance with the art of painting. It is, however, as if these supreme artists proceeded from no very full knowledge but a definite feeling of the deeper truth of the Madonna problem. Very beautiful experiences arise in us when we stand before the so-called *Pieta* of Michaelangelo in St. Peter's in Rome, where the Madonna is sitting with the corpse across her knees—thus the Madonna is at the age when Christ had already passed through death but is portrayed with all the beauty of youth. In Michaelangelo's day it was a much discussed question why at her age he had given the Madonna this youthful beauty. When asked about it he replied how it was well known that virgins long preserve the freshness of youth—and this is no mere belief but spiritually derived knowledge. Thus why should he not be right in representing the Mother of God at this age still with all the freshness of youth? It is a remarkable conception here expressed by Michaelangelo! Although it is not openly expressed by Raphael, nevertheless we feel it to be there in his pictures. We can, however, understand this conception only by going far back into the times when what meets us in the Madonnas as unconscious art was still outwardly living. We might go very far back, and actually we should find the Madonna problem all over the world. We might go to old India and there find the Goddess with the Krishna child at her breast; in a Chinese cult we might find similar pictures.

"We will not, however, go back into these far-off regions; but keep the representations repeated so impressively in olden times and which is given us again with such beauty in the Madonna. We will turn to the representations of Isis with the child Horus. These representations which have grown entirely out of Egyptian wisdom may in a certain sense be the key for the correct understanding of the portrayal of the Madonna. Here, it is true, we must direct our attention to the nature of the wisdom that led to this remarkable figure of the Egyptian Goddess, fix our attention on what this wisdom, expressed in the Isis Osiris saga, means to us. For when we understand it aright, this saga leads us deep into the actual problem of humanity. Wherever we look in the religion of Egypt, the saga of Osiris is still what is most significant and full of content—this King who in primordial times ruled as if in a golden age among men, and married his sister, Isis, who brought happiness and blessing to mankind. He stood before the eyes of ancient Egypt as a human King of divine power and divine virtue; and he ruled until he was killed by Set, his evil brother. He was killed in a strange way. At a banquet the evil brother Set, in later times called Typhon, caused a chest to be made, and craftily induced Osiris to lie down in it, when the lid was quickly closed. The chest was then thrown into the water and swept away to the unknown. His sorrowing spouse Isis seeks everywhere for her husband, after long searching finally discovering him in Asia. She brings him back to Egypt where he is dismembered by his evil brother Set, his fragments being interred in many graves. Hence the great number of tombs of Osiris in Egypt. Osiris now becomes King of the Dead, as previously he was King of living men on earth. From that other world a ray pierces the head of Isis and she gives birth to Horus who becomes the ruler of this world.

"According to the Egyptian legend Horus is the posthumous son of Osiris. Horus, who has come into existence as the result of impregnation from the world beyond, is ruler of the earthly world of the senses; Osiris is ruler of the realm of the dead. Whereas the soul while enclosed in a body is subject to the rulership of Horus, when it abandons the body—so the *Egyptian Book of the Dead* testifies it enters the realm of Osiris, itself becomes an Osiris. The *Egyptian Book of the Dead* describes in what a deeply impressive way the soul is arraigned before the tribunal in these words: 'And thou, O Osiris, what hast thou done?' Thus the soul by passing through the gate of death itself becomes an Osiris.

"According to the old Egyptians, then, we look towards two realms, the realm perceived by the senses, the realm of Horus, and the realm into which the soul enters after death where Osiris holds sway. But at the same time we know that according to the old Egyptian initiates, the initiate who had acquired the faculty of clairvoyance already in his lifetime entered the same region which otherwise can be entered only after death—that he could be united with Osiris. The initiate therefore himself became an Osiris. He tore himself from the physical, renounced all habits of the physical plane, all passions and desires, cleansed himself of the physical, became a purified soul and as such was united with Osiris.

"Now what does this legend tell us? It is a childish idea to maintain that this legend is supposed to represent the yearly course of the Sun round the Earth. The learned ones of the Earth in council have created the legend that Osiris is the Sun, whose disappearance signifies his conquest by nature's wintry powers said to be Set, the evil brother Typhon. And in Isis we have the representation of the Moon who seeks the Sun in order to be irradiated by his light. Only those who spin theoretical myths about nature out of their own minds can make such statements. The truth is that this is the external, pictorial expression of a most profound truth.

"What is this age when Osiris ruled over men? It was the time when men were still beings of soul and spirit dwelling in the world of soul and spirit among beings who also had their being in soul and spirit. When, therefore, the realm of Osiris is spoken of, it is not the physical realm that is meant; but a realm of the past in which man held sway as a being of soul and spirit. And the brother, the enemy of Osiris, is that being who enveloped man in a physical body, who densified part of this spirit and soul being into the physical body. Now we see how the once purely spiritual Osiris was laid in a chest. This chest is simply the human physical body. But because Osiris is a being who in accordance with his whole nature cannot descend so far as the physical world, who is meant to remain in the divine spiritual world, the laying in the chest, the human body, has for him the same meaning as death.

"Here, then, is represented in a wider sense the passage from the realm of soul and spirit to the physical evolutionary epochs of humanity. Osiris could not enter this physical realm; he died to the external physical world and became King in the realm the soul enters on leaving the physical world of the senses, or on developing clairvoyant powers. Hence the initiate is in his soul united with Osiris.

"What has remained to man from that realm of soul and spirit, to man who did not withdraw like Osiris from the physical sense world but entered into it? What has remained to him? It is his soul, his being of spirit and soul that will always draw him onwards to the original source of spirit and soul—to Osiris. This is the human soul dwelling within us, Isis, in a certain sense the eternal feminine who draws us onward to the realm out of which we are born.

"Isis, when she is purified and has laid aside all that she has received from the physical, is impregnated from the spiritual world and gives birth to Horus, the higher man, who is to be victorious over the lower human being. Thus we see Isis as the representative of the human soul, as that in us which as the divine spiritual is born of the universal Father and has remained within us, seeking Osiris and only finding him through initiation or death. By conjuring this Osiris and Isis saga in a picture before our soul we are looking into the realm that lies behind the physical world of the senses, into a time when man was still among the Mothers, the primordial grounds of existence, when Isis was not yet enclosed in the physical body but still united in the golden age with her spouse Osiris.

"Then there is revealed to us the most beautiful flower of mankind, the highest human ideal, which is born out of the human body impregnated by the eternal world-Spirit. Hence how could it be other than the most sublime ideal, the highest peak of humanity, the Christ Himself—for He is the ideal of what they represent—Who would naturally enter the realm of the Mothers. In Goethe's *Faust* we meet with three Mothers seated on golden tripods—three Mothers. The human soul has passed through its evolution during the ages when it was not as yet in a human body. What we today have as human conception and human birth appears to us only as final emblem and symbol of the earlier form of the same thing."

Goethe's Faust from the Standpoint of Spiritual Science, Rudolf Steiner, Lecture, Strassburg, January 23, 1910, GA 272

"Who or what are the 'Mothers'? One could speak for hours to explain what they are. Here we need only say that the Mothers were for spiritual science at all times that which man learns to know when his spiritual eye is opened…

"…Finally we touch that Great Fact, which Goethe incorporated into his final words: the 'Eternal-Feminine.' It is a sin against Goethe to say that here he means the female sex. He refers to that profundity signifying the human soul as related to the mystery of the world; that which deeply yearns as the eternal in man, the Eternal-Feminine which draws the soul to the eternally immortal, the eternal wisdom, and which gives itself to the 'Eternal-Masculine.' The Eternal-Feminine draws us towards the Eternal-Masculine. It has nothing to do with something feminine in the ordinary sense. Therefore can we truly seek this Eternal-Feminine in man and woman: the Eternal-Feminine which aspires to the union with the Eternal-Masculine in the Cosmos, to become one with the Divine-Spiritual that inter-penetrates and permeates the world towards which Faust strives. This mystery of man of all ages pursued by Faust from the beginning, this secret to which Spiritual Science is to lead us in a modern sense, is expressed by Goethe paradigmatically and monumentally in those five words at the conclusion of the second part of Faust represented as a Chorus Mysticus; that everything physical surrounding us in the sense world is Maya, illusion—*a symbol only of the spiritual.* But this spiritual we can perceive if we penetrate that which covers it like a veil. And in it we see attained what on Earth was impossible of attainment. We see that, which for the ordinary intellect is indescribable, transformed into action as soon as the human spirit unites with the spiritual world. 'The ineffable wrought in love.' And we see the significance of the moment when the soul becomes united with the Eternal Masculine of the cosmic world. That is the great secret expressed by Goethe in the words:

> Everything transient
> Is just a parable
> Here the inadequate
> Becomes an attainment;
> The indescribable
> Here it is done;
> The Eternal Feminine
> Lifts us on high.

"How could Goethe say: 'I have now completed my life's work. It is now almost immaterial what I may do during the rest of my life on Earth.'—He sealed up the second part of *Faust*, and only after his death was it given to humanity, and this humanity will need to concentrate deeply upon Spiritual Science in order to penetrate the mysteries of this powerful work…"

Mystical Knowledge and Spiritual Revelation of Nature: Perception of Spirits, **Rudolf Steiner, Dornach, August 14, 1915, GA 252**

"The interior of the female organization—what is bodily and physical as well as what expresses itself as soul in connection with the physical body—all this bears the marks of Saturn, Sun, and Moon periods in the most eminent sense. It is not for nothing that the Bible tells us how the Elohim took dust and used it to form the 'Adam,' the Man—'dust' here meaning the earthly element; which only appeared on Earth for the first time, such as air and water. The first thing that happens is that the male aspect coming out of the Cosmos [i.e., the Earth], is added to the macrocosmic aspect that the woman brings over from the Saturn, Sun, and Moon evolutions. This earthly polarity of maleness and femaleness is shrouded in a deep mystery. Of course, what has just been said refers only to what brings the masculine and the feminine to expression within the human organization. And this mystery is connected with the whole world of the Earth; with the capacities that the woman possesses only as woman during Earth evolution; with the fact that the macrocosmic aspect of the Saturn, Sun, and Moon evolutions is carried over within the woman and is taken up into the microcosm of the woman, whereas the macrocosm of the immediately preceding part of Earth evolution is taken up into the microcosm of the man. What is female and what is male carry the whole Cosmos within themselves in quite a special way. And if I have often said here that we human beings in general bear the whole macrocosm within ourselves, this means that the female and the male organizations each bear it within themselves in a different way.

"A cosmic thought dawns on Goethe as he brings the Penitent Woman to the Mater Gloriosa. For what is the

Mater Gloriosa for him? She is the one who has carried the everlasting effects of the [Old] Saturn, [Old] Sun, and [Old] Moon periods over into the Earth period in the purest way, has left them untouched by what is earthly and united herself with the macrocosm by being allowed to prepare the Christ for the Earth. The macrocosmic aspect—the eternal within the feminine—draws upward and on… "

Spiritual Wisdom in the Early Christian Centuries, Rudolf Steiner, Dornach, July 16, 1922, GA 213

"I have said on many occasions that at the time when medieval culture had reached its prime, two streams of spiritual life were flowing through the ripest souls in European civilization—streams which I have described as knowledge through revelation and knowledge acquired by reason, as we find it in Scholasticism. Knowledge through revelation, in its more scholastic form, was by no means a body of mystical, abstract or indefinite thought. It expressed itself in sharply defined, clear-cut concepts. But these concepts were considered to be beyond the scope of man's ordinary powers of cognition and must in every case be accepted as traditions of the Church. The Church, by virtue of its continuity, claimed the right to be the guardian of this kind of knowledge.

"The second kind of knowledge was held to be within the scope of research and investigation, albeit those who stood wholly within the stream of Scholasticism acknowledged that this knowledge acquired by reason could not in any sense be regarded as knowledge emanating from the super-sensible world.

"Thus when medieval culture was at its prime, it was realized that knowledge no longer accessible to mankind in that age must be preserved as it were by tradition. But it was not always so, for if we go back through the Middle Ages to the first Christian centuries we shall find that the characteristics of this knowledge through revelation was less sharply emphasized than they were in medieval culture. If one had suggested to a Greek philosopher of the Athenian School, for instance, that a distinction could be made between knowledge acquired by reason and knowledge through revelation (in the sense in which the latter was understood in the Middle Ages), he would have been at a loss to know what was meant. It would have been unthinkable to him that if knowledge concerning super-sensible worlds had once been communicated to a man by cosmic powers, it could not be communicated afresh. True, the Greeks realized that higher spiritual knowledge was beyond the reach of man's ordinary cognition, but they knew too that by dint of spiritual training and through Initiation, a man could unfold higher faculties of knowledge and that by these means he would enter a world where super-sensible truth would be revealed to him.

"Now a change took place in Western culture between all that lived in the centuries when Greek philosophy came to flower in Plato and Aristotle, and the kind of knowledge that made its appearance about the end of the fourth century A.D. I have often referred to one aspect of this change by saying that the Mystery of Golgotha occurred in an age when very much of the old Initiation-wisdom was still living in men. And indeed there were many who applied their Initiation-wisdom and were thus able, with super-sensible knowledge, to realize the significance of the Event on Golgotha. Those who had been initiated strained every nerve to understand how a Being like the Christ, Who before the Mystery of Golgotha had not been united with earthly evolution, had passed into an earthly body and linked Himself with the evolution of man. The nature of this Being, how He had worked before His descent to the Earth—such were the questions which even at the time of the Mystery of Golgotha men were trying to answer by means of the highest faculties of Initiation-wisdom.

"But then we find that from the fifth century A.D. onwards, this old Initiation-wisdom which had lived in Asia Minor, Northern Africa, in Greek culture, had spread over into Italy and still further into Europe, was less and less understood. People spoke contemptuously of certain individuals, saying that their teachings were to be avoided at all costs by true Christians. Moreover, efforts were made to obliterate all that had previously been known of these individuals...

"My only object in saying this is to show that in the present age there is little real understanding of Platonic philosophy. Modern intellectualism is incapable of it. Nor is it possible to understand the tradition which exists in regard to Plotinus— the so-called Neo-Platonic philosopher Plotinus 1. was a pupil of Ammonius Saccas 2. who lived at the beginning of the third century A.D. It is said that Ammonius Saccas gave instruction to individual pupils but left nothing in writing. Now the reason why the eminent teachers of that age wrote nothing down was because they held that wisdom must be something living, that it could not be passed on by writing but only from man to man, in direct personal intercourse. Something else—again not understood— is said of Ammonius Saccas, namely that he tried to bring about agreement in the terrible quarrels between the adherents of Aristotle and of Plato, by showing that there was really no discrepancy between the teachings of Plato and Aristotle.

"Let me try to tell you in brief words how Ammonius Saccas spoke of Plato and Aristotle. He said: Plato belonged to an epoch when many human souls were treading the path to the spiritual world in other words when there was still knowledge of the principles of true Initiation. But in more ancient times there was no such thing as abstract, logical thought. Even now (at the beginning of the third century A.D.) only the first, elementary traces of this kind of thinking are making their appearance. In Plato's time, thoughts evolved independently were unknown. Whereas the Initiates of earlier times gave their message in pictures and imaginations, Plato was one of the first to change these imaginations into abstract concepts and ideas. The great spiritual picture to which Plato tried to lift the eyes of men was brought down in more ancient times merely in the form of imaginations. In Plato, the imaginations were already concepts—but these concepts poured down as it were from the world of Divine Spirit. Plato said in effect: the Ideas are the lowest revelation of the Divine-Spiritual. Aristotle could no longer penetrate with the same intensity into this spiritual substance. Therefore the knowledge he possessed only amounted to the substance of the ideas, and this is at a lower level than the picture itself. Nevertheless, Aristotle could still receive the substance of the ideas in the form of revelation. There is no fundamental difference between Plato and Aristotle—so said Ammonius Saccas—except that Plato was able to gaze into higher levels of the spiritual world than Aristotle.—And thereby Ammonius Saccas thought to reconcile the disputes among the followers of Aristotle and Plato.

"We learn, then, that by the time of Plato and Aristotle, wisdom was already beginning to assume a more intellectual form. Now in those ancient times it was still possible for individuals here and there to rise to very high levels of spiritual perception. The lives of men like Ammonius Saccas and his pupil Plotinus were rich in spiritual experiences and their conceptions of the spiritual world were filled with real substance.

"Naturally one could not have spoken to such men of outer Nature in the sense in which we speak of Nature today. In their schools they spoke of a spiritual world, and Nature—generally regarded nowadays as complete and all-embracing—was merely the lowest expression of that spiritual world of which they were conscious.

"We can form some idea of how such men were wont to speak, if we study Iamblichus, 3. a man possessed of deep insight and one of the successors of Ammonius Saccas. How did the world appear to the soul of Iamblichus? He spoke to his pupils somewhat as follows:—If we would understand the universe let us not pay heed to space, for space contains merely the outward expression of the spiritual world. Nor let us pay heed to time, for only the illusory images of cosmic reality arise in time. Rather must we look up to those Powers in the spiritual world who are the Creators of time and of the connections between time and space. Gazing out into the expanses of the Cosmos, we see how the cycle, repeated visibly in the Sun, repeats itself every year. But the Sun circles through the Zodiac, through the twelve constellations. It is not enough merely to observe this phenomenon, for three hundred and sixty heavenly Powers are working and weaving therein, sending forth the Sun-forces which flood the whole universe accessible to man. Every year the cycle is repeated. If these Powers alone held sway, there would be three hundred and sixty days in a year. But there are, in fact, five additional days, ruled by seventy-two sub-heavenly Powers, the planetary Spirits. I will draw (on the blackboard) this pentagonal figure, because one to five is the relation of seventy-two to three hundred and sixty. The five remaining days in the cosmic year which are abandoned, as it were, by the three hundred and sixty heavenly Powers, are ruled by the seventy-two sub-heavenly

Powers. But over and above the three hundred and sixty-five days, there are still a few more hours in the year. And these hours are directed by forty-two earthly Powers.—Iamblichus also said to his pupils: The three hundred and sixty heavenly Powers are connected with the head-organization of man, the seventy-two sub-heavenly Powers with the breast-system (breathing-process and heart) and the forty-two earthly Powers with the purely earthly system in man (e.g. digestion, metabolism).

"In those times the human being was given his place in a *spiritual* universe, whereas nowadays we begin our physiological studies by learning of the quantities of carbon, hydrogen, nitrogen, sulfur, phosphorus, limestone, etc., within the human organism. We relate the human being to a *lifeless* nature. But Iamblichus would have taught how the organism of man is related to the forty-two earthly Powers, the seventy-two sub-heavenly or planetary Powers, and the three hundred and sixty heavenly Powers. Just as today man is said to be composed of earthly substances, in the time of Iamblichus he was known to represent a confluence of forces streaming from the spiritual universe. Great and sublime was the wisdom presented in the schools of learning in those days, and one can readily understand that Plotinus—who had reached the age of twenty-eight before he listened to the teachings of Ammonius Saccas—felt himself living in an altogether different world. He was able to assimilate some of this wisdom because it was still cultivated in many places during the first four centuries after the Mystery of Golgotha. With this wisdom men also tried to understand the descent of the Christ into Jesus of Nazareth and the place of Christ in the realms of the spiritual Hierarchies, in the great structure of the spiritual universe.

"And now let me deal with another chapter of the wisdom taught by Iamblichus. He said: There are three hundred and sixty heavenly Powers, seventy-two planetary Powers, forty-two earthly Powers—in all, four hundred and seventy-four Divine Beings of different orders. Look to the Far East—so said Iamblichus—and you will there find peoples who give names to their Gods. Turn to the Egyptians and to other peoples—they too name their Gods. Phoenicians, Greeks, Romans—all will name their Gods. The four hundred and seventy-four Gods include all the Gods of all the different peoples: Zeus, Apollo, Baal—all the Gods. The reason why the peoples have different Gods is that one race has chosen twelve or maybe seventeen Gods from the four hundred and seventy-four, another race has taken twenty-five, another three, another four. The number of racial Gods is four hundred and seventy-four. And the highest of these Gods, the God who came down to Earth at a definite point of time, is Christ.

"This wisdom was well suited to bring about reconciliation between the different religions, not as the outcome of vague sentiment but of the knowledge that the different Gods of the peoples constitute, in their totality, one great system—the four hundred and seventy-four Gods. It was taught that all the choirs of Gods of the peoples of ancient times had reached their climax in Christianity and that the crown of wisdom was to understand how the Christ Being had entered through Jesus of Nazareth into His earthly activity.

"And so, as we look back to an earlier Spiritual Science (which although it no longer exists in that form today, indeed cannot do so for it must be pursued today in a different way), the deepest respect grows up within us. Profound wisdom was taught in the early Christian centuries in regard to the super-sensible worlds. But knowledge of this spiritual universe was imparted only to those who were immediate pupils of the older Initiates. The wisdom might only be passed on to those whose faculties of knowledge had reached the stage where they were able to understand the essence and being of the different Gods.

"This requisite of spiritual culture was recognized everywhere in Greece, in Egypt and in Asia Minor. It is, of course, true, that remnants of the ancient wisdom still existed in Roman civilization. Plotinus himself taught for a long time in Italy. But a spirit of abstraction had crept into Roman culture, a spirit no longer capable of understanding the value and worth of *personality*, of *being*. The spirit of abstraction had crept in, not yet in the form it afterwards assumed, but adhered to all the more firmly because it was there in its earliest beginnings.

"And then, on the soil of Italy at the beginning of the fourth century A.D. we find a School which began to oppose the ancient principle of Initiation, the preparation of the individual for Initiation. We see a School arising which gathers together and makes a careful record of everything originating from ancient Initiation-wisdom. The aim of this School—which lasted beyond the third on into the fourth century—was to perpetuate the essence of Roman culture, to establish historical tradition as against the strivings of individual human Beings. As Christianity began to find its way into Roman culture, the efforts of this school were directed to the elimination of all that could still have been discovered by means of the old Initiation-knowledge in regard to the presence of Christ in the personality of Jesus.

"It was a fundamental tenet of this Roman School that the teaching given by Ammonius Saccas and Iamblichus must not be allowed to pass on to posterity. Just as in those times there was a widespread impulse to destroy the ancient temples and altars—in short to obliterate every remnant of ancient Heathendom—so, in the domain of spiritual life, efforts were made to wipe out the principles whereby knowledge of the higher world might be attained. To take one example: the *dogma* of the One Divine Nature or of the Two Divine Natures in the Person of Christ was substituted for the teaching of Ammonius Saccas and Iamblichus, namely, that the individual human being can develop to a point where he will understand how the Christ took up His abode in the body of Jesus. This dogma was to reign supreme and the possibility of individual insight smothered. The ancient path of wisdom was superseded by dogma in the culture of the Roman world. And because strenuous efforts were made to destroy any teaching that savored of the ancient wisdom, little more than the names of men like Ammonius Saccas and Iamblichus have come down to us. Of many other teachers in the Southern regions of Europe not even the names have been preserved. Altars were destroyed, temples burnt to the ground and the ancient teachings exterminated, to such an extent indeed that we have no longer any inkling today of the wisdom that lived in the South of Europe during the first four centuries after the Mystery of Golgotha.

"Again and again it happened, however, that knowledge of this wisdom found its way to men who were interested in these matters and who realized that Roman culture was rapidly falling to pieces under the spread of Christianity. But after the extermination of what would have been so splendid a preparation for an understanding of the Mystery of Golgotha, it was only possible to learn of the union of Christ with Jesus in the form of an abstract dogma laid down by the Councils and colored by the Roman spirit. The living wisdom was wiped out, and abstraction, albeit working on in the guise of revelation, took its place.

"History is well-nigh blank in regard to these things; but during the first centuries of Christendom there were a number of men who were able to say: 'There are indeed Initiates—of whom Iamblichus was one. It is the Initiates who teach true Christianity.

To them, Christ is Christ indeed, whereas the Romans speak merely of the *Galileans*.' This expression was used in the third and fourth centuries A.D. to gloss over a deep misunderstanding. The less men understood Christianity, the more they spoke of the Galileans; the less they knew of the Christ, the more emphasis they laid on the human personality of the 'Galilean.'

"Out of this milieu came Julian, the so-called Apostate 4. who had absorbed a very great deal from pupils of men like Iamblichus and who still knew something of the spiritual universe reaching down into every phenomenon of Nature. Julian the Apostate had heard from pupils of Iamblichus of the spiritual forces working down into every animal and plant from the three hundred and sixty heavenly Powers, the seventy-two planetary Powers and the forty-two earthly Powers. In those days there were still some who understood what was, for example, expressed in a most wonderful way in a deeply significant legend related of Plotinus. The legend ran: There were many who would no longer believe that a man could be inspired by the Divine Spirit [Sophia] and who said that anyone who claimed to have knowledge of the Divine-Spiritual world was possessed by a demon. Plotinus was therefore carried off to the temple of Isis in Egypt in order that the priests might determine the nature of the demon possessing him. And when the Egyptian priests—who still had knowledge of these things—came to the temple and tested Plotinus before the altar of Isis, performing all the ritual acts still possible at that time, Lo! instead of a demon there appeared the Godhead Himself!

"This legend indicates that in those times men still acknowledged that at least it was possible to prove whether a good God or a demon was possessing a human being.

"Julian the Apostate heard of these things. But on the other side there came insistently to his ears the words of a writing which passed into many hands in the Roman world during the first Christian centuries and was said to be a sermon of the Apostle Peter, whereas it was actually a forgery. In this document it was said: Behold the godless Hellenes! In very creatures of nature they see the Divine-Spiritual. This is sinful, impious. It is sacrilege to see the Divine-Spiritual in Nature, in animal and in plant. Let no man be so sinful as to believe that the Divine is present in the course of the Sun and Moon.—These were the things that dinned in the ears of Julian, now from one side, now from another. A deep love for Hellenism grew up within him and he became the tragic figure who would fain have spoken of Christianity in the light of the teachings of Iamblichus.

"There is no telling what would have come to pass in Europe if the Christianity of Julian the Apostate had conquered instead of the doctrines of Rome, if his desire to restore the Initiation-training had been fulfilled the training whereby men could themselves have attained to knowledge of how the Christ had lived in Jesus and of His place among the other racial Gods. Julian the Apostate was not out to destroy the heathen temples. Indeed he would have been willing to restore the temple of the Jews at Jerusalem. His desire was to restore the heathen temples and he also had the interests of the Christians at heart. Truth and truth alone was his quest. And the great obstacle in his way was the School in ancient Rome of which I have spoken—the School which not only set out to exterminate the old principle of Initiation but did in fact succeed in exterminating it, wishing to put in its place recorded traditions of Initiation-wisdom.

"When the moment had arrived, it was easy to arrange for the thrust of the Persian spear which caused Julian's death. It was then that the words were uttered which have never since been understood, not even by Ibsen; but which can be explained by a knowledge of the traditions of Julian's time: 'The Galilean has conquered, not the Christ!' For at this moment of death it was revealed to the prophetic vision of Julian the Apostate that henceforward the conception of Christ as a Divine Being would fade away and that the 'Galilean', the man of Galilean stock would be worshipped as a God. In the thirtieth year of his life Julian the Apostate had a pre-vision of the whole of subsequent evolution, on into the nineteenth century, by which time theology had lost all knowledge of the Christ in Jesus.

"Julian was 'Apostate' only in regard to what was to come after. The Apostate was indeed the Apostle in respect of spiritual realization of the Mystery of Golgotha.—And it is this spiritual realization that must be quickened again in the souls of men."

Notes:

1. Plotinus: c. 204/5– 270 CE) was a Greek Platonist philosopher, born and raised in Roman Egypt. Plotinus is regarded by modern scholarship as the founder of Neoplatonism. Plotinus' most notable literary work is, *The Enneads*. The three-fold cosmology of the 'Good, the True and the Beautiful' was highly developed under his teachings and is considered to have influenced the esoteric Christian school of Dionysius the Areopagite, that was founded by St. Paul in Athens.

2. Ammonius Saccas: (175 AD–242 AD) was a self-taught Hellenistic Platonist philosopher from Alexandria, considered the forerunner of Neoplatonism, as a synthesis of Plato, Aristotle, Christian Gnosticism and ancient mystery wisdom. Through his development of what would become Neoplatonism he was the most significant influence of Plotinus, whom he taught from 232 to 242 AD.

3. Iamblichus: (c. 245–c. 325) was a Syrian Neoplatonic philosopher, descended from the Emesene dynasty, a Syrian dynasty of Priest-Kings under the Roman Empire. He determined a direction later taken

by Neoplatonism. Iamblichus was also the biographer of the Greek mystical philosopher, and mathematician Pythagoras. He studied under Anatolius of Laodicea and later studied under Porphyry, a pupil of Plotinus (the founder of Neoplatonism). Iamblichus disagreed with Porphyry about Theurgy (Divine Magic), he responded to Porphyry's criticism of the practice in his work: *On the Mysteries of the Egyptians, Chaldeans, and Assyrians*.

4. Julian the Apostate: (Latin: *Favius Claudius Julianus*; 331–June 26, 363 AD) nephew of Constantine the Great, he was the Caesar of the West from 355 to 360 and Roman emperor from 361 to 363, as well as a notable philosopher and author. His rejection of Christianity (due to its lack of depth as to the Sun Mysteries, in the form it was presented by Constantine), and his promotion of Neoplatonic Hellenism in its place, caused him to be remembered as Julian the Apostate in Christian tradition. Apostate refers to a person who renounces a religious or political belief or principle. He is also referred to as Julian the Philosopher.

Karmic Relationships, Vol. VII, Rudolf Steiner, Lecture II, Breslau, June 8, 1924, GA 239

"You look out into space—I am not going to speak now about the nature of space. Here, when you look into the water, there are bubbles everywhere—bubbles which are thinner, less dense than the water. Where the Sun stands in the sky, conditions are less dense even than space. You will say: 'but space itself is void, it is nullity.' Nevertheless at the place where the Sun is situated there is actually *less* than nullity. It should not be difficult, especially in these days, for people to think of something else that is less than nothing. If there were originally five shillings in my pocket and I spend them one by one, in the end I have nothing. But when I get into debt I have less than nothing—which is the plight of a good many people today! Very well, then: where there is space,

space alone, there is nothing; but where the Sun is there is *less* than nothing, there is a lacuna in space—and there dwell the spiritual Beings referred to in the book *Occult Science* as the Exousiai [Spirits of Form], the Dynamis [Spirits of Movement], the Kyriotetes [Spirits of Wisdom]. There they have their abode, sending their own essence and power through all creation. Among them man spends the greater part of his life between death and a new birth. In association with the Exousiai, Dynamis, Kyriotetes, with human souls karmically connected with him who have also passed through the gate of death, and with yet other Beings whose existence is hardly even conjectured, the karma for the next earthly life is worked out and formulated. Conditions in this Sun region are not as they are on Earth. Why do our clever scientists—and clever they certainly are—picture the Sun as a globe of incandescent gas? It is because a certain illusory, materialistic instinct makes them want to detect physical processes in the Sun. But there is nothing physical in the Sun. One may at most speak of physical processes in the Sun's corona, but certainly not in the Sun itself. In the Sun there is nothing like natural law, for it is a world of purest spirit. Materialists' would like to insist that the Sun too is under the sway of natural law—*but it is not so*. The only laws prevailing in the Sun are those which give effect to the karmic consequences of the Good and which operate in restoring the mutilation man has undergone as the result of his 'bad' karma when he has been transported by the Love of the Venus Beings into the Sun sphere. When the life of man between death and a new birth is described many will wonder how this very lengthy period is spent. Many things that happen on the Earth command admiration and awe, but the most sublime achievements of earthly civilization are puny and insignificant in comparison with what is accomplished in a purely spiritual way during this Sun existence, when mighty Powers are all around and within us, working to the end that our karma shall take effect in the next earthly life.

"The elaboration of part of man's karma is completed in the Venus sphere, and some part even in the Mercury sphere. Later on we shall hear of a certain well-known historical personality whose destiny in his incarnation in the nineteenth century was due to the fact that his karma was very largely wrought out in the spheres of Venus and Mercury. 1. Souls who begin to give shape to their karma in these spheres often become personalities of outstanding significance in the subsequent incarnation. But in the great majority of cases the main part of the karma for the following earthly life is worked out in the Sun sphere, where the longest period is spent. We will speak in greater detail later on but today I will give an outline of how the foundations of karma are laid, stage by stage, in the various spheres. In order not to be confused by other descriptions I have given of the life between death and a new birth, you must be clear that in moving through these spheres man enters into entirely different conditions of cosmic existence. When the time comes for him to enter the Mars sphere, he is still not altogether outside the Sun sphere; for the influences of the Sun are still active in this part of the Cosmos which was once cast off by the Earth. In the Sun sphere, man is concerned only with his moral qualities and with those attributes of his being which have remained healthy; the rest has been laid aside. It persists in him as a kind of incompleteness but this is made good in the Sun sphere. During the first half of existence in the Sun sphere we are engaged in making preparation for the appropriate physical organization of the next earthly body. During the second half of the Sun existence, in union with the Exousiai, Dynamis, Kyriotetes, and with human souls karmically connected with us, we are concerned with the preparation of the moral side of karma, the moral qualities which will then be present in the next life. But this moral part and the spiritual part of karma—for example, specific talents in one direction or another—are then further elaborated in the Mars sphere, in the Jupiter sphere and in the Saturn sphere. And in passing through these spheres we come to know what the 'physical' stars are in reality.

"To speak of a 'physical' star is not really correct. For what is a star? Physicists imagine that combustion of gas or some process of the kind is taking place in the sky. But as I said, if they could actually get there they would be amazed to find no burning gas in the Sun but actually a lacuna, a gap in space, in a condition infinitely more rarefied than any particles of earthly matter could ever be. Everything is Spirit, pure Spirit. Nor are the other stars so many bodies of incandescent, burning gas, but something entirely different. Bordering on this Earth with its physical substances and physical forces, is the universal Cosmic Ether. We are able to perceive the Cosmic Ether because, as we gaze into it, our field of vision is circumscribed and the surrounding ether appears blue. But to believe as materialistic thinkers do, that physical substances are roaming around up there in the Cosmos is just childish fancy. No physical substances are moving around; for at the place where a star is seen, there is something altogether different. The farthest reaches of the etheric would lead out of and beyond space, into the spheres where the Gods have their abode. And now picture to yourselves a certain inner relationship which may exist between one person and another and comes to physical expression. Picture it quite graphically. You are caressed by someone who loves you. You feel the caress; but it would be childish to associate it in any way with physical matter. The caress is not matter at all, it is a process, and you experience it inwardly, in your *soul*. So it is when we look outwards into the spheres of the Ether. The Gods in their love caress the world. But the caress lasts long, because the life of the Gods spans immense reaches of time. In very truth the stars are the expression of love in the Cosmic Ether; there is nothing physical about them. And from the cosmic aspect, to see a star means to feel a caress that has been prompted by love. To gaze at the stars is to become aware of the love proceeding from the Divine-Spiritual Beings. What we must learn to realize is that the stars are only the signs and tokens of the presence of the Gods in the Universe. Physical science has much to learn on its path from illusion to truth! But men will not achieve self-knowledge nor will they understand their own true being until this physical science has been transformed into a spiritual science of the worlds beyond the Earth. Science in its present form has meaning only for the Earth; for physical matter in the real sense exists only on the Earth. [The difference between *physical* and *mineral* matter must be remembered here.] And so when we depart from the Earth at death, we enter more and more into a life of purely spiritual experiences. The reason why our physical life presents an entirely different aspect in these backward-streaming experiences which continue for a third of the length of earthly existence, is that we have been permeated with the essence and substance of the Moon sphere. The preparation of karma is one of the many things that have to be accomplished in the worlds of the stars.

"In order that one set of facts may be supported by others, let me explain how such observations are made by one who is versed in modern Initiation Science. For some time now, even in public lectures, I have been describing how when a man develops the faculty of genuine super-sensible perception through the methods indicated in the book, *Knowledge of the Higher Worlds*, he looks back over his earthly life, seeing it as a kind of tableau. Everything is present *simultaneously*, in a mighty panorama of the whole of life since the birth of the 'I'; but the several epochs are in a certain respect distinct from each other. We survey our experiences from birth until the change of teeth, then again, as one complete series, the experiences occurring between the time of the change of teeth and puberty, then the experiences of the period from puberty until the beginning of the twenties, and so forth. Further concentration and application of the methods for the attainment of spiritual knowledge enable us, as we survey this tableau, to observe, firstly, our life from birth to the seventh year. But later on these pictures are allowed to fade away and we see right *through* our life; when the consciousness has been emptied of all pictorial impressions and we have achieved Inspiration, we behold the living, weaving activity of the Moon sphere in place of the tableau of early childhood from birth until the seventh year. We behold this living, weaving activity. And so Initiation in the form that is normal and right for this present age brings us knowledge of the secrets of the Moon sphere, when the pictures of our own life up to the seventh year are obliterated in the consciousness of Inspiration and we perceive what now flashes up in their place.

"Then, if we observe the tableau of life between the seventh and fourteenth years and again obliterate the pictures in the consciousness of Inspiration, we gaze into the Mercury sphere. Everything has to do with the being of man; for man is an integral part of the whole Universe. If he learns to know himself as he really is, in the innermost core of his being, he learns to know the whole Universe. And now I would ask you to pay attention to the following.—Deepest respect arises in us for the old, instinctive Initiation Science which gave things that have remained in existence to this day, their true and proper names. Designations that are coined nowadays result in nothing but confusion; for modern scholarship is incapable of naming things in accordance with reality. An unprejudiced observation of life will fill us with reverence for the achievements of ancient Initiation Science. Ancient Initiation Science knew by instinct something that is confirmed today by statistics, namely, that the illnesses of childhood occur most frequently in the *first* period of life; it is then that the human being is most prone to illness, and even to death; after puberty this tendency abates. But the healthiest period of all, the period when mortality is at its lowest, is between the ages of seven and fourteen. The wise men of old knew that this is due to the influences of the Mercury sphere and again today we may make the same discovery when through modern Initiation Science we penetrate the secrets of existence. Such things fill us with reverence for these sacred traditions of humanity.

"By looking back into our experiences from the fourteenth to the twenty-first years and obliterating the pictures in the consciousness of Inspiration, we are led to the secrets of the Venus sphere. Here again the wonderful wisdom of ancient Initiation Science comes into evidence. The human being reaches puberty; love is born. When the pictures of this period of life are illumined by Initiation Science, the secrets of the Venus sphere are disclosed. Everything I am now describing is part of the true self-knowledge which unfolds in this way.

"When the pictures of experiences occurring between the twenty-first and forty-second years of life are eliminated in the consciousness of Inspiration, we are led to the Sun sphere. Through deepened self-knowledge the secrets of the Sun sphere can be experienced in this retrospective contemplation of the events of our life between the twenty-first and forty-second years. To acquire knowledge of the Sun existence our vision must cover a period three times longer than that of the periods connected with the other planetary bodies.

"I told you that the karma of a certain well-known personality in history had taken shape paramountly in the spheres of Mercury and Venus, and you will now understand how such things are investigated. 1. We look back, firstly, into the period of our own life between the seventh and fourteenth years, and then into the period between the fourteenth and twenty-first years; when the pictures have been eliminated in the consciousness of Inspiration, light is shed upon the secrets of the Mercury sphere and the Venus sphere. Through this illumination we perceive how such an individuality worked together with the Beings of the higher Hierarchies and with other human souls, and how his subsequent earthly incarnation in the nineteenth century took shape.

"Now if the elaboration of karma has taken place mainly in the *Mars* sphere, investigation is more difficult. For if a man attains Initiation before the age of 49, it is not possible for him to look back into the period of life which here comes into question, namely, the period between the forty-second and forty-ninth years. He must have passed his forty-ninth year if he is to be able to eliminate the pictures of this particular set of experiences and penetrate the secrets of the Mars sphere. If Initiation is attained after the age of fifty-six it is possible to look back into the period between the forty-ninth and fifty-sixth years of life, when karma that is connected with the *Jupiter* sphere takes shape. And now we are at the point where the various sets of events come together in one connected whole.

"It is not until the period between the fifty-sixth and sixty-third years can be included in this retrospective vision that we are able to survey the whole range of experiences and to speak out of our own inner knowledge. For then we can gaze into the profoundly significant secrets of the *Saturn* sphere. Karmas that were wrought out mainly in the Saturn sphere operate in mysterious ways to bring men together again in the world. In order to perceive all these connections in the light of Initiation Science itself—they can of course be explained and so become intelligible—but in order to perceive with independent vision and be able to judge them, we must ourselves have reached the age of sixty-three. A human being appears in some earthly life—thus for example there is a certain great poet of whom I shall speak later—and we find that through his faculties, through his literary creations, he was giving expression to that in his karma which could have been wrought out only in the Saturn sphere.

"When we look up to the Sun, to the planetary system—and the same applies to the rest of the starry heavens for they are connected in a very real way with the being of man—we can witness how human karma takes shape in the Cosmos. The Moon, the planets Venus, Jupiter—verily these heavenly bodies are not as physical astronomy describes them. In their constellations, in their mutual relationships, in their radiance, in their whole existence, they are the builders and shapers of human destinies, they are the cosmic timepiece according to which we live out our karma. As they shine downwards from the heavens their influences have real power. This was known in the days of the ancient Mystery-wisdom but the old Astrology—which was a purely *spiritual* science, concerned with the spiritual foundations of existence—has come down to posterity in a degraded, amateurish form. Anthroposophy alone can contribute something that will enable us to perceive the spiritual connections as they truly are and to understand how through the great timepiece of destiny, human life on Earth is shaped according to law.

"From this point-of-view let us think of the human being and his karma. Those who with the help of Anthroposophy evolve a healthy conception of the world as against the unsound views prevailing today, will unfold not only quite different concepts and ideas but also quite different feelings and perceptions. For you see, if we really understand the destiny of a man, we also learn to understand the secrets of the world of stars, the secrets of the Cosmos. But nowadays people write biographies without the faintest inkling that something is really being profaned by the way in which they write. In times when knowledge was held to be sacred because it issued from the Mysteries, nobody would have written biographies in the way that is customary today. Every ancient 'biography' contained indications of the influences and secrets of the world of stars. In human destiny we can perceive, firstly, the working of the Angeloi, Archangeloi, Archai; then of still loftier Sun Beings, Exousiai, Dynamis, Kyriotetes; then of the Thrones who are concerned mainly with the elaboration of karma in the Mars sphere; then of the Cherubim who elaborate the karma belonging to the Jupiter sphere; and then of the Seraphim who work together with man at the elaboration of karma in the Saturn sphere—Saturn karma. In a man's destiny, in his karma, we behold the working of the higher Hierarchies. This karma, at first, is like a veil, a curtain. If we look behind this veil we gaze at the weaving deeds and influences of Angeloi, Archangeloi, Archai, Exousiai, Dynamis, Kyriotetes, Thrones, Cherubim, Seraphim. Every human destiny is like script on a sheet of paper. Just imagine that someone looking at the writing on the paper were to say that he can see signs - K - E - I, and so forth, but he is quite unable to combine these letters into words! As there are some twenty-two to twenty-eight letters (to be exact, about thirty to thirty-four in all) such a man could only conceive that the whole of Goethe's *Faust* is made up entirely of those thirty-four letters. He cannot read, therefore he sees only the different letters. When someone else finds a great deal more in *Faust* because he can combine the letters into the words of which this wonderful work is composed, an out-and-out illiterate with no notion of how to read may say with horror: Here is someone who actually thinks that all kinds of things are contained in *Faust*—but he is an utter fool! Yet the whole of *Faust* does actually consists of these letters. Similarly, when we observe the karma of a human being in the ordinary way, we see letters only; but the moment we begin to *read* this karma we behold the Angeloi, Archangeloi, Archai and their mutual, interrelated deeds. The destiny of an individual human life becomes the richer, the more we get beyond the thirty-four letters and find in them—*Faust!* And the picture of a human destiny is enriched beyond measure when earthly ignorance is transformed into knowledge of the Cosmic Alphabet, when we realise that the letters of that script are the signs and tokens of the deeds of the Beings of the higher Hierarchies.

"To a man who beholds it, the vista of karma as the shape taken by destiny in life is so overwhelming, so sublime and majestic that simply by understanding how karma is related to the spiritual Cosmos he will unfold quite different qualities of feeling and discernment. It will not remain so much theoretical knowledge. What we acquire through Anthroposophy should not be a mere accumulation of theoretical information but should work more and more upon our life of thought and feeling, in that it rids us of the notion that we live an earthworm's existence and makes us aware that we belong to the land of Spirits. Verily, we are citizens not of the Earth alone but of the land of Spirits. The whole existence we have spent between death and a new birth converges in that which, on Earth, is enclosed within our skin. The secrets of worlds are contained in a particular form within this encircling skin.

"Self-knowledge is by no means the trivial sentimentality of which there is so much talk nowadays. Human self-knowledge is world-knowledge. And so when friends have given me an opportunity, I have often written down for them the following lines:

> If thou would'st know thy Self,
> Look out into the Cosmic Spaces.
> thou would'st fathom the Cosmic Spaces,
> Look inwards, into thine own Self.

Note:

1. Heinrich Heine, German poet (Dec. 13, 1797–Feb. 17, 1856):

    "And now let us take an example to illustrate what has been said. In comparatively early times, not long before the founding of Christianity, a certain Initiate was incarnated in the East, in the Indian civilization. In his earthly life this individuality had poor eyesight—in describing karmic relationships one must go into details of this kind—and his perceptions remained more or less superficial. This life which was characterized by the mystical outlook typical of Indian culture, was followed by other, less important incarnations. But there was a life between death and a new birth during which the superficial experiences of the Indian incarnation were worked upon in the Mercury sphere, partly too in the Venus sphere and in the Mars sphere, in conjunction with Beings of the higher Hierarchies. In the majority of human beings the influences of *one* of the cosmic spheres are dominant in the shaping of the karma; but in the case of this particular individuality the influences of the Mercury sphere, the Venus sphere and the Mars sphere worked with almost equal strength at the karmic transformation of incipient faculties arising from the experiences of an Indian incarnation. In the nineteenth century this individuality appeared again as a somewhat complex personality, namely, *Heinrich Heine.*"

Karmic Relationships, Vol. VII, Rudolf Steiner,
Lecture III, Breslau, June 9, 1924, GA 239

The Daughter of the Divine Feminine Trinity

The nature of the Cosmic Being of Wisdom (Kyriotetes) is well documented in Anthroposophical literature. The biographical descriptions of this Being of Wisdom are a key element in Steiner's Christology. Only Steiner brings forth these revelations in our current age and leaves them as an open secret for those with 'eyes to see' and 'ears to hear.' The descent of the Being of Wisdom into the being of 'the Mother of Jesus' was unprecedented in human spiritual evolution. No greater merging of an avatar (Heavenly Sophia - Kyriotetes) with a bodhisattva (Eve - Mary) has ever happened in history before. Regarding this challenging subject Manfred Schmidt-Brabant had this to say:

> "Nowadays we would say that this Isis-Sophia is the highest spirit amongst the spirits of wisdom, the Kyriotetes, this great group of beings who permeate the whole universe, for in her is active the third aspect of the Trinity, the Holy Spirit. It was always an esoteric secret that the Holy Spirit is in fact feminine."
>
> *The Archetypal Feminine in the Mystery Stream of Humanity*,
by Manfred Schmidt-Brabant and Virginia Sease,
Temple Lodge: London, 1999 (pg. 44)

Universal Spirituality and Human Physicality: Bridging the Divide—The Search for the New Isis and the Divine Sophia, Rudolf Steiner, Lecture XIV. Dornach, December 24, 1920, GA 202

"We should remind ourselves that this is what is needed: a new content that can once again fill us with unique and distinctive feelings, that can shake and waken us as true Christians were stirred in the early centuries, feeling the Mystery of Golgotha, the appearance of Christ on Earth, to be the loftiest thing that humankind can experience on Earth. We need to rekindle something of this kind again in our souls.

"Oh, this soul of ours will be able to invoke singular feelings when it sets about experiencing the new Isis legend within modern humanity: this Isis legend of the killing of Isis by Lucifer, of our journey out into the cosmic space that has become a mathematical abstraction, or in other words the grave of Isis; of the search for this Isis by kindling within us inner powers of spiritual perception which can then replace the dead heavens with an inner life that once again shows us the stars and planets as monuments of spiritual potencies flowing and surging through space. Today we only form a true vision of the manger if we experience fully, with singular feelings, what surges in this way through space, and then look upon the being who entered the world through the child lying there. We know that we bear this child within us; but we also have to meet him with understanding. And therefore, as the Egyptian looked from his Osiris to perceive Isis, we must in turn learn to look towards the new Isis, the divine Sophia. Christ will not reappear in spirit form in the course of the twentieth century only through something occurring externally; but by virtue of human beings finding the power embodied in the divine Sophia. In modern times there has been a tendency, quite specifically, to lose this Isis power, this power of Mary; which has been deadened and killed off by everything surfacing in modern human consciousness. Newer professions of faith have at least partly eradicated a vision of Mary.

"In a sense this is the mystery of modern humanity—that basically Mary-Isis has been killed, that just as Osiris was sought in Asia she must be sought now in the broad realms of heaven by the power Christ can kindle in us when we give ourselves up to him devotedly."

In the following section, due to the importance of the concepts that are so fundamental to our subject the complete lecture is given without quotation marks, preceded and followed by a triangle.

△

The Gospel of St. Luke, Rudolf Steiner, Lecture V, Basel, September 19, 1909, GA 114

Every great spiritual stream in the world has its particular mission. These streams are not isolated and are separated only during certain epochs; then they merge and mutually fructify each other. The Event of Palestine is an illustration of one most significant fusion of the spiritual streams in humanity.

We have set ourselves the task of understanding the Event of Palestine with increasing clarity. But conceptions of the world and of life do not, as some people seem to imagine, move through the air as pure abstractions and ultimately unite. They are borne by *Beings*, by *Individualities*. When a system of thought comes into existence for the first time it must be presented by an Individuality, and when these spiritual streams unite and fertilize each other, something quite definite must also happen in the Individualities who are the bearers of the world-conceptions in question. The concrete facts connected with the fusion of Buddhism and Zoroastrianism in the Event of Palestine as described in yesterday's lecture, may have seemed very complicated. But if we were content to speak of the happenings in an abstract way and not in concrete detail, it would only be necessary to show how these two streams united. As anthroposophists, however, it is our task to give accounts of the two Individualities who were the actual bearers of these world-conceptions as well as to call attention to the contents of the teachings. Anthroposophists must always endeavor to get away from abstractions and arrive at concrete realities, so you should not be surprised to find such complicated facts connected with a happening as momentous as the fusion of Buddhism and Zoroastrianism.

This fusion necessarily entailed slow and gradual preparation. We have heard how Buddhism streamed into and worked in the personality born as the child of Joseph and Mary of the Nathan line of the House of David, as related in the *Gospel of St. Luke*. Joseph and Mary of the Solomon line of the House of David resided originally in Bethlehem with their child Jesus, as recorded in the *Gospel of St. Matthew*. This child of the Solomon line bore within him the Individuality who, as Zarathustra, or Zoroaster, had inaugurated the ancient Persian civilization. Thus at the beginning of our era, side by side and represented by actual Individualities, we have the stream of Buddhism on the one hand (as described in the *Gospel of St. Luke*), and on the other the stream of Zoroastrianism in the Jesus of the Solomon line (as described in the *Gospel of St. Matthew*). The births of the two boys did not occur at exactly the same time.

The Daughter of the Divine Feminine Trinity

I shall have to say things today that are not found in the *Gospels*; but you will understand the *Bible* all the better if you learn from investigations of the Akashic Chronicle something about the consequences and effects of facts indicated in the *Gospels*. It must never be forgotten that the words at the end of the *Gospel of St. John* hold good for all the *Gospels*—that the world itself could not contain the books that would have to be written if all the facts were presented. The revelations vouchsafed to humanity through Christianity are not of a kind that could have been written down and presented to the world once and for ever as a complete record. Christ's words are true: 'I am with you always, even unto the end of the world.' [*Matthew* 28:20] He is there not as a dead but as a *living* Being, and what He has to reveal can always be perceived by those whose spiritual eyes are opened. Christianity is a living stream and its revelations will endure as long as human beings are able to receive them. Thus certain facts will be presented today, *the consequences of which* are indicated in the *Gospels*, though not the facts themselves. Nevertheless you can put them to the test and you will find them substantiated.

The births of the two Jesus children were separated by a period of a few months. But Jesus of the *Gospel of St. Luke* and John the Baptist were both born too late to have been victims of the so-called 'massacre of the innocents.' Has the thought never struck you that those who read about the Bethlehem massacre must ask themselves: How could there have been a John? But the facts can be substantiated in all respects. The Jesus of the *Gospel of St. Matthew* was taken to Egypt by his parents, and John, supposedly, was born shortly before or about the same time. According to the usual view, John remained in Palestine, but in that case he would certainly have been a victim of Herod's murderous deed. You see how necessary it is to devote serious thought to these things; for if all the children of two years old and younger were actually put to death at that time, John would have been one of them. But this riddle will become intelligible if, in the light of the facts disclosed by the Akashic Chronicle, you realize that the events related in the *Gospels of St. Luke* and *St. Matthew* did not take place at the same time. The Nathan Jesus was born *after* the Bethlehem massacre; so too was John. Although the interval was only a matter of months, it was long enough to make these facts possible.

You will also learn to understand the Jesus of the *Gospel of St. Matthew* in the light of the more intimate facts. In this boy was reincarnated the Zarathustra-Individuality, from whom the people of ancient Persia had once received the teaching concerning Ahura Mazdao, the great Sun Being. We know that this Sun Being must be regarded as the soul and spirit of the external, physical sun. Hence Zarathustra was able to say: 'Behold not only the radiance of the physical sun; behold, too, the mighty Being who sends down His spiritual blessings as the physical sun sends down its beneficent light and warmth!'—*Ahura Mazdao*, later called the Christ—it was He whom Zarathustra proclaimed to the people of Persia, but not yet as a Being who had sojourned on the Earth. Pointing to the Sun, Zarathustra could only say: 'There is His habitation; He is gradually drawing near and one day He will live in a body on the Earth!'

The great differences between Zoroastrianism and Buddhism are obvious as long as they were separate; but the differences were resolved through their union and rejuvenation in the events of Palestine.

Let us once again consider what Buddha gave to the world. Buddha's teaching was presented in the Eightfold Path—this being an enumeration of the qualities needed by the human soul if it is to escape the harsh effects of Karma. In course of time Buddha's teaching must be developed as compassion and love by men individually, through their own feelings and sense of morality. I also told you that when the Bodhisattva became Buddha, this was a crucial turning-point in evolution. Had the full revelation of the Bodhisattva in the body of Gautama Buddha not taken place at that time, it would not have been possible for the souls of all human beings to unfold what we call 'law-abidingness'—'Dharma'—which a man can only develop from his own being by expelling the content of his astral nature in order to liberate himself from all harsh effects of Karma. The Buddhist legend indicates this in a wonderful way by saying that Buddha succeeded in 'turning the Wheel of the Law.' This means that the enlightenment of the Bodhisattva and his ascent to Buddhahood enabled a force to stream through the whole of humanity as the result of which men could now evolve 'Dharma' from their own souls and gradually fathom the profundities of the Eightfold Path. This possibility began when Buddha first evolved the teaching upon which the moral sense of men on Earth was actually to be based. Such was the task of the Bodhisattva who became Buddha. We see how individual tasks are allotted to the great Individualities when we find in Buddhism all that man can experience in his own soul as his great ideal. The ideal of the human soul what man is and *can become*—that is the essence of Buddha's teaching and it sufficed as far as his particular mission was concerned.

Everything in Buddhism has to do with *inwardness*, with human nature and its inner development; genuine, original Buddhism contained no 'cosmology'—although it was introduced later on. The essential mission of the Bodhisattva was to bring to men the teaching of the deep inwardness of their own souls. Thus in certain sermons Buddha avoids any definite reference to the Cosmos. Everything is expressed in such a way that if the human soul allows itself to be influenced by Buddha's teaching, it can become more and more perfect. Man is regarded as *a self-contained* being apart from the great Universe whence he proceeded. It is because this was connected with the special mission of the Bodhisattva that Buddha's teaching, when truly understood, has such a warming, deepening effect upon the soul; for this reason too the teaching seems to those who concern themselves with it to be permeated with such intensity of feeling and such inner warmth when it appears again, rejuvenated, in the *Gospel of St. Luke*.

The task of the Individuality incarnated as Zarathustra in ancient Persia was altogether different—in point of fact exactly the opposite. Zarathustra taught of the God *without*; he taught men to apprehend the great Cosmos spiritually. Buddha directed man's attention to his own inner nature, saying that as the result of development there gradually appear, out of the previous state of ignorance, the 'six organs' of which we have spoken, namely, the five sense-organs and Manas [Spirit-Self]. But everything within man was originally born out of the Cosmos. We should have no eye sensitive to light if the light itself had not brought the eye to birth from out of the organism. Goethe said: 'The eye was created by the light for the light.' This is a profound truth. The light formed the eye out of neutral organs once present in the human body. In the same way, all the spiritual forces in the Universe work formatively upon man. Everything within him was organized, to begin with, out of divine-spiritual forces. Hence for every 'inner' there is an 'outer.' The forces that are found within man stream into him from outside. And it was the task of Zarathustra to point to the realities that are outside, in man's environment. Hence, for example, he spoke of the 'Amshaspands,' the great Genii, of whom he enumerated six—in reality there are twelve; but the other six are hidden. These Amshaspands work from outside as the creators and molders of the organs of the human being. Zarathustra showed that behind the human sense-organs stand the Creators of man; he pointed to the great Genii, to the powers and forces outside man. Buddha pointed to the forces working *within* man. Zarathustra also pointed to forces and beings below the Amshaspands, calling them the 'Izards' or 'Izeds.' They too penetrate into man from outside in order to work at the inner organization of his bodily nature. Here again Zarathustra was directing attention to spiritual realities in the Cosmos, to external conditions. And whereas Buddha pointed to the actual thought-substance out of which the thoughts arise from the human soul, Zarathustra pointed to the 'Ferruers' or 'Fravashi,' to the 'world-creative thoughts' pervading the Universe and surrounding us everywhere. For the thoughts that arise in man are everywhere in existence in the world outside.

Thus it was the mission of Zarathustra to inculcate into men an attitude of mind particularly concerned with analyzing the phenomena of the external world, to present a view of the Universe to a people whose task was to labor in the outer world. This mission was in keeping with the special characteristics of the ancient Persians and the function of Zarathustra was to promote energy and efficiency in this work, although his methods may have taken a form that would be repellant to modern man.

Zarathustra's mission was to engender vigor, efficiency and certainty of aim in outer activity through the knowledge that man has not only shelter and support in his own inner being but rests in the bosom of a divine-spiritual world and can therefore say to himself: 'Whatever your place in the world may be, you are not alone. You live in a Cosmos permeated by Spirit, among cosmic

Gods and spiritual Beings; you are born of the Spirit and rest in the Spirit; with every indrawn breath you inhale Divine Spirit; with every exhalation you may make an offering to the Great Spirit!' Because of his special mission, Zarathustra's own Initiation was necessarily different from that of the other great missionaries of humanity.

Let us consider what the Individuality incarnated in Zarathustra was able to achieve. So lofty was his stage of development that he could make provision in advance for the next (Egyptian) stream of culture. Zarathustra had two pupils: the Individualities who appeared again later on as the Egyptian Hermes and as Moses respectively. When these two Individualities were again incarnated in order to carry forward their work for humanity, the astral body sacrificed by Zarathustra was integrated into the Egyptian Hermes. Hermes bore within him the astral body of Zarathustra which had been transmitted to him in order that all the knowledge of the Universe possessed by Zarathustra might again be made manifest and take effect in the outer world. The etheric body of Zarathustra was transmitted to Moses. And because whatever evolves in *Time* is connected with the etheric body, when Moses became conscious of the secrets contained in his etheric body, he was able to create the mighty pictures of happenings in *Time* presented in *Genesis*. In this way Zarathustra worked on through the power of his Individuality, inaugurating and influencing Egyptian culture and the culture of the ancient Hebrews that issued from it.

Through his Ego too, such an Individuality is destined to fulfil a great mission. The Ego of Zarathustra incarnated again and again in other personalities; for an Individuality of such advanced development can always consecrate an astral body and strengthen an etheric body for his own use, even when he has relinquished his original bodies to others. Thus six hundred years before our era, Zarathustra was born again in ancient Chaldea as Zarathas or Nazarathos, 1. who became the teacher of the Chaldean Mystery-schools; he was also the teacher of Pythagoras [and Cyrus the Great] and again acquired profound insight into the phenomena of the outer world.

If we steep ourselves in the wisdom of the Chaldeans with the help, not of Anthropology but of Anthroposophy, an inkling will dawn in us of what Zarathustra, as Zarathas or Nazarathos, taught in the Mystery-schools of ancient Chaldea. The whole of his teaching, as we have heard, was given with the aim of bringing about concord and harmony in the outer world. His mission also included the art of organizing empires and institutions in keeping with the progress of humanity and with order in the social life. Hence those who were his pupils might rightly be called, not only great 'Magi,' great 'Initiates,' but also 'Kings,' that is to say, men versed in the art of establishing social order in the external world.

Deep and fervent attachment to the Individuality (not the personality) of Zarathustra prevailed in the Mystery-schools of Chaldea. These Wise Men of the East felt that they were intimately connected with their great leader. They saw in him the 'Star of Humanity'; for 'Zoroaster' (Zarathustra) means 'Golden Star,' or 'Star of Splendor.' They saw in him a reflection of the Sun itself. And with their profound wisdom they could not fail to know when their Master was born again in Bethlehem. Led by their 'Star,' they brought as offerings to him the outer symbols for the most precious gift he had been able to bestow upon men. This most precious gift was knowledge of the outer world, of the mysteries of the Cosmos received into the human astral body in thinking, feeling and willing; hence the pupils of Zarathustra strove to impregnate these soul-forces with the wisdom that can be drawn from the deep foundations of the divine-spiritual world. Symbols for this knowledge—which can be acquired by mastering the secrets of the outer world—were gold, frankincense and myrrh: gold the symbol of thinking, frankincense—the symbol of the piety which pervades man as feeling, and myrrh—the symbol of the power of will. Thus by appearing before their Master when he was born again in Bethlehem the Magi gave evidence of their union with him. The writer of the *Gospel of St. Matthew* relates what is literally true when he describes how the Wise Men among whom Zarathustra had once worked knew that he had reappeared among men, and how they expressed their connection with him through the three symbols of gold, frankincense and myrrh—the symbols for the precious gift he had bestowed upon them.

The need now was that Zarathustra, as Jesus of the Solomon line of the House of David, should be able to work with all possible power in order to give again to men, in a rejuvenated form, everything he had already given in earlier times. For this purpose he had to gather together and concentrate all the power he had ever possessed. Hence he could not be born in a body from the priestly line of the House of David but only in one from the kingly line. In this way the *Gospel of St. Matthew* indicates the connection of the kingly name in ancient Persia with the ancestry of the child in whom Zarathustra was incarnated.

Indications of these happenings are also contained in ancient *Books of Wisdom* originating in the Near East. Whoever really understands these *Books of Wisdom* reads them differently from those who are ignorant of the facts and therefore confuse everything. In the *Old Testament* there are, for instance, two prophecies: one in the apocryphal *Books of Enoch* pointing more to the Nathan Messiah of the priestly line, and the other in the *Psalms* referring to the Messiah of the kingly line. Every detail in the scriptures harmonizes with the facts that can be ascertained from the Akashic Chronicle.

It was necessary for Zarathustra to gather together all the forces he had formerly possessed. He had surrendered his astral and etheric bodies to Hermes and Moses respectively, and through them to Egyptian and Hebraic culture. It was necessary for him to re-unite with these forces, as it were to fetch back from Egypt the forces of his etheric body [and astral body]. A profound mystery is here revealed to us: Jesus of the Solomon line of the House of David, the reincarnated Zarathustra, was led to Egypt; for in Egypt were the forces that had streamed from his astral body and his etheric body when the former had been bestowed upon Hermes and the latter upon Moses. Because he had influenced the culture and civilization of Egypt, he had to gather to himself the forces he had once relinquished. Hence the 'Flight into Egypt' and its spiritual consequences: the absorption of all the forces he now needed in order to give again to men in full strength and in a rejuvenated form, what he had bestowed upon them in past ages.

Thus the history of the Jesus whose parents resided originally in Bethlehem is correctly related by St. Matthew. St. Luke relates only that the parents of the Jesus of whom he is writing resided in Nazareth, that they went to Bethlehem to be 'taxed' and that Jesus was born during that short period. The parents then returned to Nazareth with the child. In the *Gospel of St. Matthew* we are told that Jesus was born in Bethlehem and that he had to be taken to Egypt. It was after their return from Egypt that the parents settled in Nazareth; for the child who was the reincarnation of Zarathustra was destined to grow up near the child who represented the other stream—the stream of Buddhism. Thus the two streams were brought together in actual reality.

The *Gospels* become especially profound when they are indicating essential facts. The quality in the human being that is connected more with will and power, with the 'kingly' nature (speaking in the technical sense), is known by those cognizant of the mysteries of existence to be transmitted by the *paternal* element in heredity. On the other hand, the inner nature that is connected with wisdom and inner mobility of spirit, is transmitted by the *maternal* element. With his profound insight into the mysteries of existence, Goethe hints at this in the words:

> From my father I have my stature
> And life's serious conduct;
> From my mother a happy nature
> And delight in telling fables.

You can find this truth substantiated again and again in the world. Stature, the outer form, whatever expresses itself directly in the outer structure, and in 'life's serious conduct'—this is connected with the character of the Ego and is inherited from the paternal element. For this reason the Solomon Jesus had to inherit *power* from the father, because it was his mission to transmit to the world the divine forces radiating through the world in *Space*. This is expressed by the writer of the *Gospel of St. Matthew* in the most wonderful way. The incarnation of an Individuality was announced from the spiritual world as an event of great significance and it was announced, not to Mary, but to Joseph, the *father*. Truths of immense profundity lie behind all this; such things must never be regarded as fortuitous. *Inner* traits and qualities such as are inherited from the mother, were transmitted to the Jesus of the Nathan line. Hence the birth of the Jesus of the *Gospel of St. Luke* was announced to the *mother*.

Such is the profundity of the facts narrated in the scriptures!—But let us continue.

The other facts described are also full of significance. A forerunner of Jesus of Nazareth was to arise in John the Baptist. To say more about the Individuality of the Baptist will only be possible as time goes on. But to begin with we will consider the picture presented to us—John as the herald of the Being who was to come in Jesus. John proclaimed this by gathering together and summarizing with infinite power everything contained in the Old Law. What the Baptist wished to bring home to men was that there must be observance of what was written in the Old Law—but had grown old in civilization and had been forgotten; it was mature—but was no longer heeded. Therefore what John required above all was the power possessed by a soul born as a mature—even over-mature—soul into the world. He was born of *old* parents; from the very beginning his astral body was pure and cleansed of all the forces which degrade man; because the aged parents were unaffected by passion and desire. There again, profound wisdom is expressed in the *Gospel of St. Luke*. For such an Individuality, too, provision is made in the Mother-Lodge of Humanity. Where the great Manu guides and directs the processes of evolution in the spiritual realm—from thence the streams are sent whithersoever they are needed. An Ego such as that of John the Baptist was born into a body under the immediate guidance and direction of the great Mother-Lodge of Humanity in the central sanctuary of earthly spiritual life. The John-Ego descended from the same holy region (*Stätte*) as that from which the soul-being of the Jesus-child of the *Gospel of St. Luke* descended, save that upon Jesus there were chiefly bestowed qualities not yet permeated by an Ego in which egoistic traits had developed: that is to say, a young soul was guided to the place where the reborn Adam was to incarnate.

It will seem strange to you that a soul without a really developed Ego could be guided from the great Mother-Lodge to a certain place. But the same Ego that was withheld from the Jesus of the *Gospel of St. Luke* was bestowed upon the body of John the Baptist; thus the soul-being in Jesus of the *Gospel of St. Luke* and the Ego-being in John the Baptist were inwardly related from the beginning. Now when the human embryo develops in the body of the mother, the Ego unites with the other members of the human organism in the third week; but does not come into operation until the last months before birth and then only gradually. Not until then does the Ego become active as an inner force; in a normal case, when an Ego quickens an embryo, we have to do with an Ego that has come from earlier incarnations. In the case of John, however, the Ego in question was inwardly related to the soul-being of the Nathan Jesus. Hence according to the *Gospel of St. Luke*, the mother of Jesus went to the mother of John the Baptist when the latter was in the sixth month of her pregnancy, and the embryo that in other cases is quickened by its own Ego was here quickened through the medium of the *other* embryo. The child in the body of Elisabeth begins to move when the mother bearing the Nathan Jesus-child approaches; and it is the Ego through which the child in the other mother (Elisabeth) is quickened. 2. (Luke 1:39–44). Such was the deep connection between the Being who was to bring about the fusion of the two spiritual streams and the other who was to announce His coming!

Events of great sublimity take place at the beginning of our era. When, as so often happens, people say that truth should be simple, this is due to indolence and a dislike of having to wrestle with many concepts; but the greatest truths can be apprehended only when the spiritual faculties are exerted to their utmost capacity. If considerable efforts are needed to describe a machine, it is surely unreasonable to demand that the greatest truths should also be the simplest! Truth is inevitably complicated, and the most strenuous efforts must be made if it is desired to acquire some understanding of the truths relating to the Events of Palestine. Nobody should lend himself to the objection that the facts are unduly complicated; they are complicated because here we have to do with the greatest of all happenings in the evolution of the Earth.

Thus we see two Jesus-children growing up. The son of Joseph and Mary of the Nathan line was born of a *young* mother (in Hebrew the word 'Alma' would have been used); for a soul of such a nature must necessarily be born of a *very young mother.* After their return from Bethlehem this couple continued to live in Nazareth with their son. They had no other children; the mother was to be the mother of this Jesus only. When Joseph and Mary of the Solomon line returned with their son from Egypt, they settled in Nazareth and, as related in the *Gospel of St. Mark*, had several more children: Simon, Judas, Joseph, James and two sisters. (*Mark* 6:3).

The Jesus-child who bore within him the Individuality of Zarathustra unfolded with extraordinary rapidity powers that will inevitably be present when such a mighty Ego is working in a body. The nature of the Individuality in the body of the Nathan Jesus was altogether different—*the most important factor there being the Nirmanakaya of the Buddha overshadowing this child.* 3. Hence when the parents had returned from Bethlehem, the child is said to have been full of wisdom—that is, in his etheric body; he was 'filled with wisdom and the grace of God was upon him.' (*Luke* 2:40). But he grew up in such a way that the ordinary human qualities connected with understanding and knowledge of the external world developed in him exceedingly slowly. A superficial observer would have called this child comparatively backward—if account had been taken only of his intellectual capacities. But instead there developed in him the power streaming from the overshadowing Nirmanakaya of the Buddha. He unfolded a depth of inwardness comparable with nothing of the kind in the world, a power of feeling that had an extraordinary effect upon everyone around him. Thus in the Nathan Jesus we see a Being with infinite depths of feeling, and in the Solomon Jesus an Individuality of exceptional maturity, having profound understanding of the world.

Words of great significance had been spoken to the mother of the Nathan Jesus, the child of deep feeling. When Simeon stood before the newborn child and beheld above him the radiance of the Being he had been unable to see in India as the Buddha, he foretold the momentous events that were now to take place; but he spoke also of the 'sword that would pierce the mother's heart.' These words too refer to something we shall endeavor to understand.

The parents were in friendly relationship and the children grew up as near neighbors until they were about twelve years old. When the Nathan Jesus reached this age his parents went to Jerusalem 'after the custom,' to take part in the Feast of the Passover, and the child went with them, as was usual. We now find in the *Gospel of St. Luke* the mysterious narrative of the twelve-year-old Jesus in the temple. As the parents were returning from the Feast they suddenly missed the boy; failing to find him among the company of travelers they turned back again and found him in the temple conversing with the learned doctors, all of whom were astonished at his wisdom.

What had happened? We will enquire of the imperishable Akashic Chronicle.

The facts of existence are by no means simple. What had happened on this occasion may also happen in a different way elsewhere in the world. At a certain stage of development some individuality may need conditions differing from those that were present at the beginning of his life. Hence it repeatedly happens that someone lives to a certain age and then suddenly falls into a state of deathlike unconsciousness. A transformation takes place: his own Ego leaves him and another Ego passes into his bodily constitution. Such a change occurs in other cases too; it is a phenomenon known to every occultist. In the case of the twelve-year-old Jesus, the following happened. The Zarathustra-Ego which had lived hitherto in the body of the Jesus belonging to the kingly or Solomon line of the House of David in order to reach the highest level of his epoch, left that body and passed into the body of the Nathan Jesus who then appeared as one transformed. His parents did not recognize him; nor did they understand his words; for now the Zarathustra-Ego was speaking out of the Nathan Jesus. This was the time when the Nirmanakaya of Buddha united with the cast-off astral sheath and when the Zarathustra-Ego passed into him. This child, now so changed that his parents did not know what to make of him, was taken home with them.

Not long afterwards the mother of the Nathan Jesus died, so that the child into whom the Zarathustra-Ego had now passed was orphaned on the mother's side. As we shall see, the fact that the mother died and the child was left an orphan is especially significant. Nor could the child of the Solomon line continue to live under ordinary conditions when the Zarathustra-Ego had gone out of him. Joseph of the Solomon line had already died, and the mother of the child who had once been the Solomon Jesus, together with her children James, Joseph, Simon, Judas and the two daughters, were taken into the house of the Nathan Joseph;

so that Zarathustra (now in the body of the Nathan Jesus-child) was again living in the family (with the exception of the father) in which he had incarnated. In this way the two families were combined into one, and the mother of the brothers and sisters—as we may call them; for in respect of the Ego they were brothers and sisters—lived in the house of Joseph of the Nathan line with the Jesus whose native town—in the bodily sense—was Nazareth.

Here we see the actual fusion of Buddhism and Zoroastrianism. For the body now harboring the mature Ego-soul of Zarathustra had been able to assimilate everything that resulted from the union of the Nirmanakaya of Buddha with the discarded astral sheath. Thus the Individuality now growing up as 'Jesus of Nazareth' bore within him the Ego of Zarathustra irradiated and pervaded by the spiritual power of the rejuvenated Nirmanakaya of Buddha. In this sense Buddhism and Zoroastrianism united in the soul of Jesus of Nazareth.

When Joseph of the Nathan line also died, comparatively soon, the Zarathustra-child was in very fact an orphan and felt himself as such; he was not the being he appeared to be according to his bodily descent; in respect of the spirit he was the reborn Zarathustra; in respect of bodily descent the father was Joseph of the Nathan line and the external world could have no other view. St. Luke relates it and we must take his words exactly:

> 'Now when all the people were baptized, it came to pass that Jesus also being baptized, and praying, the heaven was opened and the Holy Ghost descended in a bodily shape like a dove upon him and a voice came from heaven which said, Thou art my beloved Son, this day have I begotten Thee. And Jesus himself, when he began to teach, was about thirty years of age ...'

And now it is not said simply that he was a 'son' of Joseph, but: 'being *as was supposed* the son of Joseph' (*Luke* 3:21-23)—for the Ego had originally incarnated in the Solomon Jesus and was therefore not connected fundamentally with the Nathan Joseph.

'Jesus of Nazareth' was now a Being, whose inmost nature comprised all the blessings of Buddhism and Zoroastrianism. A momentous destiny awaited him—a destiny altogether different from that of any others baptized by John in the Jordan. And we shall see that later on, when the Baptism took place, the Christ was received into the inmost nature of this Being. *Then, too, the immortal part of the original mother of the Nathan Jesus descended from the spiritual world and transformed the mother who had been taken into the house of the Nathan Joseph, making her again virginal* 2. Thus the soul of the mother whom the Nathan Jesus had lost was restored to him at the time of the Baptism in the Jordan. The mother who had remained to him harbored within her the soul of his original mother, called in the *Bible* the 'Blessed Mary.'

Notes:

1. Zarathas (also Zarathos or Nazarathos), who according to Rudolf Steiner lived in the 6th century BC in the Near East, was probably the last incarnation of Zarathustra in pre-Christian times. Perhaps the greatest spiritual teacher of the initiates of the Greco-Latin culture. For example, he was the teacher of Pythagoras and some of the prophets of the *Old Testament*. It was under his influence that the king of the Achaemenid Empire Cyrus the Great (Cyrus II of Persia; Old Persian: Kūruš; c. 600–530 BC) Cyrus issued the *Edict of Restoration*, in which he authorized and encouraged the return of the Jewish people to what had been the Kingdom of Judah, officially ending the Babylonian captivity, and the Temple was restored under Zerubbabel who laid the foundation of the Second Temple in

Jerusalem that was completed in the time of the Persian king Darius I. According to the *Old Testament*, Zerubbabel was a governor of the Achaemenid Empire's province of Yehud and was the grandson of Jeconiah, the nineteenth and penultimate king of Judah who was dethroned by the King of Babylon, Nebuchadnezzar II in the 6th century BC and was taken into captivity. It was Zerubbabel who led the first group of Jews, numbering 42,360, from the Babylonian captivity to Judah in the first year of Cyrus the Great. The date is generally thought to have been between 538 and 520 BC.

2. The German words are: *und machte sie wieder jungfräulich.* (and made her a virgin again)

3. Nirmanakaya, Sanskrit: Nirmāṇakāya "manifested body, emanation body"; Tibetan: Tulku. According to Rudolf Steiner, the Nirmanakaya is an astral body that has been fully transformed into Manas.

Δ

The Gospel of John in Relation to the Other Three Gospels, Rudolf Steiner, Lecture X, *What Occurred at the Baptism?* Kassel, July 3, 1909, GA 112

"…And here we touch another profound mystery of which we are constrained to speak with awe and reverence; for the preparation needed to understand such things will come to mankind only by slow degrees.

"At the same moment in which the Spirit of Christ descended into the body of Jesus of Nazareth and the transformation occurred as described, an influence was exerted upon the Mother of Jesus of Nazareth as well. It consisted in her regaining her virginity at this moment of the Baptism; that is, her inner organism reverted to the state existing before puberty. At the birth of the Christ, the Mother of Jesus of Nazareth became a virgin.

"Those are the two momentous facts, the great and mighty influences indicated, though cryptically, by the writer of the *John Gospel*...

"...Our point of departure today was the question, What occurred at the Baptism in the Jordan? and we found that the potential capacity for vanquishing death came into the world with the descent of the Christ into the threefold sheath of Jesus of Nazareth. We saw the change that came over the Mother of Jesus of Nazareth with the coming of the Christ: through the influence exercised upon her at the Baptism she became virgin again. The assertion, then, that was to be vouchsafed mankind through the *John Gospel* is indeed true: When at the Baptism the Christ was born in the body of Jesus of Nazareth, the Mother of Jesus of Nazareth became a virgin.

"That is the point of departure of the *Gospel according to St. John*; and if you grasp it in conjunction with the mighty cosmic influence exercised in the event that occurred on the bank of the Jordan, then you will also understand that an accurate description of such an event—the first description of it—could only have been achieved by one whom Christ Himself had initiated, by the risen Lazarus 'whom the Lord loved,' thenceforth always mentioned as the disciple whom the Lord loved. It was the risen Lazarus who bequeathed us the *Gospel*; and he alone was able so firmly to weld its every passage because he had received the mightiest impulse from the greatest initiator, from Christ. He alone could point to something that later Paul, through his initiation, comprehended in a certain sense: that at that moment the germ of victory over death had entered *Earth* evolution..."

The Search for the New Isis—the Divine Sophia, Rudolf Steiner, II, ***The Quest for Isis-Sophia,*** Dornach, December 24, 1920, GA 202

"If the mystery of Christmas is to be understood, we must bear in mind that Lucifer is the power wanting to retain the world-picture of an earlier stage. Lucifer is the power trying to bring into the modern world-conception that which existed in earlier stages of human development. He wants to give permanence to what existed in earlier periods. All that was moral in earlier stages also exists of course today. (The significance of morality always lies in the present, where, like seeds for the future, it provides the basis for the creation of worlds yet to come.) But Lucifer strives to separate morality as such, all moral forces, from our world picture. He allows the laws of natural necessity alone to appear in our picture of the external world. Thus the impoverished human being of modern times is presented with a wisdom of the world in which the stars move according to purely mechanical necessity, in which the stars are devoid of morality, so that the moral meaning of the world's order cannot be found in their movements. This, my dear friends, is a purely luciferic world picture.

"Just as the Egyptians looked out into the world and saw Ahriman-Typhon as the one who takes Osiris away from them, so too, we must look at our luciferic world picture, at the mathematical-mechanical world picture of modern-day astronomy and other branches of natural science, and realize that the luciferic element holds sway in this world picture, just as the typhonic-ahrimanic element held sway in the Egyptian world picture. Just as the ancient Egyptians saw their outer world picture in an ahrimanic-typhonic light, so modern human beings, because they are ahrimanic, see it with luciferic characteristics. Lucifer is present, he is working there. Just as the Egyptians imagined Ahriman-Typhon working in wind and weather, in the storms of winter, so modern human beings, if they wish to truly understand the world, must imagine that Lucifer appears to them in the sunshine and in the light of the stars, in the movements of the planets and of the moon. The world picture of Copernicus, Galileo, and Kepler is a luciferic construction. Precisely because it arose from and corresponds to our ahrimanic forces of knowledge, its content—please distinguish here between method and content—is a luciferic one.

"When the Mystery of Golgotha took place, the divine Sophia, the wisdom that enables us to see into the world with understanding, worked in a twofold way. Divine wisdom, heavenly wisdom, worked in the revelation to the poor shepherds in the fields, and in the revelation to them because of our new knowledge. We do not lack Christ; but the knowledge of Christ, the Sophia of Christ, the Isis of Christ is lacking.

"This is what we should engrave in our souls as a content of the mystery of Christmas. We must realize that since the nineteenth century even theology has come to look upon Christ merely as the man from Nazareth. That means that theology is completely permeated by Lucifer. It no longer sees into the spiritual background of existence. External natural science is luciferic; theology is luciferic. Of course if we are speaking of the inner aspect of the human being as you can see from my previous words we could just as well say that in this theology the human being is ahrimanic. Then in the same way we must say of the Egyptians that they were luciferic, just as we say of them that their perception of the external world was ahrimanic. Modern human beings must understand the mystery of Christmas in a new way. They must realize that they must first of all seek Isis, in order that Christ may appear to them. The cause of our misfortunes and the problems of modern civilization is not that we have lost Christ, who stands before us in a far greater glory than Osiris did in the eyes of the Egyptians. It is not that we have lost him and need to set out in search of him, armed with the force of Isis. No, what we have lost is the knowledge of Christ Jesus, insight into his being. This is what we must find again with the power of the Jesus Christ who is in us.

"This is how we must look upon the content of the Christmas festival. For many modern people Christmas is nothing more than a festival for giving and receiving presents, something which they celebrate every year through habit. Like so many other things in modern life the Christmas festival has become an empty phrase, And it is just because so many things have become nothing more than a phrase that modern life is so full of calamities and chaos.

"This is in truth the deeper reason for the chaos in our modern life.

"If in this our community, we could acquire the right feelings for everything which has become mere phrases in the present age, and if these feelings could enable us to find the impulses needed for the renewals that are so necessary, then this community, which calls itself the anthroposophical community, would be worthy of its existence. This community should understand the terrible significance for our age that such things as the Christmas festival are carried forward as a mere phrase. We should be able to understand that in the future this must not be allowed, and that these things must be given a new content. Old habits must be left behind and new insights must take their place. If we cannot find the inner courage needed to do this, then we share in the lie which keeps up the yearly Christmas festival merely as a phrase, celebrating it without our souls feeling and sensing the true significance of the event. Are we really lifted up to the highest concerns of humanity when we give and receive presents every year out of habit at this festival of Christ? Do we lift ourselves up to the highest concerns of humanity when we listen to the words—which have also become a phrase—spoken by the representatives of the various religious communities! We should forbid ourselves to continue in this inner hollowness of our Christmas celebrations. We should make the inner decision to give such a festival a content which allows the highest, worthiest feelings to pass through our souls. Such a festival celebration would raise humankind to the comprehension of the meaning of its existence.

"Ask yourselves whether the feelings in your hearts and souls when you stand before the Christmas tree and open the presents which are given out of habit, and the Christmas cards containing the usual phrases—ask yourselves whether feelings are living in you that can raise humankind to an understanding of the meaning of its evolution on earth! All the problems and misfortune of our time are due to this—we cannot find the courage to lift ourselves above the empty phrases of our age. But it must happen, a new content must [be]come content which can give us entirely new feelings that stir us powerfully, just as those people were stirred who were true Christians in the first Christian centuries, and who felt the Mystery of Golgotha and the appearance of Christ as the highest which humankind could experience upon the earth. Our souls must again acquire something of this spirit.

"Oh, the soul will attain to altogether new feelings if it feels committed to experience the new Isis legend within modern humanity. Lucifer kills Isis and then places her body into the infinity of space, which has become the grave of Isis, a mathematical abstraction. Then comes the search for Isis, and her discovery, made possible through the inner force of spiritual knowledge. In place of the heavens that have become dead, this knowledge places what stars and planets reveal through an inner life, so that they then appear as monuments to the spiritual powers that weave with power through space. We are able to look at the manger today in the right way only if we experience in a unique way what is weaving with spiritual power through space, and then look at that being who came into the world through the child. We know that we bear this being within us, but we must also understand him. Just as the Egyptians looked from Osiris to Isis, so we must learn to look again to the new Isis, the holy Sophia. Christ will appear again in his spiritual form during the course of the twentieth century, not through the arrival of external events alone, but because human beings find the power represented by the holy Sophia. The modern age has had the tendency to lose this power of Isis, this power of Mary. It has been killed by all that arose with the modern consciousness of humankind. And the confessions have in part exterminated just this view of Mary.

"This is the mystery of modern humanity: Fundamentally speaking, Mary-Isis has been killed, and she must be sought, just as Osiris was sought by Isis in Asia. But she must be sought in the infinite spaces of the universe with the power that Christ can awaken in us, if we devote ourselves to him in the right way.

"Let us picture this rightly, let us immerse ourselves in this new Isis legend which must be experienced, and let us fill our souls with it. Then we will experience in a true sense what humankind in many of its representatives believes, that this new legend fills the holy eve of Christmas, in order to bring us into Christmas day, the day of Christ. This anthroposophical community could become a community of human beings united in love because they feel the need, common to them all, to search.

Let us become conscious of this most intimate task! Let us go in spirit to the manger and bring to the Child our sacrifice and our gift, which lie in the knowledge that something altogether new must fill our souls, in order that we may fulfill the tasks which can lead humankind out of barbarism into a truly new civilization.

"To achieve this, of course, it is absolutely necessary that in our circles we are prepared to help one another in love, so that a real community of souls arises in which all forms of envy and the like disappear, and in which we do not look merely each at the other, but together face the great goal we have in common. The mystery brought into the world by the Christmas child also contains this—that we can look at a common goal without discord because the common goal signifies union in harmony. The light of Christmas should actually shine as a light of peace, as a light that brings external peace, only because first of all it brings an inner peace into the hearts of human beings. We should learn to say to ourselves: If we can manage to work together in love on the great tasks, then, and only then, do we understand Christmas. If we cannot manage this, we do not understand Christmas.

"Let us remember that when we do sow discord, this discord hinders us in understanding the one who appeared among human beings on the first Christmas on earth. Can we not pour this mystery of Christmas into our souls, as something which unites our hearts in love and harmony? If we do not properly understand what spiritual science is, then we will not be able to do this. Nothing will come of this community if we merely bring into it ideas and impulses we have picked up here and there from all corners of the world, where clichés and routine hold sway. Let us remember that our community is facing a difficult year, that all our forces must be gathered together, and let us celebrate Christmas in this spirit. Oh, I would like to find words that could speak deeply into the heart of each one of you on this evening. Then each one of you would feel that my words contain a greeting which is at the same time an appeal to kindle spiritual science within your hearts, so that it may become a power that can help humanity which is living under such terrible oppression.

"Beginning with such points-of-view, I have gathered the thoughts which I wished to speak to you. Be assured that they are intended as a warm Christmas greeting for each one of you, as something which can lead you into the New Year in the very best way. In this spirit, accept my words today as they were intended, as an affectionate Christmas greeting:

> "Isis-Sophia, Wisdom of God, she has been slain by Lucifer, and on the wings of the powers of the world carried her hence into the infinite space of the universe. The willing of Christ Working in man Shall wrest from Lucifer And on the boats of Spirit-knowledge Awaken in human souls Isis-Sophia Wisdom of God."

The Search for the New Isis—the Divine Sophia, Rudolf Steiner, Lecture III, *The Magi and the Shepherds: The New Isis*, Dornach, December 25, 1920, GA 202

"Through inner enlightenment man of today experiences a mathematical, mechanistic world. It is only outstanding persons like Novalis 1. who were able to feel and give expression to the poetry and deep imagination of this inner, mathematical world. This world of which Novalis sings the praises in such beautiful language is, for the ordinary man of today, the dry world of triangles and quadrangles, of squares and—sums and differences.

The ordinary human being is prosaic enough to feel this world to be barren, dry; he has no love for it. Novalis, who was an outstanding person, sings its praises because there was still alive in him an echo of what this world was before it had drawn inwards. In those times it was the world out of which the Jupiter Spirit, the Saturn Spirit, the Spirit of Aries, of Taurus, of Gemini was perceived. It was the ancient light-filled world of stars which has withdrawn and in the first stage of its withdrawal becomes the world which seems to us to be dry, mathematical, mechanistic.

"The faculty that intensified in a different form in the shepherds in the field to a perception of the voice of the Angel in the heights has become dry, barren and feeble in us—it has become our perception of the external world of sense; with it today we perceive minerals and plants, whereas with the old faculty, although it was hardly articulate, men perceived the earth's depths or the world of men and animals.

"What today has faded into the mathematical-mechanistic universe, what was once astrology, contained such a power that the Christ was revealed to the Magi as a Being of the Heavens. What today is our ordinary knowledge through the senses, with which we see nothing but the green surface of grass, the brown skins of animals and the like—to this kind of knowledge when it was still inward, when it had not yet drawn outwards to the eyes, to the skin, there was revealed to the shepherds in the field the deep influence on the Earth, the power with which the Christ would work in the Earth, what the Christ was to be for the Earth.

"We, my dear friends, must find the way whereby the inner faculty that is now dry mathematics may intensify pictorially to Imagination. We must learn to grasp the Imagination given us by Initiation Science. What is contained in these Imaginations? They are in truth a continuation of the faculty with which the

Magi from the East recognized the approach of Christ. The Imaginations are the budding, the offspring of what the men of old saw in the starry constellations, the star-imaginations, the mineral imaginations, in gold, silver, copper. The men of old perceived in Imaginations, and their offspring are the mathematical faculties of today. The mathematical faculties of today will become those faculties which understand the Imaginations. Thus by the development of the inner faculties men will have to seek for the understanding of the Christ Being.

"But external perception must also be deepened, become more profound. External perception has itself descended from what was once the life of inner experiences, of instinct in man. The power which among the shepherds in the field was still inward, in their hearts, is today only in eyes and ears; it has shifted entirely to the external part of man and therefore perceives only the outer tapestry of the sense-world. This power must go still further outwards. To this end man must be able to leave his body and attain Inspiration. This Inspiration—a faculty of perception which can be attained today—will then, out of Initiation Science, be able to give the same as was given in the proclamation to the naïve, inner knowledge of the shepherds in the field.

"Astrology as it was to the Magi, heart-vision as it was in the shepherds. With the knowledge that comes from Initiation Science through Imagination and Inspiration modern man will rise to the spiritual realization to the living Christ. Men must learn to understand how Isis, the living, divine Sophia, had to disappear when the time came for the development which has driven astrology into mathematics, into geometry, into the science of mechanics. But it will also be understood that when living Imagination resurrects from mathematics, phoronomy [now called kinematics] and geometry, this means the finding of

Isis, of the new Isis, of the divine Sophia whom man must find if the Christ Power that is his since the Mystery of Golgotha is to become alive, completely alive, that is to say, filled with light within him."

Note:

1. Novalis: Georg Philipp Friedrich Freiherr von Hardenberg (May 2, 1772–Mar. 25, 1801), pen name Novalis, was a German aristocrat and polymath, who was a deeply spiritual poet, novelist, philosopher and mystic. An early influential figure of German Romanticism and profound leader of mankind that Rudolf Steiner made reference to on many occasions.

The Holy Sophia of the Divine Feminine Trinity

Isis-Sophia, Theosophia, Sophia, Philosophia, Anthroposophia, and the Holy Sophia are aspects of the Divine Feminine Trinity that are described in detail in the works of Rudolf Steiner. Ralph Waldo Emerson pointed out that the 'natural human intellect' was evolving over time; but he did not attribute that evolution of consciousness to a 'being.' On the other hand, throughout the body of his work Rudolf Steiner has within numerous lectures given the Biography of Isis-Sophia from Her physical birth (without a human body) in 2,100 BC, to Her etheric, astral, and ego births each 700 years thereafter, as She moves through her stages of growth along with the growth of humanity as a whole.

***Artistic Sensitivity as a Spiritual Approach to Knowing Life and the World*, Rudolf Steiner, Pt. II. *Perception of the Nature of Thought*, January 10, 1915, Dornach, GA 161**

"…Thus, we see a being weaving its way through history for whom a century is as a year…

"…And … if we wanted to, we could, I may say, write the biography of [this] being, who as regards spirituality is man's superior to the extent that a century is longer than a year…

"…Thus, the historical birth of this being amongst mankind, that is, its first contact with it, took place in approximately 2,100

BC. The beginning of the development of its etheric body was in 1,400 BC, while the development of its astral body begun in 700 BC…

"…Abraham, then, was the first man to develop within himself an inner reflection of divine wisdom [the Sophia], divine vision, in an entirely human way as a human thinking about the Divine…

"…And so out of the mists of the history of philosophy a being comes towards us to whom we look up as to a Goddess descending from the divine heights, whom we see young in ancient times and whom we see grow even if slowly, so that a century for her corresponds to a year in a human life…

"…For this is the essence of Anthroposophy, that its own being consists of what man's being consists of; and the essential quality of its activity is that man receives in Anthroposophy what he himself is and must place this before him, because he must practice self-knowledge."

Perception of the Nature of Thought, Rudolf Steiner, Dornach, January 10, 1915, GA 161

"Something lives in history which passes through the etheric body, the sentient body etc., a real, actual Being. I said in my book [*The Riddles of Philosophy*, GA 18] that in the Grecian era thought was born. But in modern times it comes to actual self-consciousness in the Consciousness-Soul: thought is an independent active Being. This could not of course be said in an exoteric book intended for the public. The anthroposophist will find it however if he reads the book and notes what was the prevailing trend of its presentation. It is not brought into it but results of itself out of the very subject matter.

"You see from this that very many impulses of transformation as regards the spiritual life are coming forward in our time. For here we see something evolving that is like a human being except that it has a longer duration of life than an individual man. The individual man lives on the physical plane: for seven years he develops the physical body, for seven years the etheric body, for seven years the sentient body etc. The Being which evolves as philosophy (we call it by the abstract name 'philosophy') lives for 700 years in the etheric body, 700 - 800 years in the sentient body (the time is only approximate), 700 - 800 years in the Sentient-Soul, 700 - 800 years in the Intellectual or Mind-Soul and again 700 - 800 years in the Consciousness-Soul. A Being evolves upwards of whom we can say: if we look at the very first beginnings of Grecian philosophy this Being has then just reached the stage of development which corresponds in mankind to puberty as Being it is like man when he has reached the 14th - 16th year. Then it lives upwards to the time when a human being experiences the events between the 14th and 21st year; that is the age of Greek philosophy, Greek thought. Then comes the next 7 years, what man experiences from the age of 21 to 28; the Christ Impulse enters the development of philosophy. Then comes the period from Scotus Erigena up to the new age. This Being develops in the following 700 - 800 years what man develops between the ages of 28 and 35 years. And now we are living in the development of what man experiences in his Consciousness-Soul: we are experiencing the Consciousness-Soul of philosophy, of philosophical thought.

"Philosophy has actually come to the forties, only it is a Being that has a much longer duration of life. One year in a man's life corresponds to a hundred years in the life of the Being of philosophy. So, we see a Being passing through history for whom a century is a year; evolving in accordance with Sun-laws though one is not aware of it.

"And then only there lies further back another Being still more super-sensible than the Being that evolves as humanity except that a year is as long as a century. This Being that stands behind evolves in such a way that its external expression is our personal destiny, how we bear this through still longer periods, from incarnation to incarnation. Here stand the Spirits regulating our outer destiny and their life is of still longer duration than the life of those for whom we must say that a century corresponds to a year.

"So, you see, it is as if we look there into differing ranges of Beings, and how, if we wished, we might even write the biography of a Being who stands spiritually as much higher than man as a 100 years is longer than a year.

"An attempt has been made to write the biography of a such a Being as had its puberty at the time of Thales and Anaxagoras and has now reached the stage of its self-consciousness and since the 16th century has entered, so to say, into its 'forties.' The biography of this Being has furnished a 'History of Philosophy.'

"From this you see, however, how Spiritual Science gives vitality to what is otherwise abstract, and really animates it. What dry-wood, for instance, is the usual 'History of Philosophy'! And what it can become when one knows that it is the biography of a Being which is interwoven in our existence but evolves by Sun-laws instead of Earth-laws!

"It was my wish to add these thoughts to what we have been considering lately about the life-forces which arise in us when we look at Spiritual Science not as a theory but seek it in the guidance to living. And it is just through Spiritual Science that we find the living. What is so unalive, so dry, and withered as the history of philosophy comes to meet us out of the mist as though we looked up to it as a Goddess who descends from divine cloud-heights, whom we see young in ancient times, whom we see grow even if with the slowness where a century corresponds to a year of human life. Yet all this becomes living—the Sun rises for us like the Sun within Earth existence itself. For just as the Sun rises on the physical plane, so do we see the ancient Sun still radiate into the Earthly world in a Being that has a longer lifetime than man. As we follow man's development on the physical plane, from birth to death, so we follow the development of philosophy by seeing a Being within it. When in this way we look at what Anthroposophy can be to us we reach the point of seeing in it not only a guide to knowledge but a guide to living Beings who surround us even though we are unaware of them."

Awakening to Community, Rudolf Steiner, Lecture V, February 22, 1923, Dornach, GA 257

"In Oriental works of art the Logos streamed downward, finding only stammering expression in human media. Our art forms must be true speech forms, voicing what nature itself would say if it could live out its potential. That is the new artistic ideal that comes to stand beside the religious ideal that looks at nature from the standpoint of its seed endowment.

"The third is our scientific ideal. That is no longer based on the feeling the Orientals had that thoughts are something whispered straight into human souls by gods. Nor can it have kinship with the Greek ideal, which felt thoughts to be inner witnesses to the divine. Nowadays we have to exert purely human forces, work in a purely human way, to develop thoughts.

But once we have made the effort and achieved thoughts free of any taint of egotism, self-seeking, subjective emotionality or partisan spirit such as colors thoughts with prejudiced opinions, once we have exerted ourselves as human beings to experience thoughts in the form they themselves want to assume, we no longer regard ourselves as the creators and shapers of our thoughts, but merely as the inner scene of action where they live out their own nature. Then we feel the largeness of these selfless and unprejudiced thoughts that seem to be our own creations, and are surprised to find that they are worthy of depicting the divine; we discover afterwards that thoughts that take shape in our own hearts are worthy of depicting the divine. First, we discover the thought, and afterwards we find that the thought is nothing less than the Logos! While you were selflessly letting the thought form itself in you, your selflessness made it possible for a god to be the creator of that thought. Where the Oriental felt thought to be revelation and where the Greek found it proof of divine reality, we feel it to be living discovery: we have the thought, and afterwards it tells us that it was permitted to express divinity. That is our scientific ideal."

Goethe's Standard of the Soul, Rudolf Steiner, Pt. I. *Goethe's Faust: A Picture of his Esoteric World Conception*, 1902, GA 22

"Man dies from the lower life in order to live again in a higher existence. Higher spiritual life is a new stage of the Becoming; time becomes a symbol of the Eternal that now lives in man. The union with the 'Eternal-Feminine' allows the child in man to come into being,—the child, imperishable, immortal, because it is of the Eternal. The higher life is the surrender, the death of the lower, the birth of a higher existence.

The birth and evolution of the being of Anthroposophia gives extraordinary insight into human development provided only by Rudolf Steiner. The mysteries of Sophia are a key in understanding our future. Our spiritual development is in the hands of this being and She treats each of us as Her child. Anthroposophia prepares our soul to be a bride for the wedding of our spiritual soul to our higher self. She helps us create the Grail vessel in the heart that is made ready for the groom who descends like tongues of flame at Pentecost. Anthroposophia is the new Pentecost of the heart that purifies the spiritual soul to step across the threshold into the spiritual world. We can only step across this abyss with the help of our spiritual midwife—*Sophia*.

Further Reflections

If the tenets of this presentation are true, we will see it come to pass that the future introduces us to beings who stand ready to bring spiritual revelation to the sincere aspirant. As we spiritually advance, so too Anthroposophia will develop and show us objectively if we are taking the right path to the spirit. Throughout the many theories concerning Sophia, the one that is right for the student will become apparent as a relationship with Her develops. As Rudolf Steiner tells us, "Each person resembles the God he or she understands." This truth is self-evident but does not remove the blinders of the student seeking the full measure of Sophia's manifestation. Your version of the Divine is limited by your personal understanding of the Divine within your own heart. The limits of your understanding of the Divine become your personal spiritual limits. You 'resemble' the God or Goddess you understand like deity worship in Eastern religions. As your understanding grows, so should your vision of the Divine.

This book is but a humble attempt to help each reader expand their view of the Divine, especially as regards the Divine Feminine Trinity. Furthermore, this is not meant to be a presentation of a 'Doctrine of Sophia'; but rather, it is an exploration of the Divine Feminine, as expressed through the works of Rudolf Steiner, that hopefully illustrates that we should not be so quick to place limits on Sophia; otherwise, those limits will become who we are and who we become. For in the final analysis, we all worship an image of the Divine based on the limits of our interpretation. On the other hand, this study is humbly meant to open a panoramic view of Sophia that will give Her a chance to 'knock at your heart' and 'objectively' present your spiritual strivings to your own consciousness. Through this spiritual dialogue, we trust that the glory and wisdom of the Divine Feminine will reveal to you the mysteries of your evolving self. It is our task in the current age to *lift the veil of Isis-Sophia and live*.

For initiates ready to step beyond ordinary time and space and the conventional, intellectual content of Anthroposophy, *The Gospel of Sophia* trilogy by Tyla and Douglas Gabriel offers just such an introduction to the Being Sophia, through three biographies that unveil the Mother, Daughter, and Holy Sophia. A path of 'labors' takes the aspirant through the twelve archetypes that comprise the Divine Feminine Trinity. In Volume 2, the path of revelation and apocalypse is unfolded to provide the aspirant with the wisdom to interpret the symbols and language associated with crossing the threshold into the spiritual world through initiation. Volume 3 of *The Gospel of Sophia: The Sophia Christos Initiation*, is a spiritual self-initiation that further advances the aspirant's process of ascension. This self-initiation process is in harmony with sacred rites and rituals of the ancient mystery schools updated with the spectrum of wisdom given by the Divine Feminine Trinity. Through the three volumes of *The Gospel of Sophia*, the aspirant can find new archetypes and spiritual icons that seed the future Sixth Epoch. The physiological, psychological, theological, philosophical, and spiritual scientific descriptions of the Sophia, who is found in the human body and the world, create a comprehensive vision of the Eternal Feminine Trinity, and explains Her place alongside the Eternal Male Trinity and human spiritual development. Thus, the injunction of our age, given to us by Rudolf Steiner, is:

"Isis-Sophia, Wisdom of God, she has been slain by Lucifer, and on the wings of the powers of the world carried her hence into the infinite space of the universe. The willing of Christ working in man, shall wrest from Lucifer, and on the boats of spirit-knowledge awaken in human souls Isis-Sophia Wisdom of God." GA 202

Sophiology and the Children of Wisdom

Sophia is Greek for 'wisdom' and is the root of philosophy (love of wisdom) and theosophy (wisdom of God). Sophia, or Wisdom, has always been imaged as feminine and is described in the *Book of Wisdom* as a "holy and intelligent spirit, unique, yet manifold, subtle, lucid, pure, clear, harmless, loving the good, eager, beneficent and kind, steady, free from care, all-powerful, all-seeing, and all-permeating." Sophia has been called a 'flawless mirror' of the divine, the means through which God creates, permeating the entire Cosmos. She is often called the 'glory of God,' the beloved, wife, bride, daughter, sister, guide, midwife, and a thousand other names.

Sophia has been theologically and philosophically described in many ways in the *Old Testament* through a long tradition of 'Wisdom Teachings.' Through this tradition, Sophia is perennially renewed by visions, revelations, direct personal experiences, and many continuing apparitions throughout the world. Archaeo-mythologists call Sophia the Magna Mater, the Triple Goddess, or Great Mother who is found ubiquitously throughout aboriginal cultures. Sophia is known as the Mother, Daughter, and Holy Sophia who is the creatrix of Birth, Death, and Rebirth—the original divine feminine trinity.

Many lovers of Sophia have attempted to describe her magnificent nature and have ultimately fallen quite short of a satisfactory explanation for such questions as: Who is the 'us' referred to in *Genesis* when God was talking to himself about the creation of the human being.

Genesis 1: 26 And God said, Let us make man in our image, after our likeness: and let them have dominion over the fish of the sea, and over the fowl of the air, and over the cattle, and over all the Earth, and over every creeping things that creepeth upon the Earth.

1:27 So God created man in his own image, in the image of God created he him; male and female created he them.

Obviously, God was not alone during creation and the original 'man' was indeed 'male and female,' just like God—a male and female god(dess). The original 'Adam' was androgynous, according to the *Bible*. Later, in *Genesis* we are told another version of the way humanity was created:

Genesis
2:7 And the Lord God formed man of the dust of the ground and breathed into his nostrils the breath of life; and man became a living soul.
2:21 And the Lord God caused a deep sleep to fall upon Adam, and he slept: and he took one of his ribs, and closed up the flesh instead thereof;
2:22 And the rib, which the Lord God had taken from man, made he a woman, and brought her unto the man.
2:23 And Adam said, This is now bone of my bones, and flesh of my flesh: she shall be called Woman, because she was taken out of Man.

2:24 Therefore shall a man leave his father and his mother, and shall cleave unto his wife: and they shall be one flesh.

According to the two different versions of the creation of humanity, the *Bible* is referring to two different times when 'God(s)' ['us' & 'our'] created a 'spiritual' Adam ['them' & 'male and female'] whom God placed in the Garden of Eden, and a second Adam from whom he took a rib to create 'Woman'—Eve. This original 'Adam,' according to the great Sophiologist Jacob Boehme, was actually united to his 'twin soul' Sophia, who Adam was separated from when the 'second creation' story came about. This separation from Sophia, the being of Wisdom, is the true cause for the 'fall' of Adam into the physical world. Becoming separated from Divine Wisdom, Sophia, is the cause for needing a reunion with Wisdom and a reconciliation and redemption of the fallen nature of Adam—all humans (male and female). It is this sacred reunion, or marriage, of the eternally pure soul (Virgin Sophia) of humanity to the spiritual bridegroom of Jesus Christ (the Lamb) in New Jerusalem as it descends from Heaven to Earth. Boehme, and many other Sophia lovers, have deemed this spiritual wedding to be the end goal and culmination of human spiritual development. Sophia is the agent of the Divine in this quest to find New Jerusalem (New Eden/Paradise) and the purification of the soul that is preparing for ascension to heavenly communion and marriage.

Jacob Boehme, like John Pordage, Jane Lead, and many others, repeatedly had direct visionary experiences of Sophia throughout their lives. These encounters with a 'real being' cannot be mistaken for fantasy or ungrounded reverie. Sophia lovers experienced her in tangible experiences that changed their lives forever. They even came to believe that they should love, caress, kiss, embrace, and even marry Sophia. They dedicated their lives to writing down every vision, dream, encounter, or revelation of the Divine Lady, the missing part of their ever-seeking soul that yearns for spirit union. In fact, there is no end to the different approaches to Sophia by such Sophianic philosophers and religious clerics as: John Pordage, Jane Lead, Gottfried Arnold, Thomas Bromley, Robert Ayshford, Ann Bathurst, Friedrich Oetinger, Georg von Welling, Jakob Wirz, Franz von Baader, Leopold Ziegler, Amos Comenius, Novalis (Friedrich von Hardenberg), Johann Wolfgang von Goethe, Friedrich Shelling, Nicholas Berdyaev, Vladimir Soloviev, Sergei Bulgakov, King Solomon, Robert Fludd, Thomas Vaughan, Rudolf Steiner, Pavel Florensky, Pierre Teilhard de Chardin, and Sergei Bulgakov, among others. Every author listed here waxes poetic about the primary importance of the love of Sophia, and yet every philosopher, theologian, or visionary paints a different picture.

After we wrote the *Gospel of Sophia* trilogy, we realized that the many versions of Sophia depicted in writings were as numerous as the people who tried to share their understanding of Wisdom's place in their lives. Some authors believed that Sophia as Wisdom was simply a part of the Father, or the Son, or the Holy Spirit or perhaps a mirror, an emanation, a creature, something created, or a thousand other descriptions that limit Sophia's domain of influence. Catholics say Sophia is an aspect of the Holy Spirit. Creationists believe Sophia, the Mother, is the created Spouse of the Father—a creature. Many others believe that Sophia, as Wisdom, is simply a part of Jesus Christ's nature. John Pordage believes that Sophia is threefold (a trinity) and serves as the agent of Wisdom for the Father, Son, and Holy Ghost. Valentin Tomberg, taking his idea from the Kabbalah and *The Zohar*, believed Sophia is a separate feminine trinity that merges (weds) with the Father, Son, and Holy Ghost separately and collectively; but always through unity and ultimately creates the 'Luminous Trinity' through this heavenly union. In other words, the Male Trinity is coincident with the Female Trinity.

Robert Graves tells us in *The Greek Myths*: "The whole of Neolithic Europe, to judge from surviving artifacts and myths, had a remarkably homogeneous system of religious ideas, based on worship of the many-titled Mother-goddess, who was also known in Syria and Libya. Ancient Europe had no gods. The Great Goddess was regarded as immortal, changeless, and omnipotent; and the concept of fatherhood had not been introduced into religious thought." Therefore, according to Graves, it is clear that the Male Trinity came long after the Female Trinity. Or as Gunther Zuntz, the renown Greek scholar has said: "The cult of the Mother Goddess is the oldest godhead perceived by humankind."

The beloved mythologist Joseph Campbell tells us in his last book, *Goddesses*, that he should have named his famous works '*The Heroine's*

Journey' and '*The Heroine With a Thousand Faces*' because he realized late in life the primacy of the Triple Goddess—Sophia. He tells us in his book *Goddesses*: "The Goddess is the axis mundi, the world axis, the pillar of the Universe. She represents the energy that supports the whole cycle of the Universe. People often think of the Goddess as a fertility deity only. Not at all—she's the muse. She's the inspirer of poetry. She's the inspirer of the spirit. So, she has three functions: one, to give life; two, to be the one who receives death; and three, to inspire our spiritual poetic realization."

This change of Campbell's heart from 'the hero' to the 'heroine' is beautifully pictured in what Rumi has to say about the divine feminine nature: "Woman is a beam of the divine Light. She is not the being whom sensual desire takes as its object. She is Creator, it should be said, She is not a Creature." Rumi and Campbell found the path of Wisdom that informed them Sophia is not a creature but a creator who is the axis of the world and works through a trinity—the ancient Triple Goddess.

The idea of two Holy Trinities is in accord with the passages of *Genesis* that say 'us and ours' and clearly indicate that the divine is 'male and female' as an androgynous, separate but equal being who fashioned the original 'Adam' in 'their' androgynous 'image.' It also seems logical that in the spiritual world, Angels and spiritual beings are not male or female; which is the exclusive curse of the material world caused by the splitting of Adam and Sophia in heaven, and later Adam and Eve in Eden. When Adam was placed in the Garden of Eden, a 'helpmate' was necessary to counteract the duality of the physical world. A Father and a Mother were both needed to birth a child in the physical world of duality. Often Sophia, as Mother, is seen as co-equal with the Father. It takes a Father and Mother to wed through spiritual union to bring forth the future New Jerusalem and the fulfillment of the spiritual evolution of humanity as the 'Divine Child' of the Father and Mother, who will 'rule the Earth with an iron scepter' and be 'taken up to God, to his throne.'

It seems that Sophiologists may be creating their own limitations of their understanding of Sophia, woman, the feminine divine, and their own ability to mother the birth of the Cosmic Christ in their heart, the New Paradise planted with Sophia's help. Every imagined limitation of Wisdom's domain, or the lack of understanding for the biographies of the three Sophias (Mother, Daughter, Holy Sophia), reveal the Sophianic philosopher's lack of spiritual development and direct communion with the living Divine Being Sophia. This is, of course, to be expected. Many male Sophia lovers comprehensively accept the fact that initially all world religions, myths, and revelations know the Divine as the Being of Birth, Death, and Rebirth. This primal Feminine Divine Trinity was the original Divine Being of the ancients that they discovered by looking at a women's ability to be a 'creator goddess' through human birth, over and over again. The female lovers of Sophia seem to develop a broader view of Sophia's domain through their personal experiences with Sophia Herself, wherein She (Wisdom) instructs them in the comprehensive nature of the Divine Feminine Trinity.

For a true lover of Sophia, reading the painfully delimiting descriptions of closed-hearted theologians trying to describe the vast nature of Wisdom is like listening to what a 'man' thinks about the opposite sex—his limited understanding of what *he* thinks a woman *is*. Essentially, any male thinker cannot understand the divine nature of the female—let alone the female nature of the goddess who is married (the consort of) to each of the male members of the Holy Trinity—Father, Son, and Holy Spirit. In Tibetan Buddhism, the female deity of Wisdom is Vajrayogini who is the 'Eternally Virgin' consort of all ten thousand Buddhas. This seems incongruent to the logical mind. The idea of the Female Divine being wedded to all spiritual seekers and all spiritual hierarchies (Buddhas, avatars, saints, etc.) is difficult for any logical mind to comprehend. Vajrayogini is always shown as naked; but if you see her as naked, you fail the spiritual test and must start over again. Male priests often fail this test outright for the shame they project onto the beautiful sight of the naked female body—the Temple of Birth and Wisdom. To see Sophia in one of her many forms as the 'Bride' of all spiritual seekers or saints and deities (Angelic hosts), is to make her the ultimate shape-shifter, or protean being, who appears as a 'spiritual chameleon' who is omnipresent. Lao Tzu tells us in the *Tao De Ching*:

> "The Spirit of the Fountain never dies. It is called the mysterious feminine. It is the root of all heaven and Earth. Frail, frail it is, hardly existing. But touch it; it will never run dry."

Obviously, the wisdom of the East knows about the Triple Goddess and her unceasing fountain of wisdom and life.

Rudolf Steiner points out, like the *Bible*, that Sophia (Wisdom) is the most necessary aspect of spiritual development that humanity currently needs to evolve and complete the quest for the Holy Grail—the heart as the throne of Sophia-Christos. Sophia brings to all seekers the direct knowledge of the cosmic nature of Christ's mission. As Steiner put it: "What is needed in our time is the Wisdom (Sophia) of Christ, the knowledge of the cosmic nature of Christ." Sophia teaches us, as a personal guide, to understand the cosmic mission of Christ's redemption of the Earth and humanity. Without a Christian cosmology, Jesus Christ cannot be understood by modern materialistic humanity. Only when Wisdom is sought out by the ever-seeking soul to find the path to the higher self, the Christened self, will the individual soul attain to the spiritual marriage of the 'Ever-Virgin Soul' to the 'Christened Spirit.'

As the lover of Sophia awakens to the Language of the Spirit and begins to communicate with the Spiritual World, she comes to know the being Sophia-Christos, or the being Rudolf Steiner called Anthroposophia. From Isis-Sophia, to Theosophia, to Philosophia, to Anthroposophia we follow the path of human intellectual development throughout history through Steiner's Sophiology. Sophia, or Anthroposophia, evolves alongside of humanity as a companion, mother, sister, lover, guide, consort, inspirer, and particularly as a bridge to the cosmic nature of Christ. Or, as the *Book of Wisdom* tells us:

> "She is a reflection of everlasting light, the flawless mirror of the divine active power, and the image of his goodness which is unchanging as she renews all things, age after age she enters holy souls and makes them friends of God and prophets; for God accepts only those who make their home with Wisdom."

Many authors insist there is a 'Path of Wisdom,' a Sophianic spiritual awakening that comes through prayer and interior attention and, sometimes, through inner vision, dreams, and revelations. These inner visionary encounters are direct experiences, not theological speculation. That is what makes Sophiology, and the Love of Sophia, so profoundly different than what churches provide. There is no need for a church or male priests if the seeker has direct inward illumination. No human arbiter is needed to experience the divine—just a loving relationship with Wisdom/Sophia who is directly connected to the Holy Trinity. Sophia becomes then, a spiritual companion who restores paradise within the human heart. Humanity is redeemed from its 'fallen condition' and is regenerated and renewed in a reunion with Heaven.

This is a transmutation to the 'virginal' state of grace that existed before the 'fall.' Once the soul has 'realized' Wisdom and made her his spouse, the soul reunites with the spiritual Sophia we all left behind in Heaven. When rejoined, the soul becomes like Sophia/Wisdom and becomes a 'virgin soul' once again in preparation for the divine marriage to the Lamb of God (Christ).

The Wisdom of the Cosmos, humanity and nature was created by the same Beings who work together with the higher spiritual hierarchies to maintain the cosmic forces that balance Wisdom's creation. The hierarchical rank that is the home of Wisdom is called the Kyriotetes (Spirits of Wisdom); they work closely with the Thrones

(Spirits of Will) who reign above them maintaining the equilibrium of the forces of the Cosmos. The Being of Wisdom (Heavenly Sophia) who works through the rank of the Kyriotetes, is the second person in the Divine Feminine Trinity, called the Daughter of Sophia. This Being of Wisdom over-lighted the Mother of Jesus and ultimately helped regenerate her soul into the 'Eternal Virgin Soul' that was readied for ascension into the New Paradise.

The Daughter of Sophia (Daughter of The Mothers or Mother) returned to her hierarchical rank after the 'Mother of Jesus' (Eve-Kadmon/Mary/Sophia) ascended into Heaven during the Assumption of the Blessed Virgin. Rudolf Steiner describes this aspect of Sophia as the 'Heavenly Sophia' working from the hierarchical rank of the Beings of Wisdom, the Kyriotetes. The Heavenly Sophia, for Steiner, is distinct from the Being he calls Anthroposophia and the Being(s) he calls The Mothers (based upon the use of that name by Goethe) who created the three elementary worlds.

We can imagine the Holy Sophia in the spiritual and intellectual development of humanity as a somewhat 'collective super-consciousness' shared by all seekers on the path of Wisdom who are ascending back to their original home. This group soul of Anthroposophia (Holy Sophia) can be seen manifesting in the phylogenic development of humanity as a philosophic development of consciousness. The path of Sophia is clearly indicated for anyone to see through the descriptions of the Daughter of Sophia attested to in the beliefs concerning Mary (Sophia), the Mother of Jesus. Mary is often deified and considered to be 'The Church' or the 'body of believers' in Jesus Christ. The trace of the Daughter of Wisdom from the hierarchy of the Kyriotetes is also well worn by the questing soul seeking Sophia. But the Mother of Wisdom herself, the creatrix being who was there (us & our) at creation as a 'creator already existing before creation' is sometimes hard for Sophiologists to see or acknowledge, even though this person in the Divine Feminine Trinity seems to be the most obvious of the three. If there was a 'first mover,' then there must have been a 'first moved.' As the *Bible* tells us: "And the Spirit of God moved upon the face of the waters"; but fails to tell us exactly who or what this 'face of the waters' really is.

Mother Sophia is the ubiquitous Great Goddess who is threefold and was worshiped long before Brahma, Vishnu, and Shiva or the Father, Son, and Holy Ghost. Sophia doesn't claim to have ever 'worked alone' during creation. Almost all creation myths tell of a primal dark being, often associated with water, that was there before creation began. Sophia/Wisdom is not a creature or a created being—she is a co-creator with the creator. It takes a Father and Mother to birth in this physical world (Holy Child) and ultimately, the divine must become 'dual' as it enters the fallen realms of the material plane from heaven.

Mother Sophia is also threefold in that she is the memory of past creations that have contributed to the existence of our material world. These prior worlds are the 'Three Mothers' of the past, the three Norns of Norse mythology, the three Fates of the Greeks, and the threefold nature of most of the goddesses and female deities found in world mythologies and religions. The Mothers have created all we know as the outside world, what Sophiologists call the four eternal elements that combine to create the quintessential element of the spirit. The Mother has birthed the Cosmos and every human being in it. She knows more about the Divine Wisdom that created us than we know ourselves. The Mother loves us as her children, the Daughter Sophia loves us as the guide to Wisdom, and the Holy Sophia (Anthroposophia) helps birth every single step we take towards Wisdom, Mother Sophia, and her Divine Feminine Trinity. Sophia wedded the Father before creation and together two trinities join to create the combined 'Eternal Trinity,' as the Hebrew Kabbalah informs us.

It seems apparent that some Sophiologists demonstrate their limitations with their abbreviated versions of Sophia as mother, sister, or lover in their truncated versions of Sophia's full cosmological manifestation. One Sophiologist has a problem with women altogether, another has problems with their own mother, while another has serious

Sophiology and the Children of Wisdom

problems with loving the opposite sex—let alone 'our neighbors as ourselves.' The spiritual limits of the author seem to be the limits of their understanding of Wisdom/Sophia. Thus, this provides the many, many different theological, philosophical, and just plain-crazy ideas that abound when Sophiologists pronounce their limited view of a Triple Goddess and a Divine Feminine Trinity.

Sophia is a new religion of the future based upon direct revelations of a living, wisdom-filled, mother-like, companion in the spirit who has never gone away since her assumption into heaven, whether under the guise of 'Mary Apparitions,' the Gaia/Mother Earth as a living being movement, or the Immaculate Virgin Mother of God as intercessor to the Holy Trinity. The Great Goddess has always been a holy trinity and now the newly evolved icon of the Divine Feminine Trinity can be gleaned by combining the various limited views of Sophia into a comprehensive cosmology that effectively advances the soul towards its true spirit.

Over time, the Holy Trinity of Father-Son-Holy Spirit became the predominant religious belief in Christianity, obscuring any reference to the Holy Trinity of Mother-Daughter-Holy Sophia. All references to the co-creative, equally important, and co-substantial nature of Sophia were obliterated and the feminine divinity was relegated by church fathers to limited expression of Her nature as Mother Gaia, Mother Mary, or some aspect of the Holy Spirit—*as merely an attribute, or metaphor*. What is needed is to understand that no matter what Sophiological opinion a theologian or philosopher has, it is the poetic voice of the visionary who brings living revelations. Once we compare these varied revelations of Wisdom, the truth about the living being of Sophia rises like the Morning Star to enkindle our heart-fire (hearth) and plant spirit-seeds in the New Garden of Paradise, Eden Regained. Re-enthroning the Divine Feminine Trinity is necessary in our age as the Eternal Virgin Soul joins together in the divine marriage of the purified Soul to the awaiting Spirit (Virgin to Christ – Sophia-Christos) who will give birth again to the living Imagination of the 'Luminous Holy Trinity' shining in heaven as Father/Mother Divine.

Sophiologists—Lovers of Sophia
Jacob Boehme (Böhme 1575–Nov. 17, 1624)

Boehme was one of the most influential Sophiologists who believed he had visitations from Sophia a few times throughout his life. These direct experiences convinced Boehme he was communicating with a divine being who knew his inner self better than he knew it himself. Boehme wrote such works as: *The Aurora, The Three Principles of the Divine Being, Forty Questions on the Soul, The Signature of All Things*, and the *Mysterium Magnum*. One could say that many Sophianic authors are simply a footnote to Boehme's Sophiology. According to his own personal account, Boehme had his first vision of spontaneous enlightenment that was triggered by catching a tiny reflection of the sun in a shiny piece of pewter in 1600; subsequently, around twelve years later, Boehme began to write his first manuscript for his own use, *Morgenröte im Aufgang* (*"Morning redness upon Rising"*). A manuscript copy of the unfinished work was lent to Karl von Ender, a nobleman, who had copies made and began to circulate them. Subsequently a friend gave it the name *Aurora* (sometimes translated into English as "The Day-spring").

As Boehme tells us in *On the Virgin Wisdom*: "I cannot comprehend and hold the Virgin (because my mind falls into sins) yet the Spirit of the World shall not always hold the mind captive." But through Sophia's interventions Boehme was able to find the path to Wisdom and meet Sophia directly as he tells us: "And when I laid upon the mountain toward the north, so that all the trees fell upon me, and all the storms and winds beat upon me, and the Antichrist opened his jaws to devour me, then she came and comforted me, and married herself to me." Who is this vision of the divine that has made herself the wife of Boehme? He tells us more in the following description: "The Virgin is present before God and inclines herself to the spirit from which the virtue proceeds, out of which she (the chaste Virgin) is; this is God's Companion to the honor and joy of God; she appears or discovers herself in the wonders of God." Already we can start to see the Divine Vision is be lowered to the ideas of the material plane. This goes further in Boehme's physical desire for his bride Sophia: "You will gain the love of a kiss of the noble Sophia in the holy name Jesus, because she stands before the soul's door and knocks and warns the sinner of Godless ways. So, if he desires her love she is willing, and kisses him with a ray of her sweet love, through which the heart experiences joy." Sophia the divine has been brought down to the terrestrial images of sexual desire and pleasure. Or as Boehme has said: "Out of his lust, Adam lost the Virgin (Sophia) and in his lust he received the woman. But the Virgin still awaits him, and if he only should desire to enter into a new birth, she would receive him again with great honor. But the noble Virgin shows us the Door, and how we must enter again into Paradise."

It is obvious that the Christian/Catholic habit of degrading woman to a 'creature' is implied in Boehme's description of his relationship with Sophia. Boehme clearly separates the woman, who 'ate the fruit of the tree of knowledge' and offered it to Adam, and his pristine image of Sophia who is far, far above a common woman: "But the Wisdom of God is the Eternal Virgin, not woman: she is immaculate purity and virtue and stands as an image of God and likeness of the Trinity." In clearly separating 'woman' from 'Sophia" Boehme becomes superfluous with his praise that shines a spotlight on the chasm between the divine feminine and the human feminine. It reminds the reader of the 'curse of Eve' that has been the bane of women since the gender roles were switched from matriarchal to patriarchal. This misunderstanding of woman and the divine feminine smells of male priests in dresses demanding that only a man can be the bridge to the divine.

Boehme does mention frequently that the many different qualities of Sophia/Wisdom make her seem similar to the Male Holy Trinity.

He makes many analogies to this similarity in his works: "This All-Wisdom of God, who is the Virgin of beauty and an image of the Trinity, is in herself an image of man and the Angels and has her origin in the center of the cross, like a flower springing forth from the spirit of God." Or again in another context, "The Virgin is eternal, uncreated, and unborn: She is the All-Wisdom of God and a likeness of Divinity." Boehme all but clearly says that Sophia is a trinity unto herself. But something holds him back from crowning Sophia and placing her on the proper throne of the Divine Feminine Trinity.

Even though Boehme vacillates between total worship of Sophia and downgrading Wisdom's place in the divine cosmology, he does define the central role of Sophia in the spiritual development of the aspirant: "The image of God is human-virgin, not man or woman. Accordingly, the Fire-soul must be tempered in the fire of God and become brighter than pure gold, for it is the husband of the noble Sophia, out of the woman's seed. It is of the tincture of fire, just as Sophia is of the tincture of light. When the tincture of fire is completely purified, Sophia will be restored to it, Adam will again embrace his supremely honorable Bride, who was taken away from him at the time of his first sleep, and will become neither man nor woman, but only a branch on the jeweled tree of Christ that stands in God's paradise."

Jacob Boehme does not solve for us the 'mysterious conjunction' of soul to Sophia, the union of man and woman, or the question of whether there is a male and a female trinity that needs to wed. Boehme, like so many other Sophiologists, falls short of rounding off a complete Sophia-Christos Cosmology that can lead humanity into a future where the Wisdom of our world merges with the Love of Christ's world. From androgyne in heaven to androgyne in New Jerusalem, even though a marriage is involved, seems to be leaving something out of the picture. Too many questions arise from Boehme's incomplete cosmology that can't quite find a wholesome, untinged place for woman and divine woman—who supposedly teaches the seeker to became androgynous. This obvious missing piece to the puzzle led many other Sophiologists to accept Boehme's ideas with objections which later become newly imagined aspects of the mystery of the Threefold Sophia/Wisdom. Boehme leads us nearly as far as any other Sophianic thinker but can't resolve the gender issue when it comes to the spiritual world: "Humanity's rebirth as androgyne will mean acceptance within oneself of the whole of nature, the genuine revelation of man as microcosm. In the truth-birth of the integral human, both God and nature will be within and not outside him." This insight places the kingdom of God and Sophia in the human heart where the true tempering of humanity takes place.

Jacob Boehme's notion of the seven fountain spirits forming Eternal Nature, the material counterpart of the Virgin Wisdom, has parallels in the earlier ideas of Paracelsus who contemplated the essence of nature in terms of the four wombs (matrices, mothers) of fire, air, water, earth; and a tripartite scheme reflecting the Trinity (Father, Son, Holy Spirit).

For Paracelsus, a human being consists of three essences: body, soul, and spirit. Alchemically, these correspond to the *tria prima* ('three primes' or principles): solid, permanent element (salt); a combustible element (sulfur), and a fluid and changeable element (mercury). Salt represented the body; sulfur represented the soul (the emotions and desires); mercury represented the spirit (imagination, moral judgment, and the higher mental faculties). Jacob Boehme in his *Incarnation* refers to "Seven Mothers, out of which the substance of all Substances arises."

One of the key concepts in the theosophical tradition is the notion of the spiritual marriage of the Soul, or bridegroom, to Sophia. Clearly based on earlier German mystical traditions this is addressed by Boehme in *Christosophia*, or *The Way to Christ* (1624): "An Earnest, resolute will must pursue this, or it will not be Attained; for if the soul wishes to obtain Christ's conqueror's crown from the noble Virgin Sophia, it must court Her with Great love-desire. It must pray for it to Her in Her holiest of Names and must come before Her in highly chaste humility."

Hildegard of Bingen (1098–1179)

Hildegard of Bingen was a German Benedictine abbess and polymath active as a writer, composer, philosopher, mystic, visionary, and as a medical writer and practitioner. She founded the monasteries of Rupertsberg (c. 1150) and Eibingen (1165, replacing an Augustinian foundation of 1148). She wrote theological, botanical, and medicinal works, as well as letters, hymns, and antiphons for the liturgy. She also wrote poems, while supervising miniature illuminations in the *Rupertsberg Manuscript* of her first work about 26 visions she had entitled, *Scivias*; from the Latin phrase *Sci vias Domini* 'Know the Ways of the Lord' (1151 or 1152).

> "Antiphone for Divine Wisdom Sophia! You of the whirling wings, circling encompassing energy of God: You quicken the world in your clasp. One wing soars in heaven, one wing sweeps the Earth and the third flies all around us. Praise to Sophia! Let all the Earth praise her!"

> "And the Virgin of the Wisdom of God is the spirit of the pure element, and is therefore called a Virgin, because she is so chaste, and generates nothing; yet as the flaming spirit in man's body generates nothing, but opens all secrets, so also here; the Wisdom (or the eternal Virgin) of God opens all the great wonders in the holy element, for there are the essences, wherein the fruits of Paradise spring up."

Robert Fludd (1574–1637)

The English physician, scientist, and religious philosopher, Robert Fludd quotes often from the books of *Wisdom and Sirach (Ecclesiasticus)* in his writings. In the beginning of his *Sophia cum Moria* (1629) he invokes Wisdom (Sapientia) as his muse. In the Bodleian Library (University of Oxford) there is a manuscript in Fludd's hand entitled *Truth's Golden Harrow* (1682) in which he refers to Wisdom as feminine and as a person.

Another little-known English writer, Matthew Fowler (1617-1683) preached a sermon in Shrewsbury on biblical Wisdom which was published in pamphlet entitled *Sophia, or The Properties of Heavenly Wisdom*.

In the Bodleian Library, Oxford University, there is a unique copy of *Aurora Sapientiae, or The Dawn of Wisdom* (1629), attributed to Robert Ayshford, which reveals the existence of a theosophic circle in England in the 1620s, and therefore predates by several decades the emergence of the first major English theosophic circle around John Pordage in the 1650s. This book refers to Wisdom as feminine and expounds three principles of 'the Mystery of Wisdom.'

John Pordage (1607-1683)

John Pordage was an Anglican priest, astrologer, alchemist, and Christian mystic. He founded the 17th-century English Behmenist group, which would later become known as the Philadelphian Society when it was led by his disciple and successor, Jane Lead. In *Theologia Mystica*, Pordage describes a spiritual journey through the Sophianic cosmology of the three worlds of the 'Dark-Fire World,' the 'Fire-Light World' or common human experience, and the 'Light-Fire World' or paradise.

Portage published such works as: *The Fruitful Wonder, Theologia Mystica, Em griindlich philosophischei Sendschreiben, Vier Tractatlein*, and *Truth appearing through the Clouds of Undeserved Scandal*. A group of followers came to Pordage, including Ann Bathurst, led by Mrs. Jane Lead, who experienced a number of visions and later published them in her book *A Fountain of Gardens*. The group incorporated as The Philadelphian Society for the Advancement of Piety and Divine Philosophy in 1694. They rejected the idea of being a church, preferring the term society, and none of the members ceased their membership in existing churches. Mrs. Lead's visions were a central part of the group. Around 1694, she became a Christian Universalist. Many of the Philadelphian Society's views and writings, particularly those by

Jane Lead, remained influential among certain groups of Behmenists, Pietists, Radical Pietists, Christian mystics, and Esoteric Christians, such as the Society of the Woman in the Wilderness, and the Harmony Society, among others.

John Pordage hosted a circle of women mystics in Bradfield in Berkshire, where he was the rector. Later, the rectory became a communal house with contacts with other mystics and was a nodal point on a network that was linked to similar groups in London and elsewhere. Much of what is known about this Bradfield circle derives from the opposition it aroused, the anger of a Reading clergyman, Christopher Fowler, who engineered the ejection of Pordage from his Bradfield post in 1654. Reinstated after the Restoration, Pordage and his group nonetheless kept a low profile after this, eventually moving to London in 1668 after the death of his first wife.

Whilst Pordage wrote substantially in English throughout his life, his manuscripts have not survived. However, they were translated into German and some were published in German language editions. His only publications in English are: *A Treatise of Eternal Nature with Her Seven Eternal Forms* (1681), and *Theologia Mystica* (1683). Sophia was written in English and translated into German, then retranslated back into the original English. Sophia is written in diary form, a practice that Pordage seemed to encourage amongst members of his group. Through daily recordings of his visionary discoveries, Pordage allows the reader to chart the spirit's progress and journey. The diary consists of twenty-two entries. In Sophia, Pordage uses a diaristic form of his revelatory experiences as a technique to impart his teachings, recording the spiritual progress he makes towards understanding the nature of wisdom. He describes revelations relating to the creation of the new, magical Earth, the manifold powers of vegetation, and how one should develop the soul to enter an Eden-like environment: "…and in this paradise the soul-spirit receives the chalice of wisdom wherein is the elixir of life and the vegetablisitic quintessence."

Pordage was surrounded throughout his life by women visionaries. His first wife, Mary, was a key member of the original Bradfield group and may have been the first to experience visions. Other visionaries in this first circle include Mrs. Flavel, Mary Pocock, and Margaret Pinder, who experienced a number of visions.

Pordage's London circle included Joanna Oxenbridge and Ann Bathurst (1638- 1704). The best known of the women visionaries associated with Pordage was Jane Lead.

Sophia, by John Pordage

"The Holy Virgin reveals the New Jerusalem in the heart and soul of the newly reborn man. It is possible for the hidden door of Sophia to open so one can then meet the Virgin Sophia directly and experience peace. When the soul-spirit finally sinks down into itself the gate of the Depth of Wisdom is immediately thrown open to it and it is led into the holy eternal Principle of the Light-World. Then Wisdom is presented to him in the form of a sphere and the harmony of the microcosm with the macrocosm is demonstrated to him."

"Through four gates one must pass: the Gate of Conviction, The Gate of Destruction or Purification, the Gate of Dissolution, and the Gate of New Creation. Then comes the Day of Wisdom when Wisdom prepares her children by her fiery smelting oven which she has erected in their souls and spirits for the transfiguration of Mount Zion and the New Jerusalem. Endure the fire within until it has completely burned out all the evil seeds of astrayness, the Dragon and the Beast. I saw that this was the foundation and ground of the New Creation which was to be formed within me."

"Sophia is an invisible energy, pure energy, yea nothing other than pure energy; a sheer, pure act or working, a weaving motion; a sharp, quick, penetrating, circulating, working energy; an active, efficacious, and mighty energy. Thereupon Wisdom said to me: I wish to dwell with you upon this New Earth, to walk and talk with you here, and be found nowhere else but here. Here in my heart, in the midst of this New Earth, Wisdom has planted a central fire in order to ignite, to warm, to digest and to let spring forth that which here hand shall sow in this New Earth."

"Wisdom fed this New Earth with the clear, crystalline Water of Life like a river. Here were now fruits and herbs of Paradise that my eternal man was now to eat and live. These fruits were peace, love, gentleness, humility, unity, harmony, patience, brotherly love, purity, innocence, uprightness, constancy, loyalty, hope, faith, heartiness and other such heavenly herbs that are filled with divine energy and oil. Through these fruits eternal life and immortality flow."

"Just as Wisdom had formed my New Earth within me, she desired to proceed to create a New Heaven in my eternal spirit where she would shine like the Morning Star. She showed me how my inward New Earth depended upon the upper bodies and heavenly influences of my New Heaven within. Wisdom had become my motivator, my guide, my inner impulse, my penetrator, my life, my energy and my effectuator. She is my oil, my energy, my elixir, my gentleness, my joy and pleasure, my fecundity, my everything."

Theologia Mystica (1683) by John Pordage

"The third wonder which was presented to my intellectual sight was God's Wisdom, concerning whom I shall speak under these three heads. First, I shall speak of the birth and nativity of the Wisdom of God. Secondly, of its nature. Thirdly and lastly, of its office. First then, as to the birth and nativity of Wisdom, we are to know that it springs and flows from God's Eternal Eye, as from its Eternal root and original, and here it is fixed as in its proper seat and center; for it is by this Wisdom, that all the desire and motions of the Deity are most wisely ordered, conducted and governed, for it proceeds from and is seated in the same Eye with his desiring mind, and willing will, these three are in one another and penetrate through one another, and make up but one inseparable, indivisible power. I say that all three exist in the Eye as one power, yet distinguishable, and without the least disorder or confusion; the first is the wisdom, then the mind, and next the will; for as the wisdom proceeds from the Eye, so the mind proceeds from the wisdom, and the will from the mind."

"The Divine Wisdom is a flowing, moving power, a moving motion immediately proceeding from God's Eternal Eye. God's Wisdom is a bright ray or glance issuing from the Eye of Eternity; therefore, she is termed the brightness or clarity of the Godhead, and a pure breath or efflux from the majesty of the Almighty. We can say nothing of her but that she is the brightness and glance of the Eye of Eternity; who as she proceeds from the Eye, so she is moved by, and only by the same; for she is a mere passive bright shining virtue, that swiftly passeth through and pierceth all things, by reason of her high purity and subtlety, which can be compared with nothing better, than to a lustrous shining glance, being perfectly passive and moving only according to the motion of the Eye of the Father, which makes her more swift and piercing than anything whatsoever."

"In the first place this Wisdom is co-essential with the Holy Trinity: Because it hath been said it proceeds from the Trinity, as an outgoing ray, glance or brightness; now nothing doth immediately proceed from God, but what is of the nature and essence with him, and consequently what can this bright shining glance from the Eye of the majesty be else, but pure Deity, as proceeding from, and fixed in the Eye of Eternity."

"The second essential property of this Divine Wisdom is this, that she is coeternal with the ever-blessed Trinity. God was never without his Wisdom, nor the Eye of Eternity without this glance and bright ray which proceedeth from it; for else God could not have been an all-wise and all-knowing God."

"The third and last essential property of the Divine Wisdom, is her virgin purity, which consists in this, that she is free from all desire, will and motion of her own. She desires and wills nothing, but as the Eternal mind, and Will, desires and wills in her; she moves not, but as she is moved, and acts not, but as she is acted by the Spirit of Eternity."

"This flaming heart of Love is the sole object to which her regard is fastened continually: she receives nothing into herself but this divine Love, from the heart of God."

"What is the office of Wisdom in the Still Eternity? She is a revealer of the mysteries, and hidden wonders of the Deity. She is an enlightener of the Still Eternity. She is the golden key of the Eternal Eye, by which all the wonders of the Trinity are unlocked. I speak of Wisdom's existence with the Holy Trinity, in the Still Eternity, before ever Eternal Nature was brought forth."

Jane Lead (1624–1704)

Jane Lead joined Pordage's circle in 1663 and led the group after his death; which by then was known as the Philadelphians or Philadelphia Society. Jane Lead had many visions of Eternal Wisdom as Sophia, including a sequence of visions recorded in her published diary, *A*

Garden of Fountains (1670). In the first vision, Sophia said to her: "Behold I am God's Eternal Virgin-Wisdom, whom thou hast been enquiring after; I am to unseal the Treasures of God's deep Wisdom unto thee." Three days later, Sophia appeared again, radiant and wearing a crown, saying: "Behold me as thy Mother, and know thou art to enter into a Covenant, to obey the New Creation-Laws, that shall be revealed unto thee. A New Jerusalem, a castle all completed. A realm no enemy will ever have defeated, A Maiden who was raised as high as any goddess. This, Virgin, is your soul when she is God's beloved."

A Fountain of Gardens, A Personal Diary of her Spiritual Experiences and Encounters with the Godhead during 1677. By Jane Lead, 17th Century Prophetess of God

"My thoughts were much exercised upon Solomon's Choice, which was to find out the Noble Stone of Divine Wisdom; for by acquainting myself with her, all desirable good in Spiritual things would meet upon me. The Report and Fame that Solomon gave of Wisdom, did much excite me to seek her Favor and Friendship; demurring in myself from whence she was descended, still questioning whether she was a distinct Being from the Deity or no? Which while in this debate within my Mind, there came upon me an overshadowing bright Cloud, and in the midst of it the Figure of a Woman, most richly adorned with transparent Gold, her hair hanging down and her Face as the terrible Crystal for brightness; but her Countenance was sweet and mild. At which sight I was somewhat amazed; but immediately this Voice came, saying, Behold I am God's Eternal Virgin-Wisdom, whom thou hast been enquiring after; I am to unseal the Treasures of God's deep Wisdom unto thee, and will be as Rebecca was unto Jacob, a true Natural Mother; for out of my Womb thou shalt be brought forth after the manner of a Spirit, Conceived and Born again: this thou shalt know by a New Motion of Life, stirring and giving a restlessness, till Wisdom be born within the inward parts of thy Soul."

"Now after three days, sitting under a Tree, the same Figure in greater Glory did appear, with a Crown upon her Head, full of Majesty; saying, Behold me as thy Mother, and know thou art to enter into Covenant, to obey the New Creation Laws, that shall be revealed unto thee. Then did she hold out a Golden Book with three Seals upon it, saying, Herein lieth hidden the deep Wonders of Jehovah's Wisdom, which hath been sealed up, that none could, or ever shall break up, but such as of her Virgin-Offspring shall appear to be; who will her Laws receive, and keep, as they shall spring daily in the New Heart and Mind. This Appearance, and Words, was wonderfully sweet and refreshing in my Soul; at which I bowed and prostrated at her Feet; promising to be obedient to all her Laws."

"So, after six days the Vision appeared again, with a Train of Virgin-Spirits, and with an Angelical Host; and called to me to come and see the Virgin Queen, with her first-born Children; asking me, Whether I was willing to be joined amongst this Virgin Company? At which I replied, All willing to offer up myself most free: Then immediately I was encompassed about with this Heavenly Host, and made a Spirit of Light. Then these Words from the Virgin proceeded, saying, I shall now cease to appear in a Visible Figure unto thee, but I will not fail to transfigure myself in thy mind; and there open the Spring of Wisdom and Understanding, that so thou mayest come to know the only True God, in and by the formation of Christ, the anointed Prophet in thee; that shall reveal great and wonderful things unto thee, that are to be made known, and public, in its time and day: Therefore be watchful, and to thy Mother Wisdom's Counsel give good heed, and thou shalt greatly prosper, and succeed the Prophets and Apostles to perfect what was left behind, for completing as to Christ the Fulness of God's great Mystery: So go on, and nothing fear, or doubt; for I thy Glass for Divine Seeing shall evermore stand before thee."

"The Mind of Wisdom thus opened itself in me, as I waited in my Spirit upon her, she did shew me what Key would open the Great Mystery, which lay deeply hid in myself. It was wrought and carved out of such pure Gold, as had passed through many Fires; many Keys I had tried, but could not turn in this secret enclosed Lock, but still it shut upon me, though I thought I had that Key which was compounded of such Metals, as would have made its entrance, as Love, Faith, Patience, Humility, which with strong Supplication and Prayer, I presented, as the Key of the work."

"I knew nothing by myself, as to those working Properties from Nature, and Creature, and the Wheel of the Motion standing still, another moved from a Central Fire; so that I felt myself Transmuted into one pure Flame. Then heard I her Voice thus; Sequester and draw out of thy Animal Sensitive Life, that is too gross: I cannot appear till that disappear."

"I have learned to observe her Time and Seasons; I witness her opening as in the twinkling of an Eye, a pure, bright, subtle, swift Spirit, a working Motion, a Circling Fire, a penetrating Oil."

"Oh, how little did I understand, till Wisdom unsealed and opened her Testimony, lighting my Lamp from her Seven Pillars of Fire, which now go before me, that my Way may no more be dark: Who hath made good her Promise; for I felt her strong Impulse, and her Furnace prepared, burning as an Oven."

"Then she with her Flaming Heart did present herself to me. Out of which Heart sprouted forth a Tree, with Twelve Branches having upon the Root of it engraved, GOD is the Pith, Life and Virtue, that maketh the Heart thus Fruitful, in various opening and quickening Powers, giving forth according to each Branch, a different and peculiar Fruit. Then said she to me, Here doth lie the Mystery: do thou it come and see, how out of the Flames these Branches put forth green and palpable Fruits, that are not yet grown, yet thou with Patience must still wait till to perfection of ripeness they be grown in thee; then of the first Fruits of this Tree thou shalt bring to thy God as an Offering, who will accept it as a pure Offering. So that there is no need of anything more to be done but to watch the Fire, that it may never go out, until it be finished, and be kept in a gentle nourishing Heat, till it come to its Perfection."

"But know, you have a Mother of a higher degree, that is more true and natural to your Spirits: and she would now you should come to understand, and know her to be the Everlasting Wisdom of the Mighty God, that can do much above Nature and Creature for you: Who would have you desert all other, and hear, and learn from her mouth; from which doth drop the Law of Love and Kindness."

The Revelation of An Essay Towards the Unsealing, Opening, and Discovering the Seven Seals, the Seven Thunders, and the New Jerusalem State, by Jane Lead

"Now to proceed to what the Lord hath opened to me, from this Figure of the Woman, who is represented here as travailing in Birth; intimating to us that as by a Woman, a sinful Offspring was brought forth, in which Sorrow, Sin and the Curse had Dominion; so from this Eternal Virgin-Wisdom, a Birth is to be born, in which nothing but Joy, Life, Blessing and Eternal Power and Dominion shall take place. This Virgin, Adam had in himself, before ever Eve was taken out of him; but she withdrew as soon as Adam looked Outward, as if he were not sufficient of himself to increase and multiply for the replenishing of Paradise, God having created him Male and Female in himself."

"Now we are advanced one step higher towards Wisdom's heavenly Throne, from whence her Golden Sceptre is stretched forth to lay hold on, which passeth through and beyond every elementary Cloud, which the sensitive Life hath raised, so as we could not see our way to that sparkling Rock of the Deity; for which cause the bright Sun now shines from her Eternal Orb, through the dark Clouds, that we might see every ascending degree, twisting and winding so intricately, that without a Guide expressly sent down from that Sphere, there is no possibility ever to come to any one of her Gates which lead to the New-Jerusalem."

The Laws of Paradise Given forth by Wisdom To A Translated Spirit, by Jane Lead

"The First Commandment: Thou shalt own, and bear witness to the True God, manifested through his Virgin Wisdom, as come to restore Nature to its own Eternal Originality, which consisted in Light, Purity, and Power: And thou shalt have no other God live in thee but Jehovah, whose Arm alone hath redeemed, and brought thee into thy Primitive Liberty, and Sovereignty again, through the Internal Dying, as the acceptable Propitiation."

"The Fifth Commandment: Here thou art required to honor thy Eternal Father, and Wisdom, thy true Natural Mother, which hath brought thee forth, and up, to that stature and degree in which thou now art: hence no less is expected from thee; and as my Fear and Love is with thee, so my Honor must be thy great Concern; that so length of days may be thy Blessing from thy Father, and Me, for evermore."

"But to answer to the thoughts of thine Heart, which saith, Oh! my Mother, wherein, and how may I come to laud and honor God my Father, and Wisdom, my Mother, according as thy First-born Son, my Pattern, hath in his Paradisiacal Body done, while he was in this World. Consider thy Jesus then in his high and holy Calling, from his Birth to his Ascension, holding forth one pure Act of Glorifying his Father, in observing the Law of Wisdom his Mother, from whose Eternal Virgin Nature he had his Existence: And now know, that as thou hast had thy Birth from me, so thou art in the same Line to run parallel: having passed through the Birth-death, answerable to him that was before thee, whom thou art to follow after in hallowing that Great name, which is secret, and known but too few."

"Then spake Wisdom's Spirit in me, What hast thou seen here but the Magical Eye, which is an All-seeing globe, that includeth all Light, Power, and Might within its Circle, so that there is no need to go out for any Supply, for that all lieth within the compass of this All-generating Eye: And like as thou didst see it rise in a Moment, so shall it give new Existencies from its own in the twinkling of an Eye. This is the manner of Paradisiacal Living, quite different from the Way of the Inhabitants of the Outward World. But to thee that art come out and separated from these, my Counsel is, that thou entirely rest and depend upon this Divine Magical Eye, and never wander out from it; so will it become to thee thy Basket and thy Store: So will it be to thee thy Fountain-blessing, and thou shalt need to know no more, and to take care of no more, than what this will give forth to thee. For it is an endless Procreating Source that still puts forth New Births altogether Supernatural, to which belongs a pure, sublime, organic Body, having highly irradiated Senses, with uncorrupted, and divine Rationality, such as is grounded upon what is Seen and Known by This Eye. Hence may be demonstrated the Singularity of those Holy Beings, which are generated from this Source and Origin."

Ann Bathurst (1638–1704)

Ann Bathurst was a member of Pordage's London circle who, in a diary entry for September 1679, describes her spiritual marriage with Sophia as the fulfillment of her life.

Gottfried Arnold (1666–1714)

Another Sophianic thinker was Gottfried Arnold, a German theologian and professor of church history and author of over fifty books. His book entitled: *The Mystery of the Holy Sophia* (1700) is divided into two parts. In part one, Arnold, whilst obviously influenced by Boehme and Pordage, quotes extensively from *Proverbs*, *Sirach*, and the writings of the early Christian writers and mystics on Wisdom. In part two, Arnold presents to the reader his 'poetical proverbs' in praise of Wisdom, inspired by the *Song of Songs* in the *Old Testament*. These poems show Arnold's belief in a personal Sophia who is his "Queen, his friend and his bride." In the first part of his book, he devotes an entire chapter to "a subject so important, certain and essential," namely the spiritual marriage with Sophia.

Arnold defines Sophia: "Sophia is an eternal Being, which before all creatures, with the Holy Trinity, is eternal, and remains forever in eternity. She is above the Angels; the eternal wisdom has her root alone in the Godhead itself, and through her Being it reveals itself. Sophia is not a Person outside the Trinity. The spirit of Jesus and the spirit of Sophia are not separate. The eternal Sophia urges men through being reborn to return to completeness in Paradise, to which she will lead them."

In Gottfried Arnold we find a philosopher who was able to combine a profound knowledge of Wisdom based on the writings of the previous two thousand years, with the personal knowledge of Wisdom as Sophia based on personal introspection and contemplation. But Arnold did not speculate on Sophia, nor did he have a personal, direct revelation of her. His work is excellent as historical scholarship but falls short of 'knowing' Sophia in her many forms.

One of Arnold's best poems praises Sophia as his strength:

> Let reason laugh
> So very much at my simplicity:
> Even more will I sing
> About the object of my love.
> O Sophia, my strength
> O She is my heroine,
> And everything that I need.
> And without Her know I
> Myself to be unprepared for battle
> Be Thou mine, Thou Heroine, Thou,
> God's pure life.
> Let me be suspended unharmed
> In peace that is assured.
> Hold me tightly to You
> Protect me with your cloak!
> And when the enemy's power mounts,
> So, fight and be victorious in me!

Johann Georg Gichtel (1638–1710)

Moving from Germany in 1668 to escape persecution, Gichtel spent the rest of life teaching and writing in Amsterdam, establishing The Angelic Brethren. He is best known for his editing of Boehme's writing, the *Theosophia Revelata*, and for his own letters, published in the *Theosophia Practica*. Gichtel's major contribution to theosophy was to develop the language of Theosophic/Sophianic practice.

Gichtel believed that Sophia tests all those who seek her. The heavenly Sophia plays with all her wooers, and tries them, whether they are serious; for where there is no honest earnestness, the marriage is long delayed. This renewal of the spiritual marriage was also to occur for the remaining members of the Angelic Brotherhood in the decades after Gichtel's death. Like other mystics before and since, Gichtel believed in inner contemplation where "if we are attended by this teacher within us" assuredly "we should require no teacher without us." For Gichtel this inner teacher was Sophia.

Novalis (1772–1801)

Georg Friedrich Philipp von Hardenburg (Novalis) was born May 2nd, 1772, in Oberwiederstedt, Prussian Saxony, into a family of Protestant Lower Saxon nobility. His father was the director of a salt mine. He was the eldest son in a large family, consisting of ten children beside himself. As he had from birth been of poor health and wholly self-absorbed, he appeared in the first years of life to be a child who was removed and distance from his surroundings. A serious illness struck him down in his ninth year, confining him to his bed for months. Suddenly, after the illness, his inner faculties developed creating a remarkable memory, concentration, and a gift of observation wrought with a deep religious and artistic sense. Novalis had an open and profound relationship with Sophia.

Fragments
"In the bosom of the heavenly bride, Sophia, the birth of the Christ Spirit comes to pass within the human soul."

"When I believe that Sophia is about me and may appear, and while I act in keeping with this faith, she is about me indeed and at last surely does appear to me—in precisely the place where I thought I was myself, within me."

"I have a beloved, Sophia—Philo-Sophia is her name."

Klingsor's Fairy Tale
"The kingdom of eternity is founded,
By love and peace all strife has been impounded,
The dreams of pain are gone, to plague us never,
Sophia is priestess of all hearts forever."

Louis Claude de Saint-Martin (1743–1803)

Saint-Martin was a French philosopher, known as 'le philosophe inconnu,' ('the unknown philosopher') the name under which his works were published; he was very influential in various European mystical and theosophical movements and became the inspiration for the founding of the Martinist Order. He was the first to translate the writings of Jacob Boehme from German into French. His later years were devoted almost entirely to the composition of his chief works and to the translation of Boehme. His published letters show that he was interested in spiritualism, magnetic treatments, magical evocation, and the works of Emanuel Swedenborg.

Man: His True Nature and Ministry
"I have no doubt she may be born in our center, I have no doubt that the Divine Word can also be born there by her means, as he was thus born in Mary. All the saints and all the elect share this Sophia. The Spirit of Jesus and the Spirit of

Wisdom are not two different spirits; but rather are one spirit and one inseparable Essence."

Friedrich von Schiller (Nov. 10, 1759–May 9, 1805)

The Veiled Image at Saïs
A youth, whom wisdom's warm desire had lured
  To learn the secret lore of Egypt's priests,
  To Saïs came. And soon, from step to step
  Of upward mystery, swept his rapid soul!
  Still ever sped the glorious Hope along,
Nor could the parch'd Impatience halt, appeased
  By the calm answer of the Hierophant —
  "What have I, if I have not all," he sigh'd;
  "And giv'st thou but the little and the more?
  Does thy truth dwindle to the gauge of gold,
  A sum that man may smaller or less small
  Possess and count—subtract or add to—still?
    Is not TRUTH one and indivisible?
    Take from the Harmony a single tone
    A single tint take from the Iris bow —
  And lo! what once was all, is nothing—while
    Fails to the lovely whole one tint or tone!"

.

  They stood within the temple's silent dome,
And, as the young man paused abrupt, his gaze
    Upon a veil'd and giant IMAGE fell:
    Amazed he turn'd unto his guide—
      "And what
  Towers, yonder, vast beneath the veil?"
        "THE TRUTH,"
      Answered the Priest.
    "And have I for the truth

Panted and struggled with a lonely soul,
And yon the thin and ceremonial robe
That wraps her from mine eyes?"

.

Replied the Priest,
"There shrouds herself the still Divinity.
Hear, and revere her best: "Till I this veil
Lift—may no mortal-born presume to raise;
And who with guilty and unhallow'd hand
Too soon profanes the Holy and Forbidden —
He," says the goddess. —
"Well?"
"SHALL SEE THE TRUTH!"
"And wond'rous oracle; and hast thou never
Lifted the veil?"
"No! nor desired to raise!"
"What! nor desired? O strange, incurious heart,
Here the thin barrier—there reveal'd the truth!"
Mildly return'd the priestly master: "Son,
More mighty than thou dream'st of, Holy Law
Spreads interwoven in yon slender web,
Air-light to touch—lead-heavy to the soul!"

.

The young man, thoughtful, turn'd him to his home,
And the sharp fever of the Wish to Know
Robb'd night of sleep. Around his couch he roll'd,
Till midnight hatch'd resolve —
"Unto the shrine!"
Stealthily on, the involuntary tread
Bears him—he gains the boundary, scales the wall,
And midway in the inmost, holiest dome,
Strides with adventurous step the daring man.

.

Now halts he where the lifeless Silence sleeps
In the embrace of mournful Solitude; —
Silence unstirr'd—save where the guilty tread
Call'd the dull echo from mysterious vaults!

High from the opening of the dome above,
Came with wan smile the silver-shining moon.
And, awful as some pale presiding god,
Dim-gleaming through the hush of that large gloom,
In its wan veil the Giant Image stood.

With an unsteady step he onward past,
Already touch'd the violating hand
The Holy—and recoil'd! a shudder thrill'd
His limbs, fire-hot and icy-cold in turns,
As if invisible arms would pluck the soul
Back from the deed.
"O miserable man!
What would'st thou?" (Thus, within the inmost heart
Murmur'd the warning whisper.) "Wilt thou dare
The All-hallow'd to profane? No mortal-born"
(So spake the oracular word)—"may lift the veil
Till I myself shall raise!" Yet said it not —
The same oracular word—"who lifts the veil
Shall see the truth?" Behind, be what there may,
I dare the hazard—"I will lift the veil" —
Loud rang his shouting voice—"and I will see!"
'SEE!'
A lengthen'd echo, mocking, shrill'd again!
He spoke and rais'd the veil! And ask'st thou what
Unto the sacrilegious gaze lay bare?
I know not—pale and senseless, stretch'd before

> The statue of the great Egyptian queen,
> The priests beheld him at the dawn of day;
> But what he saw, or what did there befall,
> His lips reveal'd not. Ever from his heart
> Was fled the sweet serenity of life,
> And the deep anguish dug the early grave
> "Woe—woe to him"—such were his warning words,
> Answering some curious and impetuous brain,
> "Woe—for her face shall charm him never more!
> Woe—woe to him who treads through Guilt to TRUTH!"

Harmonist Movement (1805)

The followers in the Harmonist Movement lived their lives for Sophia in every way. One could say that they were a true 'religion of Sophia.' They would become enraptured with their pursuit of Sophia to the point that they actually thought they physically encountered Her in many ways. Some believed that Sophia would convey a spiritual kiss that would vouchsafe their souls. They truly loved Sophia in all aspects of their lives and believed She became physical in Her manifestations.

> *Harmonist's Hymn Number 394*
> Sophia, from your glances rapture flows into my heart
> When a friendly love delights my soul;
> O the pure instincts your charm arouses in me;
> This flame feeds the blessed heavenly love.
> Beloved, let me experience the gentleness and faith if we were united,
> With your sweet caress many an anxious hour would flee,
> My wounds would be healed,
> Pure fire would be drawn to love.
> Your demeanor reveals that your heart treasures me;
> What joy, what rapture when you are close to me.

Dip your brush into the rays of the Sun to paint me your lovely picture;
Your lips and cheeks scarlet
Should my mouth and heart be pressed thereon,
My soul and spirit would be refreshed.
O your walk is without care; your work is the joy of love;
Gentle and white as the lily is your sign on my breast,
For the hand of harmony is the throne of love complete;
Beloved, if you live with us, you are our spiritual Sun.

H. P. Blavatsky (Aug. 12, 1831–May 8, 1891)

Blavatsky tends to be the most comprehensive philosopher of comparative religions available, and often has the most succinct but far-reaching opinion on spiritual topics. Most of the descriptions we have presented up to this point are summarized in her sweeping statements. From the primal divinity to the being of love, Sophia is described in many of her forms found in sacred scripture. This is enigmatic, just as Sophia's evolution is a conundrum, her nature ever-changing. Blavatsky doesn't pin a final definition on Sophia because She is evolving alongside humanity. She cannot be described comprehensively without framing the description within its own historical perspective. A brilliant scholar, Blavatsky does not limit Sophia. She finds Her many aspects in a variety of Goddesses.

The Secret Doctrine
"The Gnostic Sophia, 'Wisdom' who is 'the Mother' of Ogdoad, is the Holy Ghost and the Creator of all, as in the ancient systems. The 'father' is a far later invention. The earliest manifested Logos was female everywhere—the mother of the seven planetary powers. The various Cosmogonies show that the Archaic Universal Soul was held by every nation as the 'Mind' of the Demiurgic Creator; and that it was called the

'Mother,' Sophia with the Gnostics (or the female Wisdom), the Sephira with the Jews, Saraswati or Vach, with the Hindus, the Holy Ghost being a female Principle. The female Soul of the World or the 'Great Deep;' the deity, from which these two in one have their being, is ever concealed and called the 'Hidden One,' connected only indirectly with Creation."

"The Spiritual substance sent forth by the Infinite Light is the first Sephira or Shekinah: Sephira exoterically contains all the other nine Sephiroths in her. Esoterically she contains but two. These two Sephiroths called, Father, Abba, and Mother, Amona [Aima], are the duad or the double-sexed logos from which issued the other seven Sephiroths. In the Kabala, Sephira is the same as Shekinah, and is, in other synthesis, the wife, daughter, and mother of the 'Heavenly man,' Adam Kadmon, and is even identical with him, just as Vach is identical with Brahma, and is called the female Logos. Moreover, she is called 'the Mother of the Veda, since it is through her power that Brahma revealed them, and also owing to her power that he produced the Universe'; i.e., through speech, words, and numbers. Again, as goddess of Speech and of Sound, and a permutation of Aditi—She is Chaos, in one sense. At any rate, she is the 'Mother of the gods.' Whether as Aditi, or the divine Sophia of the Greek Gnostics, she is the mother of the seven sons: the 'Angels of the Face of the Deep,' or the 'Great Green One' of the 'Book of the Dead.'"

Johann Jacob Wirz (1778–1858)

The little-known Swiss visionary, Johann Jacob Wirz began to receive visions of Sophia as divine Wisdom in 1823, these forming the basis of the beliefs of the Nazarene Community. His understanding of Wisdom is very much in the earlier tradition of journals he kept, much as Pordage and Gichtel had done a century earlier. Many of these entries are in the form of a dialogue between Wirz and his Mother, Wisdom, as in this entry for February 8, 1836: "Wisdom spoke: Endeavour to practice and hold what your Mother, heavenly Wisdom, has said to you. It is certainly difficult to travel forth in nature, wherein you dwell, on the superior way without interruption, and to make all hindrances into favorable circumstances; but faith, practiced in weakness, develops faith, until it finally becomes power. You have last night, on the end of the year, engaged in a new promise for your heavenly Mother. This she has heard better than you hear your own voice. She has taken your vow and today answers you as follows, 'Blessed are the souls that do not pledge alone to the holy Wisdom, but rather through the vow long to become wholly owned by her. To them she will be in everything.'"

Anna Bonus Kingsford (Sep. 16, 1846–Feb. 22, 1888)

Anna Kingsford was an English anti-vivisectionist, vegetarian and women's right campaigner who wrote many books including, *The Woman Clothed with the Sun, The Virgin of the World, The Perfect Way*, and numerous other writings. She was the first English woman to obtain a degree in medicine. She founded the Food Reform Movement, studied Buddhism and Gnosticism and finally became active in the Theosophical movement in England, becoming president of the London Lodge. She founded the Hermetic Society with Edward Maitland. Kingsford had many visions of Sophia and held direct communication with Sophia throughout her life.

> *Concerning the Mysteries*
> "In the Trinity of the Unmanifest, the Great Deep, or Ocean of Infinitude—Sophia—corresponds to Mary and has for Spouse the creative Energy of whom is begotten the Manifestor, Adonai, the Lord. This 'Mother' is co-equal with the Father, being primary and eternal. In Manifestation the 'Mother' is derived, being born of Time and has for Father the Planet-

God, for our planet Iacchos so that the paternity of the First Person of the Trinity is vicarious only. It is said that the Blessed Virgin Mary is the Daughter, Spouse, and Mother of God."

Vladimir Solovyov (Jan. 28, 1853–Aug. 13, 1900)

Vladimir Solovyov's entrance into Sophiological studies is inextricable from a series of religious experiences he had, the first of which occurred on the Feast of the Ascension when he was nine years old. Later, in the British Museum, he had a second experience as a vision of one he called his 'eternal friend' who instructed him to meet her in Egypt. He traveled to Egypt and there met her once again in the desert. He recorded these experiences with her in his autobiographical poem, *Three Meetings*. Solovyov calls Sophia 'the guardian Angel of the world' and the agent of 'pan-unity' and connects Sophia to Christ, the Virgin Mary, and the 'church.'

> "All in azure did my empress
> Appear today before me.
> My heart beat in sweet rapture
> And my soul began to shine
> With quiet light in rays of the dawning day.
> But in the distance, burning low
> The cruel flame of the Earthly fire still glowed."

Rudolf Steiner (Feb. 27, 1861–Mar. 30, 1925)

Steiner gives us many excellent descriptions of Sophia in our time and throughout history. Dr. Steiner was clairvoyant; but also was a spiritual scientist who taught others how to develop the forces to create new spiritual sense organs that can perceive Sophia. His descriptions make distinctions that other writers tend to blend together or mix into a generalized picture of Sophia. Sophia has distinct aspects that evolve together with humanity, and they are united in a way that is seldom described. As the greatest prophet of Sophia in our times, Steiner's insights are profound and far-reaching.

The Search for the New Isis
"It is not on account of something happening by itself from without that Christ will be able to appear again in his spiritual form in the course of the twentieth century; but rather through human beings finding the force represented by the Holy Sophia. The tendency in recent times has been to lose precisely this Isis force, this Mary force, which has been stamped out through that which has arisen within the modern consciousness of humanity. And the more recent confessions have partly obliterated a perspective concerning Mary."

"To a certain extent this is the mystery of modern mankind, that basically Mary-Isis has been killed, and that she must be sought again, sought in the widespread heavenly realms with the power which Christ is able to kindle within us when we devote ourselves to him in the right way. Man has learned to relate to the Sophia through his Consciousness-Soul, to associate her directly with human beings. This happened during the Consciousness-Soul Period [1,414 AD-3,574 AD]. The Sophia has therefore become the Being that elucidates man. Once having entered into humanity, she has to take up this human nature and set it objectively before mankind. She detaches herself again but takes with her what man is and places herself outside him, no longer merely as Sophia but as Anthroposophia, as that Sophia who has passed through the soul of man, through man's being, and henceforth bears this being of man within herself."

"Just as the Egyptians looked from Isis to Osiris, so we must learn to look again to the new Isis, the Holy Sophia. The Christ will appear in spiritual form during the 20th century, not through an external happening, but inasmuch as human beings find that force which is represented by the Holy Sophia. The present age has the tendency to lose this Isis-force, this force of the Mary. It was killed by all that arose with the modern consciousness of mankind [materialism]. New forms of religion have in part exterminated just this view of Mary. This is the mystery of modern humanity. The Mary-Isis [Sophia] has been killed, and she must be sought in the wide space of heaven, with that force that Christ can awaken in us. What we need in our time is not knowledge of Christ, it is the Wisdom, the Sophia, of Christ."

"Isis Sophia, Wisdom of God:
Lucifer has slain her,
And on the wings of the world-wide Forces
Carried her hence into Cosmic space.
Christ-will
Working in humanity,
Shall wrest from Lucifer
And on the boats of Spirit-knowledge
Call to new life is souls of humans
Isis-Sophia, Wisdom of God."

A. E., George William Russell (Apr. 10, 1867–Jul. 17, 1935)

A. E. gives the most complete description of Sophia helping the faithful soul attain Imagination, Inspiration, and Intuition that can be found outside of spiritual scientific authors. He uses simple language to create fantastic imagery that paints the reality of Sophia working with our souls. We recommend that everyone read his book *The Candle of Vision* as a master plan for the development of the soul awakening to the spirit.

The Candle of Vision
"Of the Mother of the gods, I have already said she is the first spiritual form of matter, and therefore Beauty. As every being emerges out of her womb clothed with form, she is the Mighty Mother, and as Mother of All she is that divine compassion which exists beyond and is the final arbiter of the justice of the gods. Her heart will be in ours when ours forgive."

Pavel Florensky (Jan. 21, 1882–Dec 8, 1937)

Pavel Florensky was a priest and theologian in the Russian Orthodox Church. He was a gifted mathematician, scientist, and electrical engineer who also made an impact on art history and linguistics. Florensky's 1914 book, *The Pillar and Ground of Truth*, is a mystical treatise, theological meditation, and a book of emblems. In *Letter Ten: Sophia*, he explains Sophia's nature and her relationship with the Holy Trinity.

The Pillar and the Foundation of Truth
"Sophia is the Great Root of the whole creation. Sophia is the first-created being of the creaturely world, with the creative love of God. In relation to the creaturely world Sophia is the Guardian Angel of the world, the Ideal nature of the world. If Sophia is the entire Creation, then the soul and conscience of creation, humanity, is above all Sophia. If Sophia is all of humanity, then the soul and conscience of humanity, the Church, is above all Sophia. If Sophia is the Church, then the soul and conscience of the Church, the Saints, is above all Sophia. If Sophia is the Church of Saints, then the soul and conscience of the Church of Saints is the Intercessor and Mediatrix on behalf of the creation before the Word of God, who judges and divides creation in two, the Mother of God, is

once again above all Sophia. But the true sign of the Blessed Mary is manifested in her Virginity, the beauty of her soul."

Andrej Belyj (Oct. 26, 1880–Jan. 8, 1934)

Belyj was a Russian novelist, Symbolist poet, theorist, and literary critic. He was a committed anthroposophist and follower of Rudolf Steiner. His novel *Petersburg* was regarded by Vladimir Nabokov as the third-greatest masterpiece of modernist literature. The Andrei Bely Prize is one of the most important prizes in Russian literature. His poems were set to music and performed by Russian singer-songwriters.

Belyj had a profound relationship with Sophia. Through his insight concerning Sophia, he describes her as "the door of love opening from heaven to earth that can inform all love," as he implies in the last sentence of the selection below. His belief in the heavenly marriage gives equal credence to Sophia and makes her a co-creator with Christ. Here is the true nature of the soul and spirit uniting as one beautifully displayed.

> *Selected Essays*
> "The ideas of the world and mankind coincide conditionally for us. The idea of the world may be called the world soul. The world soul, Sophia according to Soloviev, is perfect humanity, eternally enclosed in the divine nature of Christ. Here the mystical nature of the church coincides with the image of the eternal feminine, the bride of the Lamb. Here are the Alpha and Omega of true love. Christ's relation to the church—that of the bridegroom to the bride—is an unfathomable universal symbol. This symbol illuminates every ultimate love."

Sergei Bulgakov (Jul. 28, 1871–Jul. 13, 1944)

Sergei Bulgakov was a Russian Orthodox priest, philosopher, and theologian who created a comprehensive cosmology of Sophia. Bulgakov believed Sophia was an integral part of creation and identifies Sophia as the 'ousia' [true being] of the Trinity and a kind of fourth hypostasis called the Virgin. She is simultaneously created and divine and is seen as the 'world soul.' Even the church itself is seen as an aspect of Sophia. His book, *Sophia the Wisdom of God: An Outline* is considered to be one of the most complete theologies of Sophia that explains the difference between a created and an uncreated being.

> *The Pillar and Foundation of the Truth*
> "God the Father creates the world by Sophia, which is the revelation of the Son and the Holy Spirit. The divine Sophia, as the revelation of the Logos, is the all-embracing unity, which contains within itself all the fullness of the world of ideas. In Sophia, the fullness of the ideal forms contained in the Word is reflected in creation. The primary foundation of the world is rooted in the divine Sophia. Thus, God created the world by the Word and by the Holy Spirit, as they are manifested in Wisdom. Wisdom in creation is ontologically identical with its prototype, the same Wisdom that exists in God. It exists by the power of his Godhead, even though this Wisdom exists outside of God. The created world is none other than the creaturely Sophia. God communicates Sophia, the creaturely Sophia, to creation. This great being [Sophia], both royal and feminine, who is she, then but the truest humanity, the purest and most whole of beings, the macrocosmic whole, the living soul of nature and of the Universe eternally united and uniting in the process of time with the Divine and unity with all that is."

Nikolai Berdyaev (Mar. 18, 1874–Mar. 24, 1948)

Berdyaev was deeply influenced by Solovyov and was a close friend of Bulgakov. Berdyaev made significant contributions to religious existentialism with his visionary eschatological thought. He placed great emphasis on the nature of 'the church' as a manifestation and body of Sophia. Berdyaev was also greatly indebted to the works of

Jacob Boehme but is basically a mystic philosopher who developed a thorough complementary philosophy of Sophianic thought.

> *Freedom and Spirit*
> "The Divine Wisdom is the eternal Virgin and not woman, she is unsullied purity and chastity and she appears as the image of God and the image of the Trinity. The Virgin is from all eternity, she is uncreated and unbegotten; she is the Divine Wisdom and the image of Divinity. Wisdom is eternal virginity and not eternal femininity, for the wisdom-cult is that of the Virgin and not that of the feminine principle which is the result of division and the Fall. That is why the cult of Wisdom is almost identical with that of the Virgin Mary, the Mother of God."

Valentin Tomberg (Feb. 26, 1900–Feb. 24, 1973)

Tomberg was a Russian esotericist who was, at one time, a follower of Dr. Rudolf Steiner, the founder of Anthroposophy. Tomberg extracted the best from Steiner, Papus, and Louis Claude de St. Martin et al. to create his anonymous book: *Meditations on the Tarot: A Journey into Christian Hermeticism*. In it he describes a threefold Sophia, or divine feminine trinity.

> *Meditations on the Tarot: A Journey into Christian Hermeticism.*
> "It is she—the 'Virgin of light' of the *Pistis Sophia*, the Wisdom Sung of by Solomon, the Shekinah of the Kabbalah, the Mother, the Virgin, the pure celestial Mary—who is the soul of the light of the three luminaries, is, as a whole, the aspiration to participation in knowledge of the Father, Son, and Holy Spirit, and the Mother, Daughter, and Holy Soul. No one understands the Holy Trinity but by Mary-Sophia. The light of the Holy Trinity became flesh in Mary—Sophia—the light. The *Zohar* puts forward the idea of the luminous Holy Trinity as the combination of the male and female Trinities combined.

This 'dogma of the heart' [Sophia] is so powerful that the time will come when it will result in official recognition from the Church [Roman Catholic] and will be formulated raising maternal love to the level of the Luminous Holy Trinity."

Pierre Teilhard de Chardin (May 1, 1881–Apr. 10, 1955)

Pierre Teilhard de Chardin was a French Jesuit priest, scientist, paleontologist, theologian, philosopher, and teacher. He was Darwinian in outlook and the author of several influential theological and philosophical books. He took part in the discovery of Peking Man and conceived the vitalist idea of the Omega Point and developed the concept of the Noosphere. He was not well received by Catholic theologians or scientists, bordering on accusations of heresy. His love of Sophia was hidden in his writings during his life and only came to surface after his death. The poem, *The Eternal Feminine* is one of the most profound declarations of Sophia ever written.

> *The Eternal Feminine*
> "When the world was born, I came into being. Before the centuries were made, I issued from the hand of God—half-formed yet destined to grow in beauty from age to age, the handmaid of his work. Everything in the Universe is made by union and generation—by the coming together of elements that seek out one another, melt together two by two, and are born again in a third. Through me, all things have their movement and are made to work as one. I am the beauty running through the world, to make it associate in ordered groups: the ideal held up before the world to make it ascend. I am the Eternal Feminine. I was the bond that thus held together the foundations of the Universe. I am the single radiance by which all this is aroused and within which it is vibrant. I am the Church, the bride of Christ. I am Mary the Virgin, mother of all humankind."

Thomas Merton (Jan. 31, 1915–Dec. 10, 1968)

Merton was an American Trappist monk, writer, theologian, mystic, poet, social activist, and scholar of comparative religion. In 1949, he was ordained to the Catholic priesthood and was a member of the Abbey of Our Lady of Gethsemane (Kentucky), living there from 1941 to his death. Merton wrote more than 50 books, mostly on spirituality, social justice, and a quiet pacifism, as well as scores of essays and reviews. Among Merton's most enduring works is his bestselling autobiography, *The Seven Story Mountain*.

> *Hagia Sophia*
> "There is in all visible things an invisible fecundity, a dimmed light, a meek namelessness, a hidden wholeness. This mysterious Unity and Integrity of Wisdom, the Mother of all, 'Natura naturans.' There is in all things an inexhaustible sweetness and purity, a silence that is a fount of action and joy. It rises up in wordless gentleness and flows out to me from the unseen roots of all created being, welcoming me tenderly, saluting me with indescribable humility. This is at once my own being, my own nature, and the Gift of my Creator's Thought and Art within me, speaking as Hagia [Holy] Sophia, speaking as my sister, Wisdom."

"Wisdom cries out to all who will hear. When the helpless one awakens strong at the voice of mercy, it is as if Life his Sister, as if the Blessed Virgin, (his own flesh, his own sister), as if Nature made wise by God's Art and Incarnation were to stand over him and invite him with unutterable sweetness to be awake and to live. This is what it means to recognize Hagia Sophia."

"All the perfections of created things are also in God; and therefore, He is at once Father and Mother. As Father he stands in solitary might surrounded by darkness. As Mother

His shining is diffused, embracing all His creatures with merciful tenderness and light. The diffuse shining of God is Hagia Sophia. We call her His 'glory.' In Sophia His power is experienced only as mercy and as love. Hagia Sophia in all things is the Divine Life reflected in them, considered as a spontaneous participation, as their invitation to the Wedding Feast. Sophia is His manifestation in radiant splendor! She is the inexhaustible fountain of kindness, and source of creative realizations of the Father's glory."

"Now the Blessed Virgin Mary is the one created being who enacts and shows forth in her life all that is hidden in Sophia. Because of this she can be said to be a personal manifestation of Sophia, Who in God is Ousia [Greek: substance; essence] rather than Person. Natura in Mary becomes pure Mother. In her, Natura is as she was from the origin of her divine birth. In Mary Natura is all wise and is manifested as an all-prudent, all-loving, all-pure person: not a Creator, and not a Redeemer, but perfect Creature, perfectly Redeemed, the fruit of all God's great power, the perfect expression of wisdom in mercy."

Sergei O. Prokofieff (Jan. 16, 1954–Jul. 26, 2014)

Prokofieff was born in Moscow in 1954, where he studied Fine Arts and Painting at the Moscow School of Art. At an early age he came across the work of the Austrian-born philosopher and founder of modern Spiritual Science, Rudolf Steiner, and soon realized that his life was to be dedicated to Christian esotericism. He worked for many years in Dornach, Switzerland as a director of the Anthroposophical Society.

Prokofieff wrote many definitive books on Steiner's teachings, which has earned him the honor of being considered one of the greatest commentators of Steiner's opus. Prokofieff, based upon Steiner's ideas, defines the Divine Sophia as an Avatar Being after the Sun-Spirit of the Christ. This places Sophia on equal terms with Her Consort, the Son of God, Christ. This insight was gained from the works of Rudolf Steiner and his interactions with the being Anthroposophia.

Eternal Individuality
"Thus, in the figure of the Luke Mary we have a human being who was worthy of becoming the bearer of one of the highest Avatar Beings after the Sun-Spirit of the Christ Himself, of that exalted Being who in the ancient world was called the Divine Isis, and in the early Christian communities and in places where Esoteric Christianity was nurtured, the Divine Sophia."

The Heavenly Sophia and the Being of Anthroposophia
"A particular secret of the Sistine Madonna lies also in the fact that it is, so to speak, a connecting link between the past and the future. Thus, on the one hand, it points towards the Egyptian Mysteries of Isis, these being a memory of the ancient Lemurian age when human beings were still in direct communion with this Goddess, and, on the other hand, to the future mysteries of the Divine Sophia, shining towards us from the future in the image of the Virgin clothed with the Sun [Sophia]."

"For this reason, in the lecture of 3 February 1913 Rudolf Steiner spoke about the connection between the metamorphosis from the Sophia to Philosophia and finally to Anthroposophia and the historical development of the three members of man's being in Earthly evolution from the Intellectual or Intellectual-Soul, the Consciousness-Soul and the Spirit-Self, during, respectively, the Fourth, Fifth, and Sixth Post-Atlantean Epochs. However, the supersensible being, Anthroposophia is already beginning to prepare humanity today for the future receiving of the Spirit-Self (once she has in her own development begun the ascent to this higher member). Thus, in Rudolf Steiner's words it is also possible to see an indication as to how the course of two periods of seven hundred years (2100-700 BC), still as the Sophia, she prepared the Fourth Post-Atlantean Epoch; and how during two further periods (from the birth of Christ to the year 1400), as Philosophia, she prepared the Fifth, and from our time until 3500, as Anthroposophia, the Sixth Epoch."

Tyla Gabriel, N. D.

Tyla Gabriel is a board-certified naturopath as well as an internationally known entrepreneur in education and business. She holds a graduate degree in Humanities from Florida State University, where she began her life-long studies in religion, mythology, and philosophy, eventually leading her to the path of Anthroposophy. As a philosopher and theologian, her writings and teachings on the pivotal role of the Divine Feminine Trinity have broken ground that is tantamount to a new revelation of the divine that necessitates a complete revisiting of our approach to the world and ourselves.

Tyla's *Gospel of Sophia* trilogy is the testament of an aspirant of Sophia who has been given self-initiation with the assistance of the Divine Feminine Trinity as guide and teacher. From the first revelations of Sophia through the Hawaiian volcano goddess Pele, to the Etheric Christ experience several years later, Tyla has followed the luminous path of study and communion with Sophia-Christos to become an initiate of Sophia. Her teachings about the being Sophia are the result of living Moral Imaginations given to her by spiritual beings that inspired her over many years, guiding her to active, Moral Intuitions that unveil the hidden nature of the Triple Goddess—Sophia.

The Gospel of Sophia, A Modern Path of Initiation
"The Gospel of Sophia contains the wisdom of Christ. In fact, the shared descent into matter of Christ and Sophia is one of the most hidden mysteries of all as the role of the Divine Feminine Trinity has been marginalized in Christianity. But over time, we have witnessed—and are still seeing—Sophia recognized more and more because Her presence has never waned. She has never abandoned us. Sophia, as the Great Mother, has never turned Her back on human prayers and spiritual yearning. She moves through the aspiring human soul, guiding each aspirant along the path to revelation. Just as Joseph Campbell has written in the excerpt from Goddesses, "the Divine Feminine was the substance of thought and practice behind all ancient mysteries." Indeed, these mysteries were maintained by female priestesses, mid-wives, and healers. They constitute a science of the same forces of life that were observed in birth, death, and rebirth—the original trinity of the divine. The mysteries of Sophia are the mysteries of our time." I couldn't imagine how I could have been so blind as to not see Her before. Sophia became a personal friend. A mother. A guide. I no longer had to enter an underground cave to witness Her. She was both in me and all around me. All of the schools of thought and secret spiritual organizations I had ever been initiated into started to make sense."

"The more I read, the more I found Her description. Sophia became accessible in my waking life and in my dreams. Mysterious, mystic visions started to emerge, cloaked in symbols and promptings that led me further up the Holy Mountain of the Great Mother where I built a spiritual dwelling for my higher self. Sophia began to speak through other people to me, and I could feel Her working through their spirit. She was everywhere. All people. All things. Her nature spoke from each of them. After a while, the entire world became a book of knowledge that I was rewriting with a wisdom bursting forth from every aspect of life. There was nowhere I looked that I didn't see Sophia, and, therefore, me. Myself."

The Nature of Sophia
"A mystery of unity and integrity runs through the visible and invisible worlds. Rich with fertility and fruitfulness, acting as the Mother of All, this great mystery is known as Wisdom or Sophia. As a spiritual being, Her inexhaustible sweetness and purity is the very fount of love and joy. With grace and humility, She generates a silent gentleness from the unseen root of all creation that flows tenderly between all things."

"She, Sophia, is my own being, my own nature of thought and breath, my sister spirit who speaks to me. Her voice awakens me from my slumber. With her whispers, I am born anew from Her deep womb. Her soft voice rouses me from dreams. The unity of the spiritual world calls me from the separate self, which is so alone and isolated in the gravity and suffering of this Earth, this grave. Her voice breaks the spell of Eden. I am suddenly cast out, seeking Her face everywhere as my beloved."

"The kiss of Eve transforms into the blessing of Sophia. The wisdom of the ages has progressed from Time's dawn into the future destiny of paradise regained. Sophia speaks to all who will listen. The small. The innocent. The humble. Into Her loving arms each night we entrust our very life, and each new day She awakens us with spirit refreshed. Sophia takes our hand and leads us across the threshold between waking and sleep. Then, She returns us to the dawn mist of a new day where acts of creation are present everywhere around us as a reminder of Her workings."

"Sophia is so close. She seems like our own flesh and blood, our divine breath. Her mercy receives us as Her child, precious beyond imagination. As Nature, like the greatest of trees, She incarnates to stand over us as a canopy of shelter for the budding self."

"Oh Sophia, Great Goddess of Wisdom, you speak through everything, yet are so silent in the waking world. When I wake, your visage becomes blurred. You wither into a dream where I weigh myself against the world. Difficult it is to hear the subtle whisper of mercy and grace unless our senses have been awakened in dreams to break through matter's delusions. When we abandon ourselves to sweet sleep in the arms of Sophia, She will awaken us to Her wonders. Her tenderness will draw forth the love of all others, and moral heart-flames will bathe the soul."

"Then, even in daylight, we will see the pure simplicity that all is one consciousness, a single ongoing force spreading throughout the world as Wisdom that embraces everything as offspring of a loving Mother."

"The heavenly world rejoices at the awakening of a soul that receives the light of spirit into the clear silence of the heart. It calls us to adorn ourselves with the eternal. Sophia speaks to us among the myriad distractions of the world as one voice. We must hear Her. Light has fallen to the Earth. Her children return this light to heaven by deeds of moral love: light from light, love from love."

"Sophia tends Her children like a garden, always attentive and protective of new growth that blossoms into fruit. The kindest, most loving gardener imaginable, She reveals the glory and power of Her children to grow unshakably towards the light. At the same time, She also is the fertile darkness of the soil from which life springs eternal, an unknown mystery that sprouts seeds into magnificent forms. In time, She brings forth creation, death, and rebirth in the natural world. This miracle alone demands awe, wonder, and reverence. Such a great Queen, Her Throne is the fulcrum of creation where all things find their center, their true orientation."

"Only the humblest heart can be open and empty enough to receive Her presence, the sustaining pulse of all created worlds. Hidden and protected from the profane, She is naked and transparent to the humble one—for his self, through Her, stands visible and tangible. The admixture of Sophia's wisdom and the developing spiritual self are intertwined into one tree with leaves of devotion reaching for the light of Christ."

"Sophia is the gardener who tends the seeds that will blossom into a promise of our higher self—the one that Christ gave us. More tender and precious is this fruit of the spirit to Sophia than any other. Humans were created from nothingness in the timeless realm of Wisdom. Therefore, we are the aim of all creation. Through conscious self-development, we can realize that fully."

"With Sophia's help, the human bodily constitution becomes the altar and laboratory of conscious spiritual development. Each time we experience Wisdom's message through Sophia, we discover revelation in ourselves. Sophia plays with Her children in the world through seen and unseen manners. She calls forth Her qualities: Wisdom, Consciousness, Revelation, Humility, Meekness, Kindness, Purity, Mercy, Tenderness, Light, Life, and Eternal Love. In this way, She teaches us how to mirror the spirit. With Her guiding wisdom, we reflect the spontaneous participation of the human and divine in a wedding feast of soul to spirit."

"Sophia exists in everything, just as air receives Sunlight, delivering life to all in need. As a grail-offering of spiritual love, She unites all things. Knowing Her is to know communion of the spirit, to celebrate a thanksgiving of vitality, forever glorious. She, too, is filled with gratitude that all wise creatures praise Her name. We are all invited to this spiritual wedding of Sophia to Christ. It is our own wedding. This feast is the undying source of creative Imaginations. It leads to radiant splendor and nourishing life in the etheric body of the human and the Earth. The marriage is a heavenly gift of light, life, and love that replenishes dying etheric bodies. As death is conquered, Nature is renewed through this alchemical marriage of the Queen to the King, our soul to our spirit—and immortality is born. As a source of mercy and grace, this is given to the striving aspirant to feed his spiritual hunger and thirst.

"Sophia helps us cleanse our soul to be ready for this alchemical feast wherein we are also taught to forgive, a truly divine quality. Love and forgiveness become the well-spring of the fountain of mercy and grace. This Fountain of Life can overturn darkness into light, gravity into levity. When divine fountains begin to spring forth in our soul, we become co-creators with Sophia, transforming our former self into a brilliant radiance that sheds the weight of praise and blame, along with all Earthly desires."

"Mary-Sophia is the one created being who perfectly embodies the hidden Sophia in her soul. She is a personal manifestation of Sophia. In her nature alights the purest mother, the origin of a divine birth. As Wisdom, Mary-Sophia has become perfect purity, prudence, love, power, and divine wisdom through mercy. She is sadness and joy redeemed through spiritual consciousness. It is she that places the crown upon Christ's head, enabling the gifts of the Cosmic Word to enter human nature. Through her embodiment of wisdom, freedom, and love, Mary-Sophia anoints Christ with the glorious crown of suffering, humility, and kindness. This is the mysterious conjunction of the human with the divine, and the enduring model for all human spiritual development. Sophia contains the wisdom of Christ. In fact, the shared descent into matter of Christ and Sophia is one of the most hidden mysteries of all as the role of the Divine Feminine Trinity has been marginalized in Christianity. But over time, we have witnessed—and are still seeing—Sophia recognized more and more because Her presence has never waned. She has never abandoned us. Sophia, as the Great Mother, has never turned Her back on human prayers and spiritual yearning. She moves through the aspiring human soul, guiding each aspirant along the path to revelation."

The Gospel of Sophia
"Just as Joseph Campbell has written in Goddesses, the Divine Feminine was the substance of thought and practice behind all ancient mysteries. Indeed, these mysteries were maintained by female priestesses, mid-wives, and healers. They constitute a science of the same forces of life that were observed in birth, death, and rebirth—the original trinity of the divine. The mysteries of Sophia are the mysteries of our time."

"Sophia, as Daughter of the Goddess, shared a body with Mary for eleven years after the crucifixion. Christian history shows that after Christ was baptized in the Jordon, Sophia over-lighted Mary with both human and divine wisdom. She dissolved all Earthly nature in that body so that it could be taken whole and complete into heaven at Her assumption. In this way, like Christ, she utilized a human body with all of its imperfections as the vehicle of consciousness for the Daughter of the Goddess."

"There is a saying in Hawaii that "Pele giveth and Pele taketh away." This refers to the function of the Triple Goddess, who rules birth, death, and resurrection. She existed before and after the more well-known trinities of Father, Son, and Holy Spirit, or Brahma, Vishnu, and Shiva, or any other of the much later, male-dominated, Sun-centered religions and cultures."

"She is the unmanifested Creatrix who has participated in all levels of existence, including the human. She descended as a Pure Virgin Soul and lived for eleven years as a human. The Holy Sophia is now growing with humanity as a sister soul. As Queen Mother, She redeemed humanity by giving birth to the Christ. She was with Christ through His three-year ministry and lived eleven years after His resurrection, teaching the apostles, in particular St. John the Divine at Ephesus in Turkey."

"Mary (Sophia) overcame death herself after the dormition period, was assumed into heaven, and now sits on Her Throne of Wisdom next to Christ Jesus and God the Father. Mary's apparitions have never ceased to appear to those with a pure heart. She nurtures, intercedes, and shows the way. She is the principle of Wisdom (Sophia) that has been hidden for thousands of years, and She has now reascended Her lost Throne of Power, comprised of the collective wisdom of all nature. By whatever name She is known—Eve, Mary, Sophia—She has resurrected the fall of the Virgin Soul into dark matter and has led Her through Wisdom to her higher Spirit-Self. We are all called to this wedding feast as brides in the great alchemical marriage."

"Eve and Adam were Virgin Souls incarnating first in Eden and then on the Earth. They continued to incarnate in the many mysterious religions of antiquity until the time of Jesus of Nazareth. Eve became Mary, the mother of Jesus. Adam became John the Baptist. Together, they stand next to Christ Jesus as Adam and Eve redeemed."

"The forces of Sophia the Daughter inspired Mary/Eve at the time of Jesus' baptism in the Jordan by John the Baptist and lived with Her for years after the descent of the Holy Spirit, even until Her Assumption into heaven."

"As the tongues of fire descended at Pentecost, the Holy Spirit that had inspired John the Baptist moved the Apostles to spread the Gospel of Peace, and Sophia the Daughter dwelt in Mary and instructed St. John the Divine. The Holy Sophia wed the Holy Spirit in this World Pentecost."

"The Most Holy Trinosophia is triple in function. She is the Mother (Creatrix), Daughter (Spirit of Wisdom), and the Holy Sophia (Collective Evolving Consciousness of Humanity)."

"Maria Sophia is the first and greatest initiate to arise complete and pure. She is the first of the Virgin Souls to return to Her spiritual home, New Jerusalem, a place which exists in the etheric atmosphere around the Earth, much like Shambhala or Heaven."

"Sophia has conquered death, resurrected, and has now returned to Her Temple of Wisdom and ascended Her mighty throne of birth, death, and resurrection. Now the Triple Goddess calls out, not the ancient injunction of the Egyptian mysteries, "I am the past, the present, and the future; no one has lifted my veil and lived," but a new invocation of Sophia (given by Rudolf Steiner): "I am the past, the present, and the future; all must lift my veil to live."

Dr. Gabriel gives us a beautiful picture of Sophia in her poem, *The Temple of Sophia Christos*, found in the *Gospel of Sophia* and presented here as another revelation of Sophia. Below this poem is a prayer to Sophia that illuminates the many aspects of Sophia which Tyla has described so comprehensively in her trilogy.

The Temple of Sophia Christos
They gathered from all parts of the world,
Launched from the golden heart of the earth,
Aiming their colorful deeds to the stars.

There, surrounded by veils of glorious majesty flowing aloft,
Like funeral pyres of living archetypes rising from spiritual
    thoughts
Gleaned from the fires of love's illuminating mind,
Rising like painted warriors dancing round the leaping-fire,
Beckoning thinking to courageous union with archetypes
    divine,
Who sacrifice their supersensible perception as new starlight,
Weaving and quivering before the breath of the solar winds,
Joyfully coloring their bursts of mighty, upward spirit-force,
Sighing with relief from suffering and bearing the hopeful
    future,
When human-angels brighten their future heavenly worlds,
With radiating, fiery love received from celestial stars above.

Sound forth the waves of luminous curtains bright,
Like thunder rippling the cold thin air of the North,
Announcing the new rainbow bridge with clarion calls.

The crown of glory shines upward the new starlight made by
    human hearts,
Encircling the poles as twin rings of colorful fires that do not
    burn.

Michael's sword of fire stands guard against unprepared souls,
So that Eden's rush of light be not vainly wasted on weak eyes.

There, Michael shines as the countenance and face of Christ,
With Sophia standing on the other side of the threshold door,
Welcoming the Soul into Spirit's home, Sophia's Temple of Wisdom.

Our Sophia

Hail Holy Mother! Know Her!
Our Mother, who art risen from the endarkened tomb!

Hail Queen of Heaven!
Seated on Your celestial Throne beside Your Son.
Thou art the One and the Many, Thrice Great Goddess!

Hail Triple Goddess of Birth, Death, and Rebirth!
Who has created and sustains all visible and invisible worlds
and lets them, in time,
Fall back into Her creative womb at the moment of death,
to be born again renewed.
Thou Who art the past, present, and future—ruling the world
with wisdom and virtue.

Thou art Three in One: Mother, Daughter, and Holy Sophia,
In co-creative union with the Father, Son and Holy Spirit,
Before time began or space whirled into manifestation,
Together with the Ground of Being that moves not.

Hail Goddess of the Seven Pillars of Virtue and Time!
Teacher of Humility—Who builds fortitude and
obedience to the spirit,

Teacher of Compassion—Who gives kindness to the heart to develop love,

Teacher of Purity—Who instills self-control through chastity and prudence,

Teacher of Generosity—Who shares justice through charity and selflessness,

Teacher of Temperance—Who ignites patience in the soul to tame desires,

Teacher of Diligence—Who births hope to engender spirit zeal and persistence,

Teacher of Patience—Who endures with kindness and faith through divine mercy.

Hail Sophia! Ruler of Wisdom and Space!
We know You as:

Creatrix—Who gives life eternal and holds all creation in Her heart,

Mother of All—Who tends Her children with loving devotion,

Goddess of Wisdom—Who thinkers have courted and loved wholeheartedly,

Goddess of Nature—Who brings untold power and strength into the world,

Goddess of Beauty—Who we hold and emulate in our soul and spirit,

Cosmic Virgin—Who is cleansed and purified as a radiant vessel of spirit,

Holy Bride—Who is ready for the alchemical wedding of soul to spirit,

The Beloved—Who is joined in spiritual union for all times to come,

Goddess of Love—Who is author of the primal force of creation,
Mother of God—Who birthed the Father, Son, and Holy Spirit,
Queen of Heaven—Who is raised back to Her primal Throne of Wisdom,
Most Holy Trinosophia—Who is Three in One, when time and space are no more,
Sophia Christos—Who is the Wisdom of Christ's cosmic nature and etheric revelation.

Hail Most Holy Trinosophia!
Bless our petition of the heart: to always draw closer to Your ways,
To Know You as Mother of all worlds, Who is the ground of the Father.
Teach us the Wisdom of Your Daughter, Who wed Christ to redeem darkness and death,
Joining Holy Sophia and the Holy Spirit in fiery union as World Pentecost,
Baptizing those who mount to higher realms witnessing the Heavenly Marriage
Of Male and Female Trinities wed as holy union divine—Sophia Christos.

BIBLIOGRAPHY

- Andreæ, Johann Valentin. *Reipublicæ Christianopolitanæ descriptio*. Argentorati: Sumptibus hæredum Lazari Zetzneri, Strasbourg, 1619.

- Andreæ, Johann Valentin. *Johann Valentin Andreae's Christianopolis; an ideal state of the seventeenth century.* translated from the Latin of Johann Valentin Andreae with an historical introduction. by Felix Emil Held. The Graduate School of the University of Illinois, Urbana- Champaign, 1916.

- Arnold, Edwin Sir. *The Light of Asia, or The Great Renunciation (Mahâbhinishkramana): Being the Life and Teaching Gautama, Prince of India and Founder of Buddhism (As Told in Verse by an Indian Buddhist)*. Kegan Paul, Trench, Trübner & Co., London, 1879.

- Avari, Burjor. *India: The Ancient Past: A History of the Indian Sub-Continent*. Routledge, New Edition, 2007.

- Barnwell, John. *The Arcana of the Grail Angel: The Spiritual Science of the Holy Blood and of the Holy Grail*. Verticordia Press, Bloomfield Hills, 1999.

- Barnwell, John. *The Arcana of Light on the Path: The Star Wisdom of the Tarot and Light on the Path*. Verticordia Press, Bloomfield Hills, 1999.

- Blavatsky, H. P. (Helena Petrovna). *Isis Unveiled: A Master-Key to the Mysteries of Ancient and Modern Science and Theology*. J. W. Bouton. New York, 1878.

- Blavatsky, H. P. (Helena Petrovna). *The Key to Theosophy: Being a Clear Exposition, in the Form of Question and Answer, of the Ethics, Science and Philosophy for the Study of Which the Theosophical Society Has Been Founded.* The Theosophical Publishing Company, Ltd. London, 1889.

- Blavatsky, H. P. (Helena Petrovna). *The Secret Doctrine: The Synthesis of Science, Religion and Philosophy.* The Theosophical Publishing Company, Ltd. London, 1888.

- Blavatsky, H. P. (Helena Petrovna). *The Voice of Silence: Being Extracts from the Book of the Golden Precepts.* Theosophical University Press, 1992.

- Bockemuhl, Jochen. *Toward a Phenomenology of the Etheric World: Investigations into the Life of Nature and Man.* Anthroposophic Press, Spring Valley, N. Y., 1977.

- Campanella, Tommaso. *The City of the Sun.* The ProjectGutenberg Ebook, David Widger, 2013.

- Colum, Padriac. *Orpheus: Myths of the World.* Floris Books. Colum, Padriac. The Children's Homer. MacMillan Co., 1946.

- Colum, Padriac. *The Tales of Ancient Egypt.* Henry Walck Incorporated, New York, 1968.

- Crawford, John Martin. *The Kalevala: The Epic Poem of Finland.* John B. Alden, New York, 1888.

- Gabriel, Douglas. *The Eternal Curriculum for Wisdom Children: Intuitive Learning and the Etheric Body.* Our Spirit, Northville, 2017.

- Gabriel, Tyla. *The Gospel of Sophia: The Biographies of the Divine Feminine Trinity,* Volume Our Spirit, Northville, 2014.

Bibliography

- Gabriel, Tyla. *The Gospel of Sophia: A Modern Path of Initiation,* Volume 2. Our Spirit, Northville, 2015.

- Gabriel, Tyla and Douglas. *The Gospel of Sophia: Sophia Christos Initiation,* Volume 3. Our Spirit, Northville, 2016.

- Gabriel, Douglas. *The Spirit of Childhood.* Trinosophia Press, Berkley, 1993.

- Gabriel, Douglas. *The Eternal Ethers: A Theory of Everything.* Our Spirit, Northville, 2018.

- Gabriel, Douglas. *Goddess Meditations.* Trinosophia Press, Berkley, 1994.

- Gebser, Jean. *The Ever Present Origin.* Ohio University Press, 1991.

- Green, Roger Lancelyn & Heather Copley. *Tales of Ancient Egypt.* Puffin Books, New York, 1980.

- Harrison, C. G. *The Transcendental Universe; Six Lectures on Occult Science, Theosophy, and the Catholic Faith.* George Redway, London 1893.

- Harrison, C. G. *The Transcendental Universe; Six Lectures on Occult Science, Theosophy, and the Catholic Faith.* Delivered Before the Berean Society, edited with an introduction by Christopher Bamford. Lindesfarne Press, Hudson, 1993.

- Hamilton, Edith. *Mythology.* Little Brown And Co., Boston, 1942.

- Harrer, Dorothy. *Chapters from Ancient History.* Waldorf Publications, Chatham, 2016.

- Hazeltine, Alice Isabel. *Hero Tales from Many Lands.* Abingdon Press, New York, 1961.

- Heidel, Alexander. *The Babylonian Genesis: The Story of Creation.* University of Chicago Press, Chicago, 1942.

- Hiebel, Frederick. *The Gospel of Hellas.* Anthroposophic Press, New York, 1949.

- Jocelyn, Beredene. *Citizens of the Cosmos: Life's Unfolding from Conception through Death to Rebirth.* Continuum, New York, 1981.

- König, Karl. *Earth and Man.* Bio-Dynamic Literature, Wyoming, Rhode Island, 1982.

- Kovacs, Charles. *Ancient Mythologies and History.* Resource Books, Scotland, 1991.

- Kovacs, Charles. *Greek Mythology and History.* Resource Books, Scotland, 1991.

- Landscheidt, Theodor. *Sun-Earth-Man a Mesh of Cosmic Oscillations: How Planets Regulate Solar Eruptions, Geomagnetic Storms, Conditions of Life, and Economic Cycles.* Urania Trust, London, 1989.

- Laszlo, Ervin and Kingsley, Dennis L. *Dawn of the Akashic Age: New Consciousness, Quantum Resonance, and the Future of the World.* Inner Traditions, Rochester Vermont, 2013

- Plato. *The Republic.* Dover Thrift Editions, 2000.

- Sister Nivedita (Margaret E. Noble) & Coomaraswamy, Ananda K.. *Myths of the Hindus and Buddhists.* Henry Holt, New York 1914.

- Steiner, Rudolf. *Ancient Myths: Their Meaning and Connection with Evolution.* Steiner Book Center, 1971.

- Steiner, Rudolf. *Christ and the Spiritual World: The Search for the Holy Grail.* Rudolf Steiner Press, London, 1963.

- Steiner, Rudolf. *Foundations of Esotericism*. Rudolf Steiner Press, London, 1983.

- Steiner, Rudolf. *Isis Mary Sophia: Her Mission and Ours*. Steiner Books, 2003.

- Steiner, Rudolf. *Man as a Being of Sense and Perception*. Steiner Book Center, Vancouver, 1981.

- Steiner, Rudolf. *Man as Symphony of the Creative Word*. Rudolf Steiner Publishing, London, 1978.

- Steiner, Rudolf. *Occult Science*. Anthroposophic Press, NY, 1972.

- Steiner, Rudolf. *Rosicrucian Esotericism*. Anthroposophic Press, NY, 1978.

- Steiner, Rudolf. *Rosicrucian Wisdom: An Introduction*. Rudolf Steiner Press, London, 2000. GA 425

- Steiner, Rudolf. *The Bridge between Universal Spirituality and the Physical Constitution of Man*. Anthroposophic Press, NY, 1958.

- Steiner, Rudolf. *The Evolution of Consciousness*. Rudolf Steiner Press, London, 1926.

- Steiner, Rudolf. *The Goddess from Natura to the Divine Sophia*. Sophia Books, 2001.

- Steiner, Rudolf. *The Holy Grail: from the Works of Rudolf Steiner*. Compiled by Steven Roboz. Steiner Book Center, North Vancouver, 1984.

- Steiner, Rudolf. *The Influence of Spiritual Beings Upon Man*. Anthroposophic Press, NY, 1971.

- Steiner, Rudolf. *The Reappearance of Christ in the Etheric*. Anthroposophic Press, NY, 1983.

- Steiner, Rudolf. *The Risen Christ and the Etheric Christ*. Rudolf Steiner Press, London, 1969.

- Steiner, Rudolf. *The Search for the New Isis the Divine Sophia*. Mercury Press, N.Y., 1983.

- Steiner, Rudolf. *The Spiritual Hierarchies and the Physical World*. Anthroposophic Press, N.Y., 1996.

- Steiner, Rudolf. *The Tree of Life and the Tree of Knowledge*. Mercury Press, NY, 2006.

- Steiner, Rudolf. *The True Nature of the Second Coming*. Rudolf Steiner Press, London, 1971.

- Steiner, Rudolf. *Theosophy*. Anthroposophic Press. New York, 1986.

- Steiner, Rudolf. *Wonders of the World, Ordeals of the Soul, Revelations of the Spirit*. Rudolf   Steiner Press, London, 1963.

- Steiner, Rudolf. *World History in Light of Anthroposophy*. Rudolf Steiner Press, London, 1977.

- Tappan, Eva March. *The Story of the Greek People*. Houghton Mifflin Co., Boston 1908.

- van Bemmelen, D. J. *Zarathustra: The First Prophet of Christ*, 2 Vols. Uitgeverij Vrij Geestesleven, The Netherlands, 1968.

- Watson, Jane Werner (Vālmīki). *Rama of the Golden Age: An Epic of India*. Garrard Pub., Champaign.

ABOUT DR. RUDOLF STEINER

Rudolf Steiner was born on the 27th of February 1861 in Kraljevec in the former Kingdom of Hungary and now Croatia. He studied at the College of Technology in Vienna and obtained his doctorate at the University of Rostock with a dissertation on Theory of Knowledge which concluded with the sentence: "The most important problem of human thinking is this: to understand the human being as a free personality, whose very foundation is himself." He exchanged views widely with the personalities involved in cultural life and arts of his time. However, unlike them, he experienced the spiritual realm as the other side of reality. He gained access through exploration of consciousness using the same method as the natural scientist uses for the visible world in his external research. This widened perspective enabled him to give significant impulses in many areas such as art, pedagogy, curative education, medicine, agriculture, architecture, economics, and social sciences, aiming towards the spiritual renewal of civilization.

He gave his movement the name of "Anthroposophy" (the wisdom of humanity) after separating from the German section of the Theosophical Society, where he had acted as a general secretary. He then founded the Anthroposophical Society in 1913 which formed its center with the construction of the First Goetheanum in Dornach, Switzerland. Rudolf Steiner died on 30th March 1925 in Dornach. His literary work is made up of numerous books, transcripts and approximately 6000 lectures which have for the most part been edited and published in the Complete Works Edition.

Steiner's basic books, which were previously a prerequisite to gaining access to his lectures, are: *Theosophy, The Philosophy of Freedom, How to Know Higher Worlds, Christianity as a Mystical Fact,* and *Occult Science.*

ABOUT THE AUTHOR, DR. DOUGLAS GABRIEL

Dr. Gabriel is a retired superintendent of schools and professor of education who has worked with schools and organizations throughout the world. He has authored many books ranging from teacher training manuals to philosophical/spiritual works on the nature of the divine feminine.

He was a Waldorf class teacher and administrator at the Detroit Waldorf School and taught courses at Mercy College, the University of Detroit, and Wayne State University for decades.

He then became the Headmaster of a Waldorf School in Hawaii and taught at the University of Hawaii, Hilo. He was a leader in the development of charter schools in Michigan and helped found the first Waldorf School in the Detroit Public School system and the first charter Waldorf School in Michigan.

Gabriel received his first degree in religious formation at the same time as an associate degree in computer science in 1972. This odd mixture of technology and religion continued throughout his life. He was drafted into and served in the Army Security Agency (NSA) where he was a cryptologist and systems analyst in signal intelligence, earning him a degree in signal broadcasting. After military service, he entered the Catholic Church again as a Trappist monk and later as a Jesuit priest where he earned PhD's in philosophy and comparative religion, and a Doctor of Divinity. As a Jesuit priest, he came to Detroit and earned a BA in anthroposophical studies and history and a MA in school administration. Gabriel left the priesthood and became a Waldorf class teacher and administrator in Detroit and later in Hilo, Hawaii.

Douglas has been a sought-after lecturer and consultant to schools and businesses throughout the world and in 1982 he founded the Waldorf Educational Foundation that provides funding for the publication of educational books. He has raised a great deal of money for Waldorf schools and institutions that continue to develop the teachings of Dr. Rudolf Steiner. Douglas is now retired but continues to write a variety of books including a novel and a science fiction thriller. He has four children, who keep him busy and active and a wife who is always striving towards the spirit through creating an "art of life." She is the author of the Gospel of Sophia trilogy.

The Gabriels' articles, blogs, and videos can currently be found at:

OurSpirit.com
Neoanthroposphy.com
GospelofSophia.com
EternalCurriculum.com

TRANSLATOR'S NOTE

The Rudolf Steiner quotes in this book can be found, in most cases, in their full-length and in context, through the Rudolf Steiner Archives by an Internet search of the references provided. We present the quoted selections of Steiner from a free rendered translation of the original while utilizing comparisons of numerous German to English translations that are available from a variety of publishers and other sources. In some cases, the quoted selections may be condensed and partially summarized using the same, or similar in meaning, words found in the original. Brackets are used to insert [from the author] clarifying details or anthroposophical nomenclature and spiritual scientific terms.

We chose to use GA (Gesamtausgabe — collected edition) numbers to reference Steiner's works instead of CW (Collected Works), which is often used in English editions. Some books in the series, *From the Works of Rudolf Steiner*, have consciously chosen to use a predominance of Steiner quotes to drive the presentation of the themes rather than personal remarks and commentary.

We feel that Steiner's descriptions should not be truncated but need to be translated into an easily read format for the English-speaking reader, especially for those new to Anthroposophy. We recommend that serious aspirants read the entire lecture, or chapter, from which the Steiner quotation was taken, because nothing can replace Steiner's original words or the mood in which they were delivered. The style of speaking and writing has changed dramatically over the last century and needs updating in style and presentation to translate into a useful tool for spiritual study in modern times. The series, *From the Works of Rudolf Steiner* intends to present numerous "study guides" for the beginning aspirant, and the initiate, in a format that helps support the spiritual scientific research of the reader.

Made in the USA
Monee, IL
12 April 2024

56841613R00193